COMPUTER-ASSISTED INSTRUCTION
and
INTELLIGENT TUTORING SYSTEMS:

Shared Goals and Complementary Approaches

TECHNOLOGY IN EDUCATION SERIES

Edited by
Raymond S. Nickerson

Nickerson/Zodhiates • Technology in Education: Looking Toward 2020

Larkin/Chabay • Computer-Assisted Instruction and Intelligent Tutoring Systems: Shared Goals and Complementary Approaches

Bruce/Rubin • Electronic Quills: A Situated Evaluation of Using Computers for Writing in Classrooms

COMPUTER-ASSISTED INSTRUCTION and INTELLIGENT TUTORING SYSTEMS:

Shared Goals and Complementary Approaches

Edited by
JILL H. LARKIN
RUTH W. CHABAY
Carnegie Mellon University

LAWRENCE ERLBAUM ASSOCIATES, PUBLISHERS
1992 Hillsdale, New Jersey Hove and London

Carol Scheftic

Editor for Content and Style
during the crucial early period of the book's development

Lawrence Erlbaum Associates, Inc., Publishers
365 Broadway
Hillsdale, New Jersey 07462

Library of Congress Cataloging-in-Publication Data

Computer-assisted instruction and intelligent tutoring systems : shared goals and complementary approaches / edited by J.H. Larkin, R.W. Chabay.
p. cm.
Includes bibliographical references and index.
ISBN 0-8058-0232-0.—ISBN 0-8058-0233-9 (pbk.)
1. Computer-assisted instruction. 2. Intelligent tutoring systems. I. Larkin, J. H. (Jill H.) II. Chabay, R. W. (Ruth W.)
LB1028.5.C5288 1991
371.3'34—dc20 91-15081
CIP

Printed in the United States of America
10 9 8 7 6 5 4 3 2 1

Contents

Introduction

Jill H. Larkin and Ruth W. Chabay, Editors
Center for Design of Educational Computing, Carnegie Mellon University

THE PURPOSE OF THIS BOOK

Two groups of individuals share a vision that computers can provide excellent instruction for large numbers of students. The first of these groups we call developers of computer-assisted instruction (CAI). This group consists predominantly of experienced teachers and educational researchers, with strong backgrounds in the subject matter of their programs. The second group we call developers of intelligent tutoring systems (ITS). This group consists predominantly of researchers in cognitive psychology and computer science who develop principles of learning and apply them in instructional programs.

Unfortunately, these groups have had few vehicles for sharing ideas or programs. Different backgrounds and settings have meant reading different journals and attending different conferences. The purpose of this book is to foster a mutual understanding of shared issues and complementary approaches so as to further powerful educational applications of computing.

The following pages first summarize the complementary, but distinct, approaches of CAI and ITS, and then discuss shared issues toward which these complementary approaches are directed.

COMPLEMENTARY APPROACHES

Central Aims

The aim of CAI programs is to address existing needs of particular groups of students. The CAI developer wants to produce the program that has the best chance of teaching effectively and applies to this end all available experience and expertise. CAI programs are specific and hand-crafted for the domain, topic, and students addressed. With these specifically tailored programs, CAI pushes the frontier of the best that can be done with current technology and imaginative techniques.

In contrast, the aim of ITS developers is to implement in programs a set of instructional principles sufficiently general to provide effective instruction for a variety of teaching tasks. ITS programs are strongly rooted in research on the psychology of learning. With large programs that provide instruction for many tasks (e.g., a significant part of a course), ITS pushes the frontier of knowledge about what general instructional techniques work and why.

Instructional Models

CAI programs do not follow a single theoretical model of instruction. In many CAI programs, the instruction emulates (in a form appropriate to the computer medium) interactions that might occur between a student and an excellent teacher. Other programs attempt to create an engaging, motivating environment that encourages purposeful exploration in a domain. A rich diversity of environments and problems is often a goal in CAI, and a suite of programs developed for a single course may vary significantly in goals, tasks, and style.

CAI programs reflect their developers' experienced beliefs about good teaching and good design for the computer medium. Some of the most interesting programs derive from developers' intuitions about activities well-suited to the medium, rather than from traditional instruction in the domain. Learning goals can be implicit in CAI, and activities may or may not be explicitly related to the tasks the student will be expected to perform after instruction.

ITS programs, in contrast, contain an explicit computer-implemented model of instruction. It is this model, and not the hand-crafted code of the developer, that determines how the program responds to the student. This model of instruction consists of two parts: (a) a *performance model* capable of performing the tasks the student is learning to perform, and (b) a *teaching model* that compares the student's actions with those of the performance model, and determines what (if any) reactions the ITS will provide to the student.

The performance model usually consists of a large set of fine-grained inference rules (although other techniques may be used in conjunction with these rules). Each rule consists of actions together with conditions under which these actions should occur. It is important that the rules be small in scope, because then they can be combined flexibly, in different ways, to do different activities. When an ITS is running, these rules are not invoked in any fixed order. Instead, at each point in time, the program searches for the rule most likely to contribute useful information to the current situation. This rule-based program architecture has had repeated success in building computer programs that apply large amounts of knowledge flexibly to a variety of tasks.

The teaching model in an ITS consists of engaging the learner in a reasoning task, and comparing the student's actions with the set of actions that can be generated by the performance model. This comparison lets the ITS identify when the student does something either wrong (according to domain knowledge) or useless in pursuit of the current task. The teaching model then determines what (if any) advice is to be offered. Furthermore, the tasks given to the student are designed so that (a) all inference rules in the performance model are required to solve the full set of tasks, and (b) each inference rule is applied in several contexts. Thus, the student has multiple opportunities to practice and acquire the knowledge represented by each rule.

In summary, CAI programs reflect experience in teaching in a particular domain, and consist of varied activities designed to help students increase domain knowledge and apply that knowledge in different contexts. ITS programs have an explicit model of the knowledge required for a domain of tasks, and the activities they include provide systematic practice in using all relevant knowledge.

Program Structure

CAI programs are interaction centered, reflecting the CAI model of instruction in which the computer is an interactive medium for instruction characteristic of excellent teachers. CAI programs are therefore built to provide a specific kind of student interaction with the computer screen. These programs start with a vision of this interaction, and then programming is done to make that vision real. CAI developers see the computer screen as a programmable interactive communications medium.

Single CAI programs are usually relatively brief (although some can be used in many ways) and deal with only a few aspects of a domain (e.g., comparing the size of fractions). A set of related programs, carefully coordinated by their developer(s), can provide instruction throughout an entire course.

In contrast, *ITS programs are knowledge centered*, reflecting the explicit model of performance knowledge on which they are based. Interaction with a student consists of the model sending a message to the interface which in turn uses its own knowledge of graphics and layout to convey the information to the student, and to convey student input back to the central model.

ITS programs are typically comprehensive, with one program, in a single format, providing most or all of the instruction for a large fraction of the material in a course. The knowledge encoded for early lessons is re-used when appropriate for later lessons, much as the student is intended to use knowledge acquired earlier, along with new knowledge to address more complex tasks. An

ITS systematically teaches a body of knowledge by providing multiple and varying opportunities for the student to learn each inference rule in the performance model.

Necessary Experience

Because CAI is interaction centered and because it takes time to learn the sensitive use of a new and difficult medium (e.g., film and television as well as the computer), many of the best CAI programs are written by people with years of experience. The authors in this book, for example, have up to 20 years experience in the computer medium.

In particular, three of the CAI chapters reflect work which began in the PLATO[1] instructional computing environment originating at the University of Illinois. This environment provided a graphics screen with nearly twice the number of pixels as the standard Macintosh, a touch interface, and the ability to back-project microfiche—all available in the early 1970's! The size of the PLATO system allowed very large courses to require several hours of computer work each week. Thus new programs could accrue hundreds or thousands of hours of student use each semester.

In contrast, ITS is based on efforts to represent explicitly the knowledge humans use in performing a set of tasks. Building such programs is an extremely difficulty task, and stresses existing principles and techniques in both psychology and computer science. Therefore, developers of ITS are usually researchers in psychology or computer science, and have extensive experience in both fields. In particular, they draw on about 20 years of research on detailed processes of the human mind, and ways of characterizing these processes through computer-implemented models.

Computer Implementation

The aim of CAI is to provide practical instruction, consisting of interactive programs that teach effectively. Therefore CAI programs are developed under heavy computational and other constraints (eloquently described in the chapter by Brackett). They must respond rapidly (to support interaction and varied graphic interactions). Without graphics and fast interaction, no CAI program described in this book could exist in anything like its current form. Yet these programs must run on affordable and widely available machines (low end Macintoshes and PCs, and the educationally ubiquitous Apple II), machines with severe memory and speed limitations.

---

[1]PLATO® is a registered trademark of The Roach Organization, Inc. The PLATO system is a development of the University of Illinois.

CAI programs are generally algorithmic in structure (i.e., describable by a flow-chart) with user input often determining branching. Programs are organized around the screen display, and interactions with students center on the display, which changes in response to various inputs from the student. Algorithmic programs can be faster and simpler than those with more complex architectures. In CAI, the most-used languages are algorithmic languages, e.g., versions of BASIC, PASCAL, and assembly language, as well as descendents of TUTOR (the PLATO programming language).

In contrast, ITS programs exploit models of knowledge and teaching. Because the human mind is complex, computational models of its functioning are complex. Implementing them requires powerful machines and the most sophisticated techniques of computer science research.

ITS programs can not be algorithmic because humans have abilities far more varied than those of any algorithmic program. Instead ITS programs have a logic based on repeatedly applying knowledge (encoded as rules) to react to a current situation. Furthermore, content of this knowledge consists not of numbers, but of symbols (words, phrases, rules). ITS systems are therefore almost always written in languages that support processing of symbols and lists (e.g., LISP, Prolog) and their rule-based extensions (e.g., GRAPES, OPS5). ITS systems use extensively techniques of "artificial intelligence," that is techniques for building large programs that can incorporate large amounts of knowledge, and use it flexibly. For efficiency, ITS programs are sometimes written (or rewritten) in C, one of the most powerful modern algorithmic languages.

Implications

The differing aims, constraints, and instructional models imply the following substantial differences between CAI and ITS programs.

CAI programs are hand-crafted using deep knowledge of the domain, the students, and the computer medium. In CAI, the interface is intuitive, and using it is part of the instructional process. Good CAI has clarity and charm. Despite their algorithmic architecture, the clever hand-crafting of interactions gives these programs the feeling of freedom of interaction. Good CAI typically has been used for many thousands of hours by varying students, although quantitative studies of its effectiveness are rare.

In contrast ITS programs are the product of an applied science. They are based on, and explicitly include, psychological principles of learning. The instruction aims to provide systematically opportunities for learning all knowledge in a carefully defined domain. These programs are often meticulously tested with student groups, and their effectiveness can be dramatic (although there are few demonstrations of continued utility in widespread use).

SHARED PRINCIPLES

The chapters in this book, each describing the development and nature of one or more instructional programs, make concrete the contrasts discussed above. However, they also illustrate a rich set of largely shared design principles for good educational computing. The following paragraphs summarize these shared principles, which appear as continuous themes throughout the chapters in this book.

Engage the student in active work on central tasks

For example, Corbett & Anderson's principles of intelligent tutoring include providing instruction in the context of active problem solving. Chabay and Sherwood, summarizing their experience-based guidelines for CAI, give the mandate "Ask, don't tell," and go on to discuss techniques for designing programs that consistently engage the student in active work. This principle is reflected by every instructional program described in this book. Students do not passively read screens of text, or simply watch graphic simulations.

Use the interface to suggest appropriate reasoning

Displays and interfaces have long been a primary focus of CAI. In particular, Dugdale provides an excellent description of the intricate interaction between the domain being taught and the intricate displays that teach it. Only recently have ITS developers given significant attention to the difficult task of designing principled and effective graphic interactions. The chapters by Reiser et. al, and by Lesgold et. al., discuss this work.

Center work on appropriate reasoning

Most of the time the student should be working smoothly and successfully on important tasks. In Dugdale's *Green Globs*, for example, students are free to write whatever equations they like, with the aim of producing a graph that will pass through "globs" placed on the screen. Any engagement in the program means thinking about the relation between equations and their graphs. The actual graph that does appear is itself immediate feedback on whether the student's thinking about this relation was accurate or not. In the ITS world, relevant, successful, active thinking is achieved by tracing inference rules used by the student, and by intervening with a correction or hint if the student moves more than a step or two away from an appropriate reasoning sequence. This does not mean the student can solve a problem in just one "correct" way—the program's inference rules always attempt to support any correct solution, and often to provide strategic advice on incorrect reasoning.

Provide prompt feedback focusing attention on erroneous thinking

For example, Dugdale's elegant CAI programs are designed so that the interface gently prohibits many irrelevant actions, and the results of relevant actions are immediately apparent. All of the ITS programs are designed to track the student's reasoning and to give increasingly detailed feedback when the student does something wrong or irrelevant. In particular, the chapter by Reiser, et., al., discusses the use of knowledge in the ITS to formulate this feedback.

Adapt instruction to individual student knowledge

Corbett & Anderson describe how ITS programs can adapt through selecting the inference rules required by the task—a small set at first, more later on. In contrast the ITS *SHERLOCK* (Lesgold, et. al.) provides a single set of problems, but uses hints to suggest inferences the student finds difficult. Dugdale's CAI adapts to students' knowledge by letting students set their own tasks, within a cleverly designed environment where involvement in any task is likely to increase skill and ability to design and solve more complex problems. Many CAI programs (e.g., Culley's earlier grammar programs), provide the student with unlimited practice, together with information on success rates. Thus students with varying initial capabilities can readily use the program as a tool to build skill.

VALUE OF INTERACTION

Although the shared instructional principles discussed above are, of course, implemented quite differently in ITS and CAI programs, there are also the beginnings of joint implementations. For example, the chapter by Culley describes how a CAI developer began explicitly to need the techniques used in ITSs. Sack and Soloway, ITS developers, discuss both their needs for the evaluation techniques of educational research, and for a program structure that provides greater student interaction.

The purpose of this book is to acquaint both ITS and CAI developers with a broad range of approaches to their common vision of broadly effective educational computing.

ACKNOWLEDGEMENTS

We wish to acknowledge, with great appreciation, the central contributions of the following individuals and organizations:

The James S. McDonnell Foundation which provided funding for the conference, held in March, 1988, on which this book is based, and for preparation of the manuscript. John Bruer, President of the Foundation, provided intellectual and moral support to complement the financial support of his organization. During initial planning for the book and conference, Jill Larkin was supported by a fellowship from the Guggenheim Foundation and by a National Science Foundation Visiting Professorship for Women.

Neither the conference nor the book would have been possible without the resources and working environment provided by Carnegie Mellon University and its Center for Design of Educational Computing. Additionally the Software Engineering Institute provided excellent facilities for a technologically complex conference.

Stanley Smith of the University of Illinois challenged and enlivened the workshop with his demonstration of innovative chemistry programs, which allow students to see and analyze real chemical phenomena using interactive videodisc technology.

Carol Scheftic served ably as the central contact with authors and as editor during the first difficult phases of manuscript preparation. Carol Scheftic and Ruth Chabay also took full responsibility for the conference leading to this book, while Jill Larkin managed to attend the sessions despite pneumonia.

Alice Huston patiently and meticulously read all of the ITS chapters, giving invaluable suggestions for making these chapters readable to an audience outside of the computer science community.

Finally, Mary McCallum provided patient expertise in proofreading, correcting endless versions of manuscripts, tracking down detailed information, and transferring materials (physically and electronically). She cheerfully took on endless extra tasks both contributing directly to this book and giving time for the editors to edit — a task more difficult than either of us had imagined.

Jill H. Larkin and Ruth W. Chabay
Pittsburgh, October, 1991

SUMMARY OF CHAPTERS AND PROGRAMS

Ch. No.	*Author*	*Program Type*	*Age Level*	*Subject matter*
1.	Dugdale	CAI	Pre College	Mathematics
2.	Culley	CAI /ITS[2]	University	Latin
3.	Corbett & Anderson	ITS	University	Programming in LISP
4.	Reiser et al.	ITS	University	Programming in LISP
5.	Chabay & Sherwood	CAI	All Levels	Design issues in CAI
6.	Brackett	CAI	Pre College	Slide presenter & scientific reasoning
7.	Lesgold et al.	ITS	Military	Electronic device troubleshooting
8.	Sack & Soloway	ITS[2]	University	Programming in PASCAL

[2]These two chapters describe programs which are not "tutors", but which use techniques of artificial intelligence.

1 The Design of Computer-Based Mathematics Instruction

Sharon Dugdale
Division of Education, University of California, Davis

INTRODUCTION

Overview

This chapter illustrates, by example, some design goals and instructional techniques devised and used during a fifteen-year software development and implementation effort for mathematics instruction.

The example instructional programs illustrate a variety of styles, sharing a common goal of encouraging students to become active, creative, independent learners. To this end, the programs minimize rote repetition of algorithms and procedures in favor of more attention to analyzing problems and developing strategies.

Three programs are presented in some detail with discussions of their features, goals, and classroom dynamics. A hypothetical fourth example is used to extend the instructional perspective to the teaching of more routine skills and to suggest considerations for defining appropriate roles for computer-implemented tutors. In conclusion, the chapter contrasts three styles of feedback in response to student errors and offers suggestions for the design of instructional materials in general.

An Introductory Remark

This chapter is about mathematics in particular, due to reservations about discussing instructional design independent of a subject matter context. Imagine entering the kitchen of a good restaurant and asking the chef, "What food preparation method do you use?" The chef would likely respond with a blank stare—not out of incompetence, but simply because the choice of a food preparation method is so obviously dependent on what particular food is being prepared, and for what audience. Similarly, in preparing knowledge for consumption, it is important to take a careful look at what is to be served, understand its inherent qualities and characteristics, and then select or devise a presentation method which best brings out its unique flavor and character.

This is not to say that a basic knowledge of general instructional design is unnecessary, any more than a basic knowledge of cooking is unnecessary for the good chef. On the contrary, a knowledge of a *variety* of methods seems useful, and the basic sense of where to use (and not use) these various methods is at least as important as the methods themselves. The sense of where to apply what methods is probably rooted more in an understanding of their function than in a strict recall of their form, and the designer who is led by a more functional approach may be better able to set aside the recipe box and do some inventive things.

Of course we can point to examples of educational software that could be improved by the strict application of generic design rules—just as we sometimes encounter food that is better doused with ketchup. This chapter is not expected to remedy such fundamental deficiencies, nor is it intended to address efficient production of routine materials. (Though there is undeniably much to be said for the consistent quality, reliability, and economy of a good fast food operation.) The purpose here is, rather, to explore issues beyond those addressed in the basic recipe books. This purpose requires a specific content, although it is hoped that the examples and discussions presented will provide insights applicable beyond the content covered here.

Background

The Fractions Curriculum

The first two examples represented here, *Sort Equivalent Fractions* and *Darts*, are from the *Fractions Curriculum* of the PLATO® Elementary Mathematics Project[1] (Dugdale and Kibbey, 1980). Developed for use on the PLATO network (Smith and Sherwood, 1976; Lyman, 1984), this curriculum covers common fractions, mixed numbers, and an introduction to decimal notation. It includes approximately 100 individual computer programs, a teacher's manual, and booklets and worksheets for students.

The management system allows a teacher to assign topics and individual activities. Based on the teacher's assignments and on individual student

---

[1] PLATO is a registered trademark of The Roach Organization, Inc. The PLATO system is a development of the University of Illinois.

background information (either stored by the programs during interaction or entered by the teacher), the management system constructs personalized student sessions. Although many session structures are possible, a typical student session might include:

1. a few minutes of review from previous material,
2. 15-20 minutes of work from a menu of currently assigned topics,
3. 5-10 minutes of work from an expanded menu which includes several general experience programs in addition to the currently assigned topics. The general experience programs are typically games and exploratory activities which provide practice with previous material, expansion of current topics, or initial exploration of new areas.

The management system provides an extensive on-line data reporting facility with which teachers and students can follow individual progress.

The curriculum offers students extensive experience using fractions and mixed numbers to manipulate interactive models, establishing a variety of representations for rational numbers and links between those representations. The models usually allow many different ways of solving problems. This provides opportunities for exploration, helps students attend to the meaning of what they are doing, and helps avoid the notion that mathematics is simply the repetition of dictated algorithms.

The curriculum provides a mix of instruction, review, practice, experience, and exploration. In many of the programs, the difficulty and complexity of the task is automatically adjusted (up or down) based on the student's performance. Completion of these programs depends on reaching a "mastery level," that is, demonstrating proficiency with problems of a complexity deemed necessary for use in succeeding materials. The mastery level number and the student's current level number are continuously displayed to keep the student informed about progress through the program.

As a pioneering effort in the use of computer networks to encourage sharing of ideas among students, the curriculum includes:

1. inter-terminal programs which allow students to interact with each other in real time from widely separated terminals, and
2. "libraries" which allow students to store their work and see products generated by other students who are working not only at other places but at other times.

Through these network facilities students share their work and ideas not only with their own classmates, but also with students in other classes and other schools (Dugdale, 1979).

Beginning in 1973, the fractions curriculum was developed in conjunction with use by students in public school classrooms. This permitted the authors to tailor the materials to the needs of students and teachers in realistic educational settings. During the 1974-75 and 1975-76 school years the curriculum was pilot tested as a regular part of the mathematics program in about a dozen classrooms, serving a total of approximately 300 students each year. The curriculum reached essentially finished form during the second of those years.

A summative evaluation done by Educational Testing Service proved these materials highly effective in both achievement and attitude improvement (Slottow, 1977; Swinton 1978). Further work and adaptations were done in conjunction with special needs programs, including work with hearing impaired students and those with other physical, emotional, or learning problems (Dugdale and Vogel, 1978).

This curriculum and related materials produced by other development teams (Seiler and Weaver, 1976; Cohen and Glynn, 1974) continue to be a regular part of the daily mathematics program for students in approximately 20 local classrooms. The materials were designed for use by students in grades 4-6 in a classroom situation where they could be integrated with the ongoing mathematics instruction on a daily basis. However, most of the activities have found broad applicability in adult education programs and numerous other settings served by the PLATO/NovaNET℠ computer network[2]. Because it was developed to take full advantage of the network capabilities, touch-sensitive display, and other features of the PLATO system, the fractions curriculum as a whole has not been transported to microcomputers more common in elementary school classrooms.

Fortunately, the theoretical results of the development effort have transferred more readily to other systems. The following design principles were distilled from analysis of the style and techniques used in many of the programs. Programs displaying these characteristics were labelled *intrinsic models.*

1. The student is given a working model to explore and manipulate.
2. The mathematics to be learned is intrinsic to the model. In other words, the model is a direct expression of the underlying mathematics.
3. Feedback is direct, relevant, diagnostic, and often graphic, so that students can tell at a glance what the error was and how it relates to a correct solution. Unnecessary verbiage and gimmicks unrelated to the mathematics are avoided.

---

[2] NovaNET has evolved from the earlier PLATO system. NovaNET is a service mark of University Communications, Inc.

4. The model provides a rich environment for exploration by students of widely varying mathematical background and ability, but students find that the more mathematics they apply, the more they are able to do.

In short, intrinsic models provide students a rich, mathematically accurate environment and the motivation to manipulate and learn from that environment. Models of this sort can engage students in formulating and using mathematical strategies in ways that were not possible before computers entered the classroom (Dugdale, 1982). Two of the programs presented in this chapter, *Darts* (from the Fractions Curriculum) and *Green Globs* (from a later development effort), are examples of intrinsic models.

Materials on Graphing and Functional Relationships

A later project applied the design principles outlined above to create software to improve students' understanding of functional relationships—concepts fundamental to further work in mathematics, science, and engineering, and an area to which the calculational and display capabilities of the microcomputer proved especially well suited (Dugdale and Kibbey, 1984). This project was one of the first efforts to use microcomputers to involve students in the exploration of graphic representations of functions, including qualitative, as well as quantitative, aspects of graphs. *Green Globs*, the third example presented here, is taken from this development effort.

Initial development of the graphing materials was done on the Color MicroPLATO system (Stifle, et al., 1979). The materials have since been revised and expanded, and derivative works have been created for IBM-PC and Apple II series microcomputers (Dugdale and Kibbey, 1983a, 1983b, 1986a, 1986b).

The materials were developed in conjunction with student use in two public high schools. Students generally worked in pairs or groups of three, actively discussing what they were doing and sharing ideas. Some students, however, became deeply engrossed in working out complicated equations and seemed more intensely involved when working alone. Observation indicated that each of these modes of use (individual and small group) provided different important learning and exploration opportunities.

Evaluation was largely formative, involving on-site observation of students and interviews with teachers and students. The materials underwent several cycles of testing and revision. In an informal two-week trial with the finished materials, students showed gains in performance on test items concerning linear and quadratic graphs (Dugdale and Kibbey, 1983).

Later efforts have extended the work with functional relationships, developing various approaches to understanding algebraic concepts and physical phenomena through functions and their graphs (Dugdale, 1986-87).

EXAMPLE 1: SORT EQUIVALENT FRACTIONS

Description

As shown in Figure 1, this is a practice program in which students sort fractions into equivalence sets. The student is given a collection of fractions and some loops to sort them into by size. A fraction can be moved into a loop or moved from one loop to another by touching the fraction and then touching the desired location on the screen.

After all of the fractions have been placed into the loops and the student has indicated that he or she is finished, the computer checks the equivalence of the fractions within each loop and responds by telling the student how many fractions are not in the correct loop. The student is asked to correct any wrong placements and may move the fractions around the screen until the problem has been solved correctly.

The program adjusts to student performance, increasing or decreasing the difficulty of discriminations, the number of fractions to sort, and the number of loops to sort them into, based on student proficiency in sorting the fractions. Completion of the exercise requires passing a specified difficulty level. The current level is shown at the bottom of the screen to keep the student informed of progress through the activity.

Discussion

This example is included here because the content objectives *appear* simple and obvious—to identify equivalent fractions and group them into equivalence sets. The exercise might be appropriately classified as "drill and practice," and the surface objectives could be met by various other computer or paper-and-pencil activities. However, upon working with the program or observing students using it, it becomes apparent that beyond this surface agenda are several unobtrusive features that foster a richer experience for the student.

First, the feedback for student errors simply tells how many fractions are not in the correct loop. Of course, the computer could just as easily tell which particular fractions are misplaced and which loops they belong in, leaving nothing for the student to figure out. The issue of how much and what kind of feedback to provide for student errors is an important one. Here, the limited feedback leaves students to diagnose their own errors. Having just finished scrutinizing each fraction to place it into a loop, few students are eager to methodically check each fraction again in order to find one or two errors. The common tendency is to scan the page and ask, "What is an easy way to spot a misfit?" Observation of students indicates that this diagnostic step is important in encouraging students to step back and look at the problem in a less

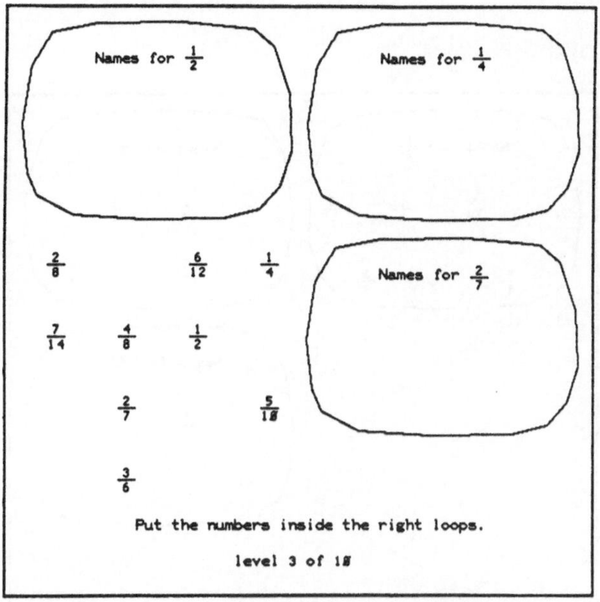

Figure 1a: Initial display from *Sort Equivalent Fractions.*

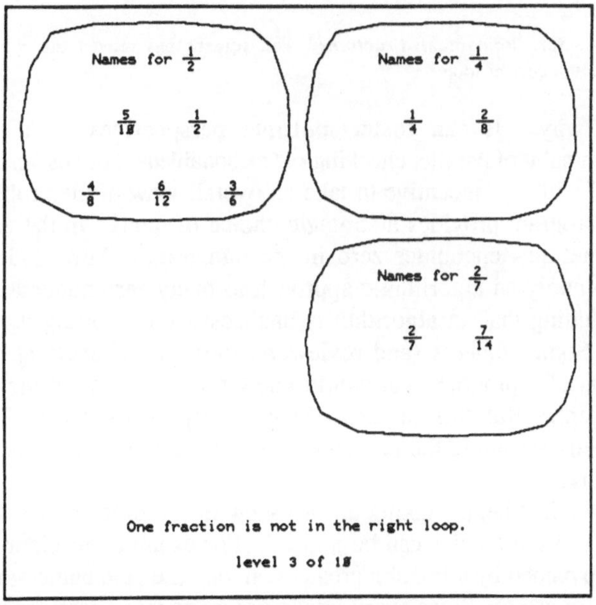

Figure 1b: *Sort Equivalent Fractions.* The student has sorted the fractions into the loops, and the computer has responded that one fraction is misplaced.

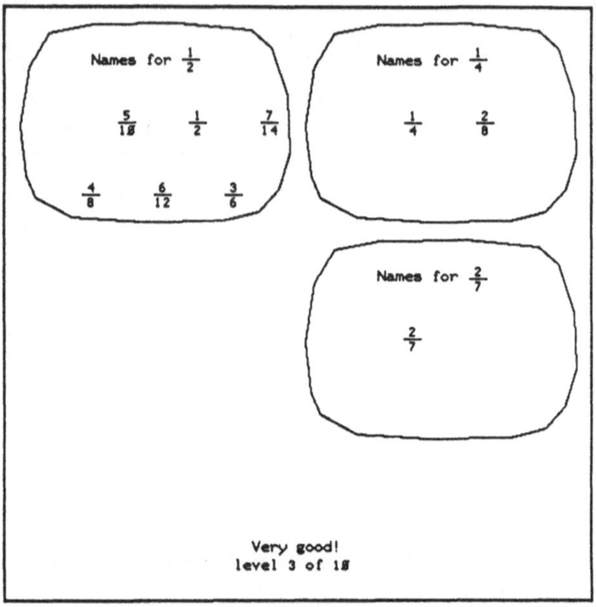

Figure 1c: *Sort Equivalent Fractions.* The student has moved the misplaced fraction to the correct loop.

mechanical way. It can foster multiple perspectives on the problem, encouraging a habit of parallel checking for reasonableness of answers.

Coupled with this incentive to take an overall view of the problem to spot errors, the program provides a strategic choice of items. In the early levels, students sometimes encounter zero in the numerator. Few students find it necessary to apply an algorithmic approach to many zero-numerator fractions before concluding that an algorithm is unnecessary for sorting the zeros into their loop. Some students (and reviewers, too) may chuckle at the lack of sophistication of a program that would know no better than to include such a trivial problem. But this apparent lack of sophistication has planted an important seed—scanning the problem for shortcuts can sometimes avoid a lot of tedious work!

Once a student begins taking an overview of the problem and looking for shortcuts, various strategies can be noticed. For example, in Figure 2 there is only one loop named by a fraction greater than one (i.e., the numerator is greater than the denominator). Since every fraction must go into a loop, no algorithmic checking is necessary to know that all of the fractions greater than one go into the $\frac{3}{2}$ loop. Although this is hardly an earthshaking mathematical revelation in itself, it can serve as a step toward more interesting ideas.

For example, factors and multiples become useful, too. If the denominator of a fraction is not divisible by 7, it does not belong in the $\frac{2}{7}$ loop. But anyone assuming that all fractions with denominators divisible by 7 necessarily do belong in the $\frac{2}{7}$ loop is in for a thought-provoking surprise. (This may have been the error in Figure 1b.) The intent is not to avoid the possibility of errors and misrules, but to treat them as conjectures to be tested and revised. Strategies are developed and refined with experience, and the insights gained in the process can be useful beyond the task at hand.

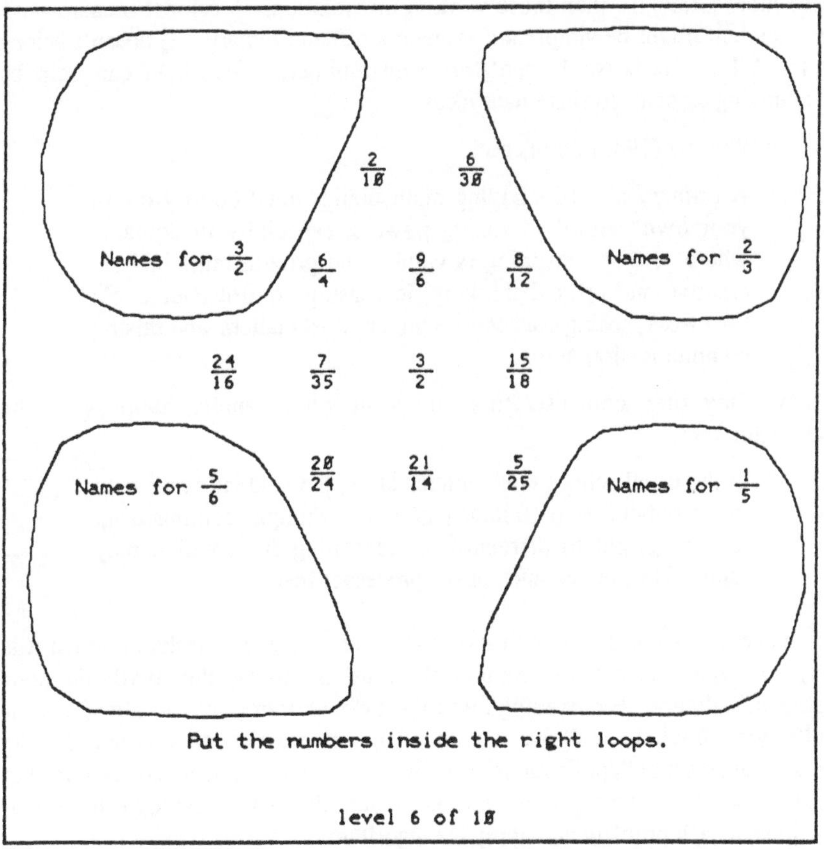

Figure 2: Sorting fractions into loops: just one loop has a value greater than 1.

Of course, different students notice different things. One student looking at the display in Figure 2 might begin by placing all of the fractions greater than 1 into the $\frac{3}{2}$ loop, while another might scan for multiples of numerators and denominators, and still another might notice that any fraction with the denominator more than twice the numerator must go into the $\frac{1}{5}$ loop (the only loop for fractions less than $\frac{1}{2}$). Students can make substantial progress on the problem using any combination of these strategies, but even taken together, these techniques are not sufficient to finish the problem. Something further is needed to decide whether $\frac{20}{24}$ belongs in the $\frac{5}{6}$ loop or the $\frac{2}{3}$ loop.

Students are generally eager to share their insights and discoveries, and students who interact with each other as well as with the computer are likely to learn more strategies than those working in isolation. A critical breakthrough for a student might be simply a classmate's offhand remark, "$\frac{15}{18}$ doesn't belong in the $\frac{2}{3}$ loop, because 15 isn't an even number." Teachers can help by encouraging students to share their ideas.

As Whitney (1986) points out,

> A primary aim of studying mathematics must be to grow in your own natural reasoning powers, especially in domains where precise reasoning is valid. The growth must include creative and critical thinking, increasing control over one's own work, seeing connections with related matters, and raising communication skills.

Whitney then contrasts this aim with what usually happens in the classroom:

> In the usual school mathematics class, the student's aim is to try to remember particular patterns of thought coming from reasoning, but to disregard the reasoning from which they came. Thus the essence of the process is lost.

Indeed, it is not uncommon to see students engaged in tasks in which it is easy to bypass any mathematical thinking by using the available non-mathematical cues. For example, when a textbook introduces an algorithm for multiplying fractions, follows it with a page of practice, then concludes the section with a set of "applications" (i.e., word problems), students do not need to make sense of the word problems to know that the task is to pick out the two fractions in each problem and apply the algorithm.

There are some subtle but critical differences between this sort of mathematics bypass and the following things that happen in using *Sort Equivalent Fractions*.

1. Students are turning an apparently routine exercise into a more varied one, rather than turning a supposedly problem-solving activity into a routine.
2. Any particular strategy is useful on only a small percentage of the problems, so flexibility and inventiveness are encouraged. In most problems there are some discriminations that are most easily approached with a more standard algorithm, and it is usually best to use a variety of strategies, including the algorithms commonly associated with equivalent fractions.
3. Students' strategies are based on the *sense* of the mathematics. For example, the ones mentioned above deal with the meaning and arithmetic of zero, the sense of fractions greater or less than one, and some ideas of multiples, factors, divisibility, and number theory. Not only are these ideas intimately associated with the sense of equivalent fractions, they have the potential for linking equivalent fractions with concepts used in other types of problems and laying intuitive groundwork for later work. Using several such ideas together can provide the student multiple perspectives on equivalent fractions and foster adaptive flexibility in approaching a problem—some bonuses not usually expected of an equivalent fractions drill.

Although students consider their strategies "tricks" to avoid the repeated application of a standard algorithm (which appears to be the purpose of the program), there is a striking contrast between the apparently intended activity and what students make of it. The process of scanning a problem for an easy solution, recognizing characteristics that can be used to shorten the problem, choosing strategies to minimize the work, and using various mathematical ideas is surely a richer experience than extensive practice of a specified procedure for comparing fractions.

To summarize, in addition to the obvious content objectives, the program is designed to foster:

1. Some strategies and mathematical ideas beyond the usual equivalent fractions material.
2. The important notion that it is worth stepping back for an overall view of the problem and choosing a strategy, instead of trudging through the exercise in a mechanical fashion.
3. An experience of success in approaching an apparently tedious and routine problem with some personally-found strategies.

EXAMPLE 2: DARTS

Description

Darts is an activity that allows the student to explore the placement of rational numbers on the number line. As shown in Figure 3, balloons are tied to a number line, and the student shoots darts at the balloons by estimating their positions on the line. Fractions, decimals, mixed numbers, and expressions using operations are all acceptable inputs.

For each number the student enters, a dart flies across the screen and lodges in the number line at the specified position, popping a balloon if it hits one. The student's input is shown beside each dart. The game continues until all of the balloons have been hit.

The program adjusts to student performance, moving to higher levels as the student gains expertise. For higher levels there is a larger distance displayed between integers and the balloons are smaller, so greater precision is required to hit the balloons.

Discussion

Classroom mathematics typically gives students little meaningful experience with estimation and approximation. Students spend nearly all of their time on problems that have one correct answer, and "close" does not count. This is, of course, not representative of the world outside of the classroom.

An important concept is that measurement is not exact, but rather an approximation that must be made accurately enough to accomplish the given purpose, within the limits of the tools at hand. The intent of *Darts* is not to have students name "exact" points on the number line, but rather to involve students in estimation. It is interesting that adults first encountering *Darts* often ask whether the darts must hit the balloons exactly in the center. Children, however, generally assume that the goal of the game is simply to hit the balloons, and that any number that accomplishes that purpose is as good as any other.

A subsequent imitation of *Darts* by other authors handles this idea quite differently. In their program, when a balloon is hit and the student's input is displayed, a second number pops out to the side where the balloon had been. This gives the impression that although the student's estimate hit the balloon, it was somehow not as correct as the "real" answer that was expected by the computer.

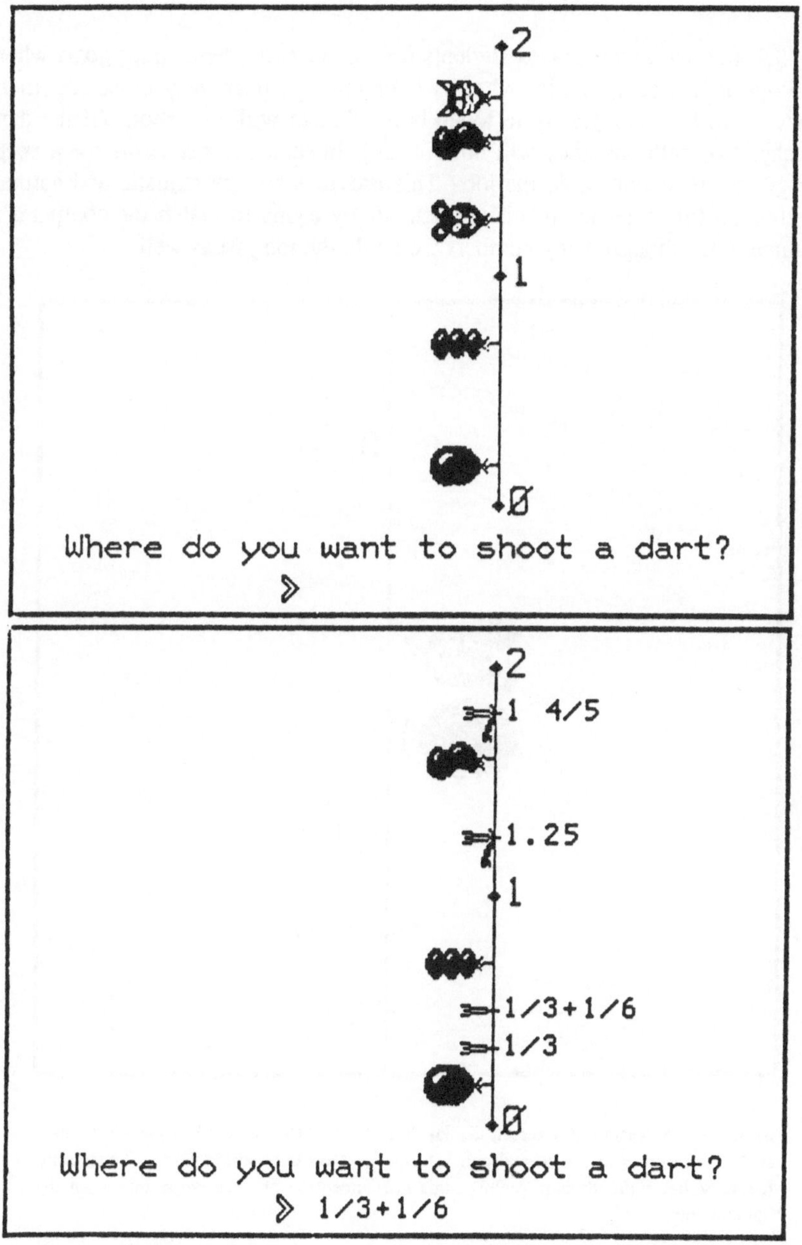

Figure 3: Displays from *Darts*. (top) The student shoots darts by telling where on the number line the darts should go. (bottom) Each dart flies across the screen and lodges in the number line, popping a balloon if it hits one. The student's input is shown beside each dart.

In contrast, *Darts* leaves students free to set more demanding goals when appropriate. For example, when two balloons appear very close together, students will sometimes try to touch both of them with one shot. (If the dart touches two balloons, they will both break.) In such cases,students see a *need* for greater precision to do the job. This provides a more realistic and natural motivation for increased precision than simply trying to match the computer's number, even though many numbers would do the job just as well.

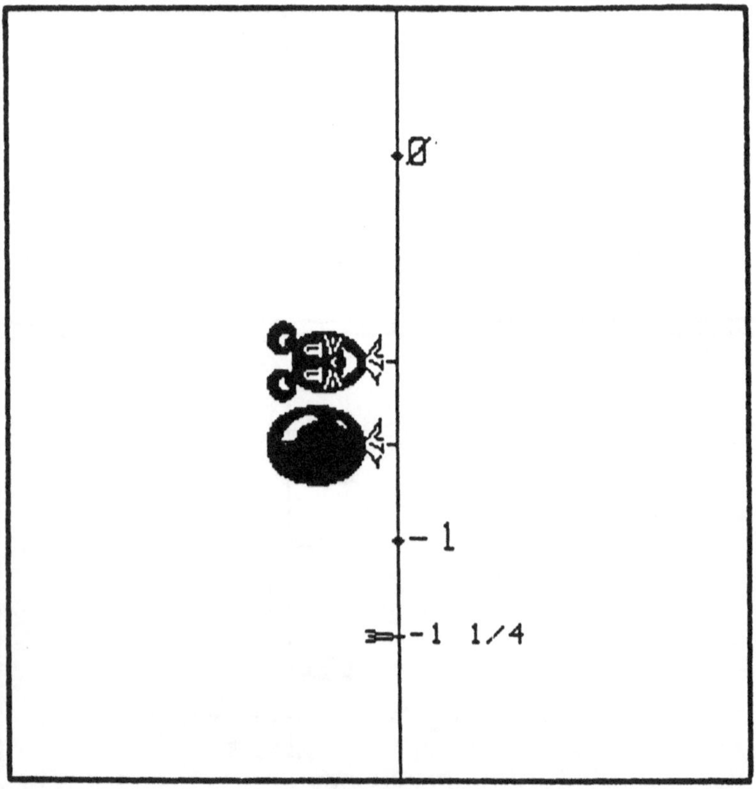

Figure 4: A portion of a screen display from Darts. The student has just shot a dart at $-1\frac{1}{4}$, expecting to hit the balloon just above -1 on the number line. The graphic feedback helps the student "debug" this misconception of negative numbers on the number line.

One critical difference between *Darts* and many math games written for computers is simply that *Darts* is actually a mathematical model. Many CAI games have a "theme" or motivation that is unrelated to the mathematics. *Darts*, however, was designed on the premise that mathematics is intrinsically interesting and useful. A student who shoots a dart is using mathematics in a much different sense from a student who writes the answer to a problem in order to see a clown jump up and down.

In *Darts*, the student's activity and the feedback offered by the computer both revolve around the mathematics. When a dart hits the number line, the student receives immediate visual feedback, not just whether the response was right or wrong, but also where the guessed number lies in relation to the target and previous guesses. For example, Figure 4 shows a common misconception about negative numbers. The student is assuming that $-1\frac{1}{4}$ is above (i.e., *larger* than) -1. Observation has shown that students frequently enter the lesson with this misconception and then quickly correct it.

The graphic, non-judgmental feedback simply reflects the student's input, essentially saying, "Here is what you did," and leaves the student to decide how it relates to what was intended.

Contrast this with possible attempts to provide verbal feedback. Something like "You hit one" or "You missed" offer nothing beyond the visually obvious. To offer anything potentially useful could require either guessing what the student had in mind or giving extensive information to choose from. For example, in Figure 5 the student has just shot a dart at $\frac{1}{3}$, and we could say something like the following:

> "If you were shooting at the round balloon, you probably forgot the whole number part. Since your previous shot was $\frac{1}{2}$, if you were shooting at the cat, you may think that larger denominators make larger fractions, which is not true. If you were shooting at the mouse balloon, you were still a little high—keep going."

Of course, we could think of additional possibilities, or we could ask the student to tell which balloon the dart was intended to hit, but it is still an awkward solution.

In fact, if we were watching the student, we might well find that *none* of our guesses have come close to what the student had in mind. He or she might have been simply asking "How big is $\frac{1}{3}$?" in order to use that distance to measure off $\frac{2}{3}$, $\frac{3}{3}$, $\frac{4}{3}$, to see which balloons might be hit by thirds. Indeed, this particular strategy was observed during the early classroom testing of Darts. The student would enter fractions of the form $\frac{1}{n}$, for increasing integer values of n. After each dart she would measure, with her fingers, the distance from 0 to $\frac{1}{n}$, then use that distance to mark off intervals up the number line, searching for balloons that could be hit with fractions of denominator *n*. She was using the computer to locate $\frac{1}{n}$, using the idea that $\frac{m}{n}$ corresponds to *m* intervals of size $\frac{1}{n}$, and defining a general algorithm for hitting all of the balloons.

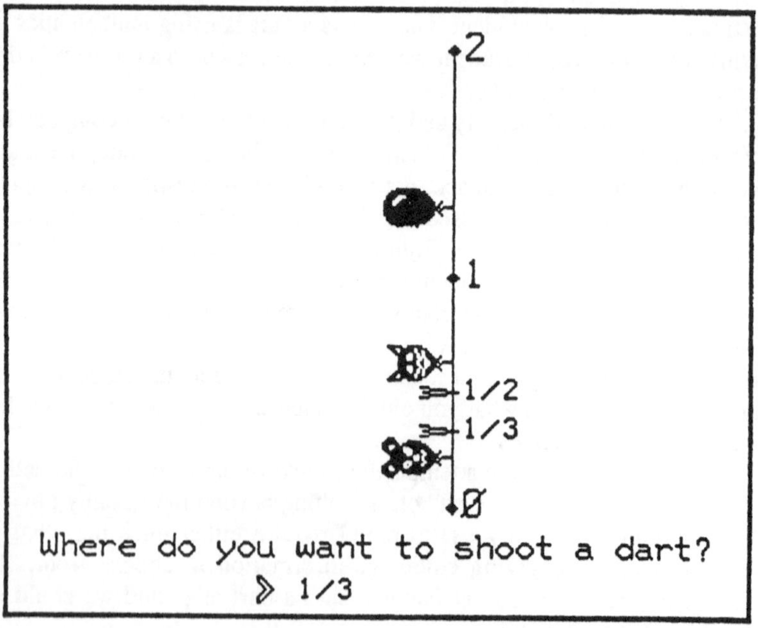

Figure 5: Screen display from *Darts*. The student has just shot a dart at $\frac{1}{3}$.

The point is that when giving feedback, even the basic assumption that the student was trying to hit a balloon may be wrong, and to respond as if the student *should* have been trying to hit a balloon could discourage some of the more interesting approaches that students have been observed to use.

Graphic feedback, reflecting the input and leaving the diagnostic thinking to the student, gives a wide bandwidth of information from which the student notices only what is relevant. That is, there is more information available than could reasonably be verbalized, including any number of unanticipated possibilities, but the student notices only that which relates to his/her particular intent.

If the student's guess is equivalent to a previous guess, both guesses are recorded, and the equivalence is shown, as illustrated in Figure 6. Students are frequently observed to briefly look startled, then say "Oh, right..." (*Darts* is often used with students who have not yet studied equivalent fractions, so it is reasonable for a student to be thinking in eighths and take a moment to recognize that $\frac{4}{8}$ really is the same as $\frac{1}{2}$.) This feedback essentially tells the student, "You used that number before, and here is what you called it last time."

The student is left to debug whatever strategy led to using the same number again with a different name.

The strategies students develop and use are numerous and varied. It is not uncommon to see a student measure the distance between integers by counting finger-widths, then use this same unit to measure the distance to each balloon. With this strategy students are frequently observed to use fractions like $\frac{9}{13}$ or $\frac{11}{17}$ with no trouble or confusion at all. One particularly careful student using this method was observed to count $12\frac{1}{2}$ finger widths between integers. She thought for a moment, then used 25ths, calling each half-finger width equal to $\frac{1}{25}$.

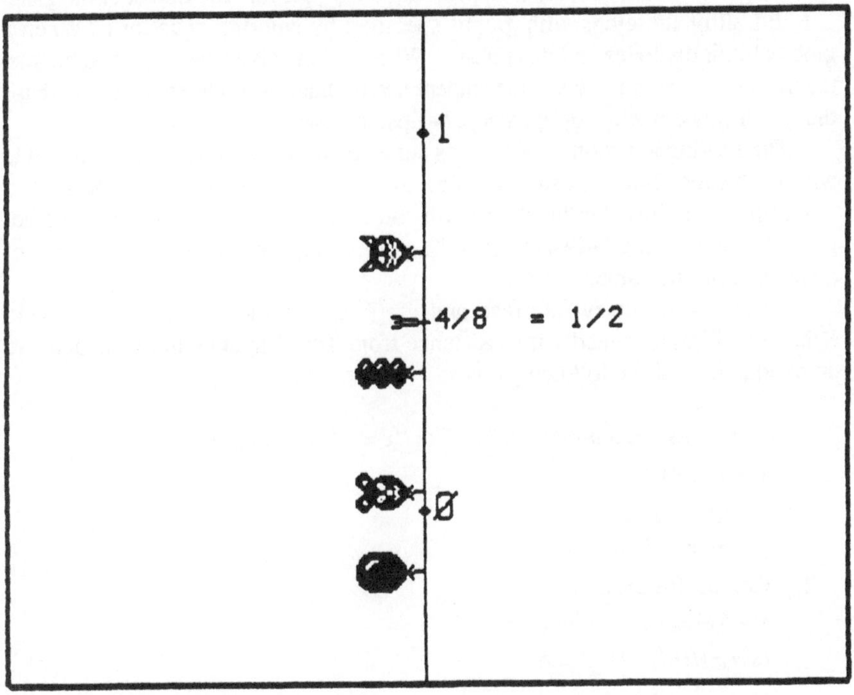

Figure 6: A portion of a screen display from *Darts*. The student has just shot a dart at $\frac{4}{8}$, only to find that $\frac{4}{8}$ is the same as $\frac{1}{2}$, where a previous dart had been shot. The lesson saves the student's previous shot and shows its equivalence with the later shot.

In applying their beginning knowledge of fractions to a *mathematically accurate* model like *Darts*, students who are beginning the study of fractions can discover and figure out ideas well beyond what is traditionally expected. They can also build a comfortable working familiarity with rational numbers that will be valuable in later work.

EXAMPLE 3: GREEN GLOBS

Description

Green Globs provides students an opportunity to use and further develop their knowledge of equations and graphs. The computer displays coordinate axes with 13 green globs scattered to appear randomly placed. The object of the game is to hit all of the globs with graphs specified by entering equations. When a glob is hit, it explodes and disappears. When a shot misses the expected targets, the display of the graph gives the student useful diagnostic information—perhaps the graph was too wide, or too steep, or upside down.

The scoring algorithm encourages students to hit as many globs as possible with each shot. For each shot, the first glob hit is worth one point, the second is worth two points, the third is worth four, and so on. For example, a five-glob shot will score 1+2+4+8+16 = 31 points. Figure 7 shows a sequence of displays from the game.

The equation entry interface and graphing routines, designed by David Kibbey and implemented with assistance from Tom Layman, allow students to enter equations of the following types:

1. Functions beginning with "y =" or "x =", for example:
   $y = x^2\text{-}3x\text{+}2$
   $x = (y\text{+}2)(y\text{-}1)3$
   $y = 3\text{+}x5\text{+}5/x\text{-}(x\text{-}1)3/(x^2\text{-}x)$
2. Conics, for example:
   $x^2\text{+}5y^2 = 30$
   $(x\text{-}4)^2/10\text{-}(y\text{+}2)^2/2 = 6$
   $x^2 = 12$
   $x(y\text{+}3) = 5$
3. Square root, absolute value, logarithmic, exponential, and trigonometric functions.

Eligible expressions are accepted in natural formats. For example, the program does not require "3*x," but accepts the usual "3x." Likewise it accepts "$\tan^2(y\text{-}\pi)$," rather than requiring something like "(tan(y-3.14))**2."

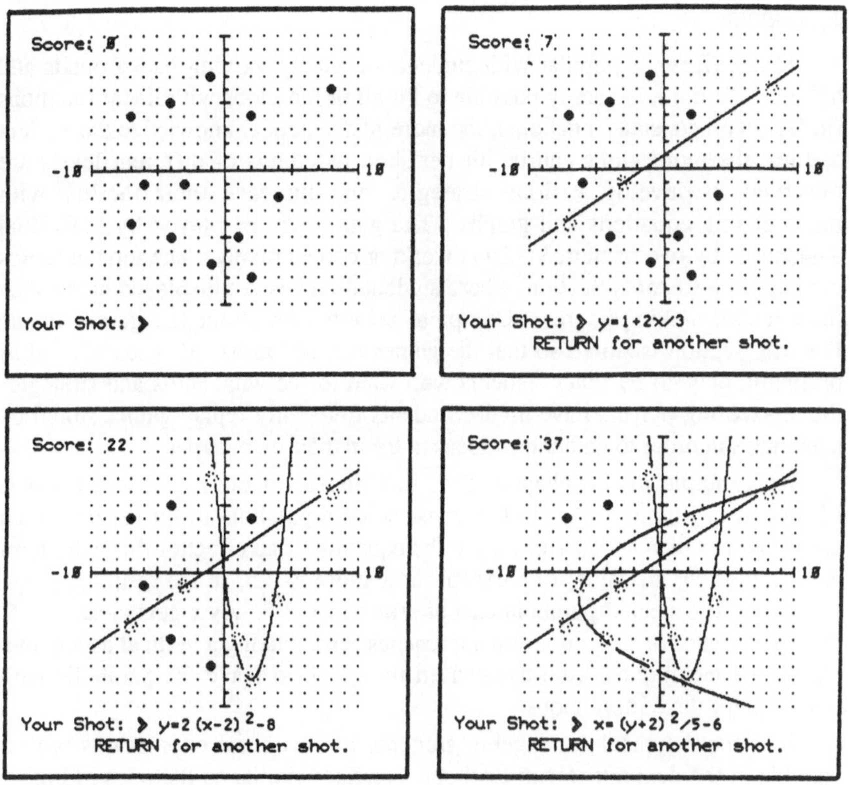

Figure 7: Sequential displays from a game of *Green Globs.* The student enters equations, which are graphed by the computer. The green globs explode as they are hit by the graphs. Shown is the initial display of thirteen globs, followed by the student's first three shots.

In addition, the program provides appropriate assistance with syntax conventions, such as parentheses around a function argument. For example, when a student types "cos" or any other recognized function, the program expects the next keypress to be either the exponent key or a left parenthesis to begin a function argument. If the student begins to type an argument without parentheses, the program not only reminds the student that the function argument must be enclosed in parentheses, the program inserts the appropriate left parenthesis and follows it with the student's entry.

Discussion

Green Globs is popular with students of widely varying backgrounds and abilities. While it is clearly possible to hit all of the globs with linear functions (in fact, with constant functions), the more mathematical knowledge the student applies, the more globs can be hit per shot. Students of different levels are observed to develop various strategies and increase their facility with manipulating equations and graphs. The game may be played by individual students or by two or more students working cooperatively. The top ten scores are kept in a Records Section, where students' names are displayed along with their record-making scores. Complete information about the games in the Records Section is stored so that the games can be "replayed" (i.e., viewed as originally played) by other students who want to see what shots and strategies the top-scoring players have used. Students frequently replay games stored by classmates in order to gather new ideas to try in their own games.

An example of the elegant ideas that appear in the Records Section is illustrated in Figure 8. Jason has constructed a parabola to hit several green globs, but has then added $1/(x\text{-}3.5)$ to the equation. The effect of this extra term is negligible for all values of x except those close to 3.5, so the resulting graph is nearly the expected parabola except around $x = 3.5$. As x gets close to 3.5, the denominator of the extra term approaches zero, making a vertical asymptote. Using this technique, Jason has caused the graph to leave the parabolic path briefly to hit three more globs.

It is more typical for algebra students to encounter expressions with a variable in the denominator in textbook exercises similar to the ones in Figure 9. The student is asked to tell for what value of the variable each expression is undefined. Following the example provided, the student figures out for what value of the variable each denominator is zero and records that value as the answer.

Contrast the student's experience in Figure 9 with that in Figure 8. The mathematical content is similar—when the denominator is zero, the function is undefined. But instead of simply telling where a given function is undefined, Jason has decided where he wants a discontinuity in the function, he has decided how to make that happen, and he has used it to accomplish something important to him. In addition, he is not concerned only with one particular x-value (where the function is undefined), but with the behavior of the *entire function*. This puts the discontinuity into a meaningful context, since the function gets very large in a positive direction on one side of the particular x-value, and very large in a negative direction on the other side of that x-value.

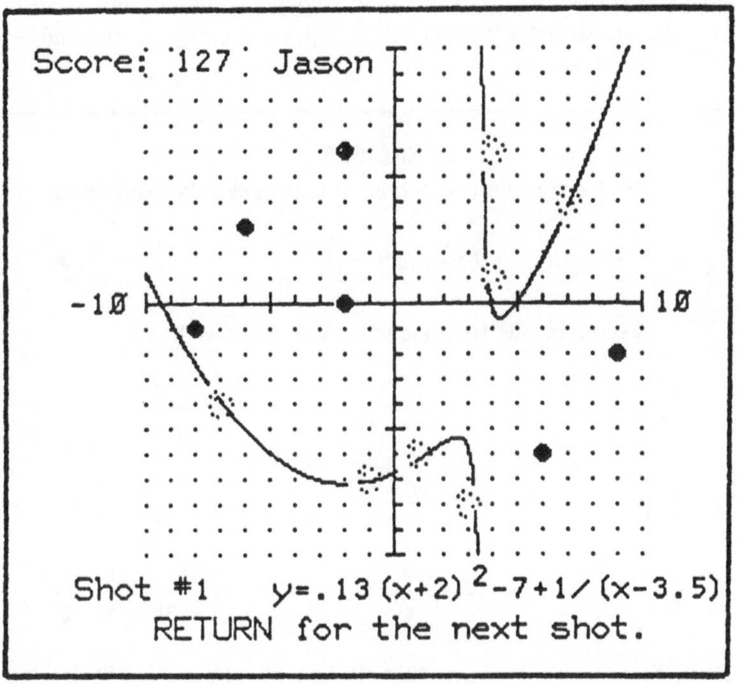

Figure 8: Screen display of a game stored in the *Green Globs* Records Section. The student's name is shown at the top of the screen. Jason has constructed a parabola to hit several green globs, but has then added $1/(x\text{-}3.5)$ to the function in order capture three more globs.

And finally, between Figure 8 and Figure 9, is there any doubt which one the student would consider an accomplishment worth saving to show to classmates, or which one the other students would want to analyze for ideas to use themselves?

Less spectacular, but no less important, are advances made, for example, by ninth grade general mathematics classes. Using just constant functions like $x = 4$ or $y = -2$, their initial strategy is simply to look for pairs of globs on a horizontal or vertical line, being careful not to hit any of these globs singly from the other direction. These students soon notice the more interesting graphs in the algebra students' games and begin replaying those games in order to find out how to make lines with different slopes, and curves, too. Of course, the equations copied from other games are not immediately useful in their own games, because the globs are placed differently. Hence, it is necessary to experiment to find out which features of the equations affect which features of the graphs. It is fascinating to see these students, generally not at all fond of mathematics, so strongly motivated to work on concepts beyond what is expected in their classwork.

EXERCISES

State the value for which each expression is undefined.

Example: $\frac{3y}{18 + 3y}$

Solution: - 6, because when y = - 6, 18 + 3y = 0

1. $\frac{5}{6m}$	5. $\frac{2k}{3k - 12}$	9. $\frac{4}{x^2 - 4}$
2. $\frac{2}{b - 4}$	6. $\frac{3n + 4}{3n + 4}$	10. $\frac{m - 3}{5m + 10}$
3. $\frac{-7}{5t}$	7. $\frac{z + 2}{z^2}$	11. $\frac{2t}{3t^2 - 5t - 2}$
4. $\frac{2x}{8 + 2x}$	8. $\frac{4y + 10}{5 - 6y}$	12. $\frac{7a}{a^2 + 8a + 12}$

Figure 9: Typical textbook exercises for rational expressions.

The scoring algorithm for *Green Globs* helps maintain interest over a wide range of performance by placing a high premium on figuring out how to hit *one more glob* on a given shot. On any one shot, the first glob hit is worth one point, the second is worth two points, the third is worth four, and so on. So, for example, a four-glob shot scores a total of 15 points, but a five-glob shot scores 31 points. Thus, the novice is well rewarded for hitting three globs on a shot instead of two, as is the expert for hitting seven instead of six.

Green Globs provides an appropriate challenge to a wide range of participants without any special adjustments for individual students—all are treated the same. Because students automatically set their own goals, the only criterion for judging the correctness of a student's input is whether it did what the student wanted it to.

The program accommodates many levels and styles, but without the sophisticated (and sometimes inadequate or inappropriate) branching frequently employed for this purpose. Note, too, that in *Green Globs* the students have extensive control over the activity and experience in a much more fundamental way than if they were simply offered a series of explicit choices by the program.

Another interesting and popular technique uses factored polynomials. As shown in Figure 10, for example, the graph $y = (x+6)(x-1)(x-7)$ can be constructed to cross the x-axis at -6, 1, and 7. Using the coordinates of a target glob not on the x-axis, students can find an appropriate factor to adjust the graph to make it hit the desired globs. Notice, however, that this technique is *not* sufficient to hit all of the globs with one shot. The catch is that the space available for typing the equation is limited by the edge of the screen. Only about four or five such factors will fit. Facing this limitation, students are observed to apply the identity $(x+a)(x-a) = x^2-a^2$ to shorten the equation and make room for more factors. For example, $(x+3)(x-3)$ can be replaced by x^2-9. This technique spreads quickly among students once it has been discovered.

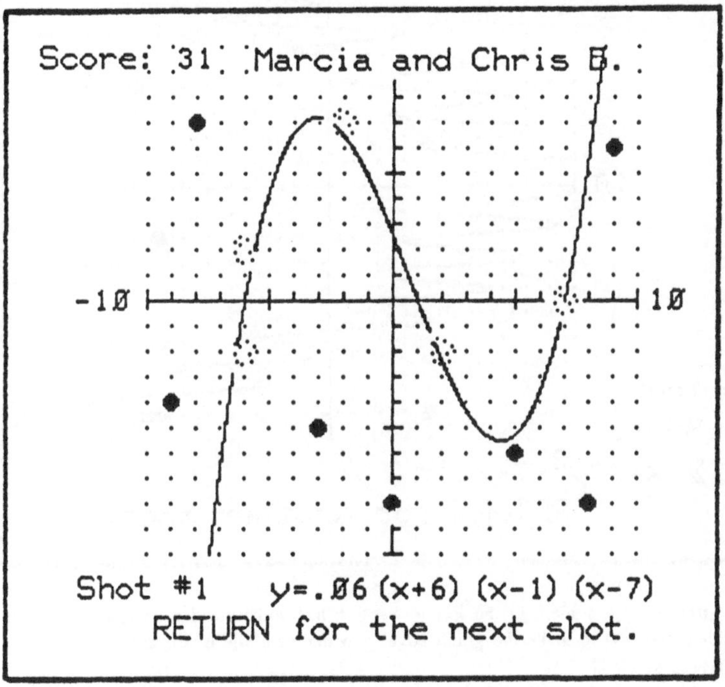

Figure 10: Using a factored polynomial, Marcia and Chris have constructed a function to cross the x-axis at three chosen points.

The traditional algebra curriculum includes extensive attention to the factoring of trinomials (expressions of the form ax^2+bx+c), which, as Usiskin (1980) points out, is time-consuming and of little practical value. The technique is applicable only to carefully chosen expressions with integer roots, and it does not generalize well to polynomials of degree greater than two. In contrast, when students build a function *from* the roots, choosing a factor for each place they want the graph to cross the axis, they are applying the important *principles* involved in factoring, but without the tedious *manipulations* that often obscure the sense of the mathematics. For the graph to cross the axis, the function value must be zero. It can be made zero when $x=a$ by including a factor of $(x-a)$, and when any factor is zero, the function is zero.

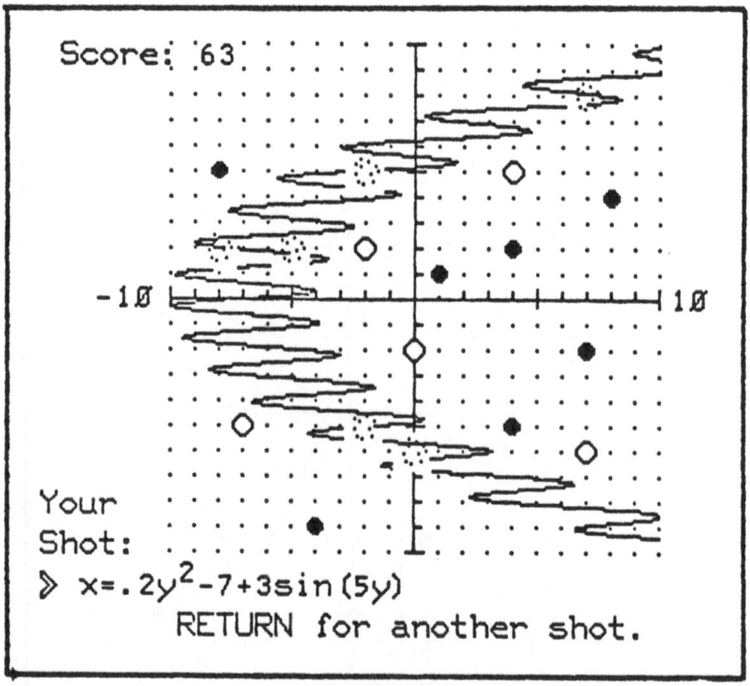

Figure 11: A student in the Expert Section has constructed a parabola and then added 3sin(5y) to make the graph cover a wider path while still avoiding the shot absorbers.

Trigonometric functions are not allowed in the *Green Globs* Novice Section because a function like $y=10\sin(10x)$ could easily hit all of the globs with one shot. In the Expert Section students can use trigonometric functions, but must avoid the five "shot absorbers" scattered among the globs. Figure 11 shows a clever use of a trigonometric function in the Expert Section. The student has constructed a parabola and then added 3sin(5*y*) to make the graph cover a wider path, while still avoiding the shot absorbers.

As is evident from the examples given above, the sharing of ideas through games stored in the Records Section exposes students to a variety of ideas and strategies. More specifically, it exposes them to interesting and creative ideas *invented by their classmates.*

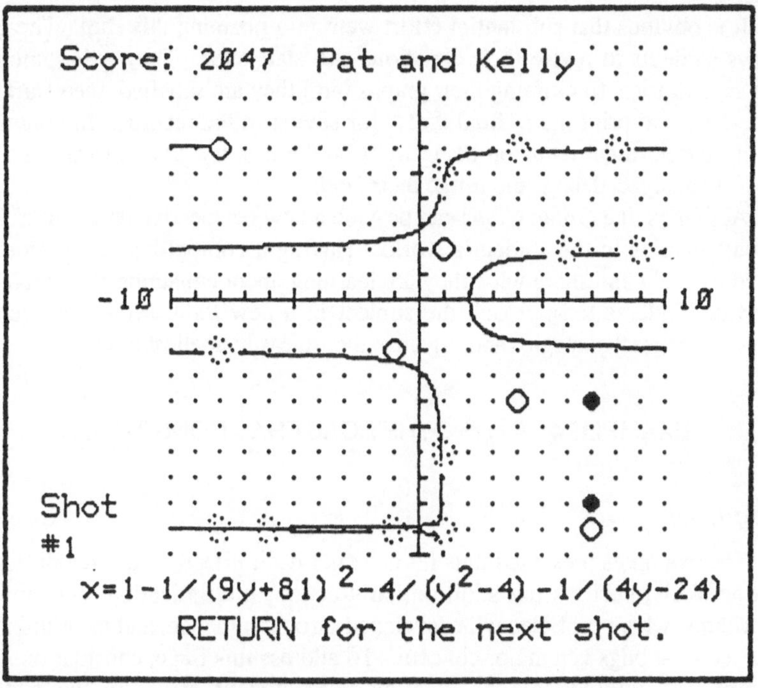

Figure 12: Two students in the Expert Section have combined various techniques to hit eleven globs with one shot.

A not-uncommon attitude is that mathematics is a dry, dull subject, completed long ago, and stored in books. When a student encounters a creative use of mathematics developed by a classmate, it can present not only a new idea, but a new perspective. The student may realize, "Mathematics can be used in interesting and creative ways—not just by ancient people I don't know, but by my classmates, and by *me*." The goal is to foster a rich environment of mathematical *thinking*, *investigation*, and *exchange of ideas*. Figure 12 illustrates the use of a combination of techniques gathered from this rich exchange of ideas. Starting with the vertical line $x=1$, these two students have added three rational terms, using the technique shown in Figure 8. They have squared the first denominator to make both branches of the graph go the same direction, thus hitting globs at (-1,-9), (-6,-9), and (-8,-9) while avoiding a shot absorber at (7,-9). In the second rational term they have combined factors (y-2) and (y+2) into (y^2-4) to save space and cause two discontinuities with one term. In addition, they have carefully chosen their coefficients to cause the "corners" of their graph to be more nearly square near (1,-9), where there was a glob to hit, and more rounded near (1,2) and (-1,-2), where shot absorbers needed to be avoided.

It is obvious that substantial effort went into planning this shot. The game allows students to revise their equations and start over. They will sometimes take several tries, fine-tuning their graphs until they are satisfied, then start their game over and print their "final draft" for saving in the records. In contrast to the more traditional focus on being right on the first try, this rewards students' efforts to analyze, debug, and refine their work.

Activities like *Green Globs* can provide a new perspective on the usefulness of mathematics in the student's world. Having a compelling environment in which to apply and share what they are learning about equations and graphs can motivate students to approach the subject in a new light, seeing the need to formulate general strategies and organize their ideas in applicable ways.

EXAMPLE 4: A HYPOTHETICAL FRACTIONS TUTOR

Description

The examples presented thus far have not dealt directly with the mastery of routine skills, such as the addition, subtraction, multiplication, and division algorithms, where proficiency is developed through practice, and the elimination of procedural bugs is a major concern. To address this issue, consider one final example, a hypothetical one, dealing with student errors in the addition algorithm for fractions.

Suppose a tutor (either human or computer) presents the problem: $\frac{1}{2} + \frac{3}{4}$, and receives from the student the answer: $\frac{2}{3}$.

Examining the student's work, the tutor might recognize the common bug of adding both numerators and denominators, as shown in Figure 13. The tutor could remind the student that when adding fractions, we first find a common denominator, then add only the numerators. The student could correct the error and then practice some more problems using the proper algorithm.

A more astute tutor might also note that this particular student error could be due to a confusion between the addition and multiplication algorithms, since the multiplication algorithm for fractions is analogous to this student's incorrect addition method (performing the specified operation on the numerators and on the denominators). After a quick check of the records to verify that this student has covered multiplication as well as addition, the tutor could point out the difference between the two algorithms and have the student practice some multiplication, too, coaching as necessary until the student exhibits proficiency in distinguishing the two operations and correctly performing the appropriate algorithm for each case.

$$\frac{1}{2}+\frac{3}{4}=\frac{1+3}{2+4}=\frac{4}{6}=\frac{2}{3}$$

Figure 13: A common error in adding fractions. The student has added the numerators, added the denominators, and reduced the result.

The above scenario requires some sophistication and diagnostic capability on the part of the tutor. The tutor's coaching not only improves the student's performance with a particular algorithm, it also deals with a likely source of confusion and reviews a related algorithm. However, it ignores a fundamental problem: that a student at this level of learning about fractions would encounter

$$\frac{1}{2}+\frac{3}{4}$$

and respond with "$\frac{2}{3}$" without seeing any reason to question that response.

Notice that in the interaction described above:

1. There is no evident expectation on the part of either the tutor or the student that the task should have any meaning in terms of the size of the particular quantities named. Addition of fractions is treated only as an abstract exercise in symbol manipulation.
2. The student appears helpless to make any judgment about the correctness of the answer, relying entirely on the tutor to say whether or not the response is correct and to instruct the student in a procedure to fix it. Further, when a new answer is produced, the student is still dependent on the tutor to say whether it is any more appropriate than the previous one.

Discussion: Improving the Tutor

How can the tutor be improved to address this apparent lack of sense and the resultant student helplessness?

It is unlikely that a student at this level really lacks any idea of how big $\frac{1}{2}$, $\frac{2}{3}$, or $\frac{3}{4}$ may be, if such quantities arise in a meaningful context. More likely, the student has developed no habit of making sense of arithmetic problems and no facility for checking answers for reasonableness.

Hence, retreating to remedial work on the size of simple fractions is not likely to be an appropriate solution. Returning to models or manipulatives to illustrate the meaning of the operation may have some merit, but this approach is often as mechanical as the algorithm itself, and it can be too cumbersome for students to find it convenient for routine use. Other procedures for verifying answers, for example subtracting one addend from the sum to verify that the result is the other addend, are tedious and prone to the same errors as the initial problem. These sorts of remediation and error detection procedures commonly focus on finding an exact answer, as if one can have no notion of what the result will be until the required procedure has been completed.

In contrast, what is needed here is a more informal, qualitative, number-sense idea of assessing reasonability, and habit of using that sense. Why struggle through formal procedures when a quick look is sufficient? For example, given the answer $\frac{2}{3}$ to the above problem, it is easy to observe that the proposed sum is less than one of the addends. Given no negative addends, it is clear that the proposed answer is too small. Or one might note that $\frac{1}{2} + \frac{3}{4}$ is bigger than $\frac{1}{2} + \frac{1}{2}$, so the answer must be greater than 1.

Given any proposed answer, it is easy to make various informal checks to decide whether it is within reasonable bounds. If the proposed answer had been larger, say 3, then different reasoning would be appropriate, perhaps finding an upper bound rather than a lower bound: because both addends are less than 1, their sum must be less than 2. Or, had the proposed answer been $1\frac{1}{4}$, one might first note that it is not obviously too large or too small, then reason informally that $\frac{1}{2} + \frac{3}{4}$ is $\frac{1}{4}$ more than $\frac{1}{2} + \frac{1}{2}$, so $1\frac{1}{4}$ is indeed the correct answer. A problem as simple as $\frac{1}{2} + \frac{3}{4}$ could have been approached in this informal way to begin with, bypassing the formal algorithm altogether.

Notice that while assessing the reasonableness of possible answers, we are exercising important mathematical reasoning skills and laying a foundation for conceptualizing and using mathematical arguments, an important aspect of what Schoenfeld (1988) refers to as "thinking mathematically." Detecting algorithmic errors provides a convenient vehicle for encouraging this sort of reasoning, since algorithmic errors often produce very inappropriate answers which are easy to spot with a few common sense checks. Procedural errors in arithmetic do not routinely lead to answers that are very close to correct, especially if the procedure is applied to a variety of problems.

There are some similarities between the mathematical reasoning skills developing here and the strategies mentioned earlier in *Sort Equivalent Fractions*. In both cases students draw upon a variety of ideas, choosing methods appropriate for the given situation. The strategies are based on the sense of the mathematics, not on complicated, meaningless procedures, and different students will take different approaches. Hence, students who interact with each other, as well as with the tutor, may develop and use more strategies than those working alone.

In addition to performing error diagnosis and algorithmic coaching procedures, a good arithmetic tutor should help students develop a *qualitative sense* of mathematics, a *variety* of useful techniques, and a *flexible* approach to problems. Such a tutor might include the following sorts of procedures in its repertoire:

1. Check for evidence of use of formal algorithms on problems that clearly do not warrant it. For example, a good tutor encountering

$$\frac{1}{2} + \frac{1}{2} = \frac{2}{4} = \frac{1}{2}$$

should recognize the evident procedural error (adding numerators and denominators, as in Figure 13), but instead of proceeding to review the algorithm, the tutor should address the bigger problem: that a student looking at $\frac{1}{2} + \frac{1}{2}$ *would choose to use a formal algorithm at all* and would have no more sense of the problem than to propose $\frac{1}{2}$ as an answer. It is not appropriate to treat such a response as simply a procedural error to be remedied by review of the algorithm.

2. Help students develop a basic facility for estimating answers. Given a problem, students could find convenient upper and lower bounds for the answer. If there is any difficulty with this, the tutor could propose possibilities for consideration, perhaps starting with suggestions quite obviously too large or too small. For example, "Could the answer be fifty? Could it be zero? Is it bigger than ten? Suppose I say the answer is two—what do you think?" Involving several students in the discussion could make a richer experience, as different students offer insights and reasons for accepting or rejecting particular choices.

The *primary* intent here is to develop a habit of recognizing answers that are too large or too small. It is reasonable to expect any student at this level to master this skill. In addition, carefully chosen suggestions and questions could help some students develop more sophisticated insights. For example, in rejecting a particular suggested integer value for an answer, one student might say it is too large, while another student might assert that the given problem could not have an integer solution "because when you add halves and thirds, there will always be some fraction left over." This student could be encouraged to investigate the more general question of what conditions must be met in order for a sum of fractions to be an integer. If this pursuit proves interesting, the tutor could suggest that someone investigate whether *squaring* a fraction can produce an integer. From here it is a small step for a student to show that if an integer is not a perfect square, then its square root cannot be expressed as a rational number.

This is not to suggest that students learning to add and multiply fractions should necessarily address the irrationality of the square root of two. Rather, it is intended to illustrate *one* possible path of student inquiry which could be fostered by a tutor that is:

a. aware of a wealth of conceptual connections between the present topic and other, perhaps more advanced, topics,
b. equipped to recognize unexpected, but promising, student insights, and
c. able to perceive and exploit opportunities to encourage students to apply their insights to related questions of appropriate complexity and interest for the particular student(s) involved.

What might emerge from any particular tutoring session depends upon what ideas students suggest in approaching the task at hand. A good tutor needs to help students develop *their own* reasoning and solution paths, and possibly even their own questions to investigate.

3. Coach students to detect and correct errors, applying effective tools for debugging defective algorithms. As more routine calculation is taken over by computers, facility with judging results and debugging algorithms may be more important skills than performing calculations. If an algorithm produces an unreasonable answer, the student could be asked to try the algorithm on a "transparent" problem (one like $\frac{1}{2} + \frac{1}{4}$, where the solution is obvious, and bugs may be easy to detect). The tutor might continue the dialogue along the following line: "Does your algorithm work? What does not make sense about it? Draw a picture and relate what your algorithm does to what is in the picture. Fix your algorithm. Try it on a different transparent problem. Does it work? Now go back to the original problem. Again, is your answer reasonable?" The tutor's suggestions here are not unlike heuristics proposed by Polya (1957).

Rules with Meaning

Of course, any procedural error in arithmetic is probably more efficiently remedied, in the short term, by reviewing the appropriate rule and practicing some problems, as was done by the hypothetical fractions tutor presented above. However, there are important issues to consider beyond the efficiency of correcting a particular procedural error.

Anyone who has faced a class of middle school students after summer vacation (or even after a chapter on a different topic) knows the difficulty of fractions algorithms surviving intact without regular use. Students usually recall many of the procedures associated with fractions: finding a common denominator, converting mixed numbers to improper fractions, cross-multiplying, inverting one of the fractions, performing the designated operation on some combination of the numerators and denominators, etc. What particular combination of procedures is necessary for a given operation is not so clearly remembered, and once a combination has been tried, there is little notion of how to tell whether the answer is reasonable. Students usually require a review of the algorithm and an example to follow.

In the long run, training students for *retention* of rote procedures seems less useful than building skills for *reconstruction* of procedures when needed. Certainly reconstruction skills are more generally useful in approaching new problems, extending algorithms to new domains, or making a reasonable attempt at problems for which an appropriate algorithm is not apparent.

Mathematics is all too often treated as simply a set of rules and algorithms to be practiced to proficiency. Note, however, that this is not an argument against algorithms and procedures. On the contrary, it is a plea for a more insightful perspective on the role and importance of algorithms in mathematics, countering the common notion that they are tedious, meaningless classroom drudgery. Students should achieve not just algorithmic proficiency, but also appropriate perspectives on the power, use, and limitations of algorithms, not studied as a list of features, but experienced as reality. Such perspectives could include:

1. Formal algorithms are a convenience. People invent them to help with complex problems and facilitate routine operations. (They are also useful for telling a computer how to do something.)
2. Some problems do not require the use of a formal algorithm. It is a good idea to assess each problem and decide how to approach it efficiently.
3. It is not necessarily more accurate or better to use a formal algorithm. In fact, automatically applying a multi-step formal algorithm without assessing the problem for more direct solutions can waste time and effort, as well as increase the risk of procedural errors.
4. Formal algorithms may not keep the sense of the problem in mind, and hence, can necessitate checking answers for reasonability. It may be necessary to look for errors or debug a faulty algorithm.
5. Algorithms can be tested or debugged by trying them on simple problems where it is easy to make sense of the procedure. This can be useful when an algorithm has been confused or partially forgotten.

Tutors that treat student errors simply as procedural bugs, which can be corrected by review of the algorithm and further practice, neglect valuable opportunities to develop important mathematical reasoning skills and leave students with a very limiting perspective of the nature of mathematics. Mathematics can be presented as a mysterious chore, or it can be an expression of reality, a language for convenient manipulation of complex models, and a rich, dynamic, useful tool.

SUMMARY AND CONCLUSION

This chapter has illustrated, by example, some design goals and instructional techniques devised and used during a fifteen-year software development and implementation effort for mathematics instruction. The common thread uniting the various individual programs is not a similarity of screen display, a standard interaction format, or even an adherence to a particular instructional style, but rather a notion of what sort of cognitive experiences a student should have in learning about the subject matter.

The examples presented exhibit a variety of instructional strategies and some common characteristics as well. For example, the style of feedback in response to student errors varies substantially from one program to another, yet the ultimate intent of the feedback is consistent: to encourage students to become active, creative, independent learners.

When the program model is itself a direct expression of the mathematical reality, as in *Darts* and *Green Globs*, student manipulation of the model can result in direct *graphic* feedback, reflecting the student's input in the context of the mathematical model. This wide-bandwidth, visual feedback provides more information than could reasonably be verbalized, but students notice only those aspects which relate to their current intent. Comparing their results with what they intended, students make successive tries, using the graphic feedback diagnostically with each iteration. Verbal feedback is used in a secondary capacity, dealing with cases where the specified dart or graph is off the screen, where a syntax error prevents processing of an input, and other instances not conveniently covered by the graphic feedback.

In contrast, the primary error feedback in *Sort Equivalent Fractions* is *verbal*, informing the student how many fractions are in the wrong loops. Yet this program, too, leaves the diagnostic thinking to the student. Instead of directly presenting strategies for the student to use, the computer takes a more subtle, indirect approach. Using problems arranged to help students realize that a rote procedural approach is not always best, the program provides students ample opportunities to "outsmart" the computer by devising strategies to avoid tedious routine.

In contrast to both of these styles, the feedback advocated for improving the hypothetical fractions tutor includes *direct coaching* in the use of particular strategies to improve performance on computational problems. Although this approach lacks the subtlety of the previous example, the suggested tutoring techniques carefully avoid building dependence on an authority to judge correctness of a solution and prescribe corrective measures. Emphasis is, rather, on coaching students in the sorts of mathematical reasoning, error detection, diagnostic, and debugging skills necessary to become independent learners. The traditional focus on *retention* is replaced by a focus on *reconstruction* skills.

Although the examples exhibit a variety of styles, a common goal is to encourage students to become active, creative, independent learners. To this end, the programs reduce the emphasis on repetition of algorithms and procedures in favor of more attention to analyzing problems and planning strategies. Rather than directly telling students what they are to learn, identifying errors, and suggesting how to correct them, these programs pose challenges and require students to do much of the development of strategies and techniques. It is important for students to gain confidence in their *own* abilities to analyze a problem and devise an appropriate strategy.

All of the examples emphasize the development of student strategies, but the techniques students use in *Green Globs* are probably the most sophisticated, sometimes requiring considerable effort in working out a problem. Further, the product of this effort can often be visually quite impressive and not easily communicated without graphics. Hence, in such a program it can be especially important, both motivationally and educationally, to provide a facility for storing students' winning strategies for others to see.

The programs do not *require* teacher involvement or classmate interaction. However, they are most effectively used in conjunction with related classroom activities and a teacher who encourages active discussion among students about their ideas and strategies in approaching the programs. An emphasis on learning from classmates can expose students to a variety of ideas and encourage them to develop their own approaches and strategies, rather than relying entirely on procedures from the textbook. This can be facilitated by a teacher who takes a role similar to that advocated for the fractions tutor, noting student insights and suggesting appropriate related questions to investigate.

In conclusion, the following suggestions are offered for the design of instructional materials in general.

1. *Design instruction around the subject matter.* Although it is not unusual for instructional designers to begin with a format or set of design rules and attempt to fit the subject matter into them, a richer experience can be achieved by designing instruction around the inherently interesting and important characteristics of the subject matter. This approach, of course, requires a variety of design techniques and an adequate knowledge of the subject matter, probably including an awareness of a wealth of conceptual interconnections and interesting related ideas.

2. *Exhibit a genuine enthusiasm for both the subject matter and the students.* Instructional materials should reflect the richness of an interesting and dynamic subject matter as well as an appreciation and respect for the student's potential to devise original and creative solutions. It is important to recognize insights of students at all ability levels and to encourage investigation of ideas which students consider their own. Extensive work with students during the development of materials can be beneficial in achieving this goal.
3. *Give careful attention to the student's experience beyond the immediate content objectives.* Learning takes place on many levels. Instructional methods impact not only students' mastery of information and skills, but also their attitudes and perspectives. It may be a simple matter to effectively train students to perform a particular procedure (and they may even enjoy the experience), but if at the same time they learn that the subject matter in general is a disjoint collection of meaningless routines, this is hardly an educational victory. Instruction should focus not only on subject matter content, but on the sorts of experiences students need in order to become creative, involved, independent learners.

ACKNOWLEDGEMENTS

The work reported on in this chapter was done while the author was at the Computer-Based Education Research Laboratory at the University of Illinois, Urbana-Champaign. The programs presented here were developed by Sharon Dugdale and David Kibbey with support from the National Science Foundation, US NSF C-723 and NSF-SED80-12449. Any views expressed herein are those of the author and do not necessarily reflect the views of the National Science Foundation.

REFERENCES

Cohen, D., & Glynn, G. (1974, June). *Description of graphing strand lessons.* Urbana, IL: University of Illinois, Computer-based Education Research Laboratory, CERL Publications.

Dugdale, S. (1979, October). *Using the computer to foster creative interaction among students.* Urbana, IL: University of Illinois, Computer-based Education Research Laboratory, CERL Publications.

Dugdale, S. (1982, March). Green globs: A microcomputer application for graphing of equations. *Mathematics Teacher.*

Dugdale, S. (1986-87). Pathfinder: A microcomputer experience in interpreting graphs. *Journal of Educational Technology Systems*, **15** (3), 259-280.

Dugdale, S., & Kibbey, D. (1980). *The fractions curriculum of the PLATO elementary school mathematics project.* (2d Ed.). Urbana, IL: University of Illinois, Computer-based Education Research Laboratory, CERL Publications.

Dugdale S., & Kibbey, D. (1983, June). *Prototype microcomputer courseware for teaching high school algebra.* Final Report to the National Science Foundation, SED80-12449.

Dugdale S., & Kibbey, D. (1983). *Graphing equations.* Iowa City, IA: Conduit.

Dugdale S., & Kibbey, D. (1983). *Interpreting graphs.* Iowa City, IA: Conduit.

Dugdale, S., & Kibbey, D. (1984). Some computer applications for the pre-college mathematics and science curriculum. In Technology in education and training: Planning and management. *Proceedings of the 6th National Conference on Communications Technology in Education and Training.* Silver Spring, MD: Information Dynamics, Inc.

Dugdale S., & Kibbey, D. (1986). *Green globs and graphing equations.* Pleasantville, NY: Sunburst Communications.

Dugdale S., & Kibbey, D. (1986). *Interpreting graphs.* Pleasantville, NY: Sunburst Communications.

Dugdale, S., & Vogel, P. (1978, October). Computer-Based instruction for hearing-impaired children in the classroom. In *American annals of the deaf,* **123** (6).

Lyman, T. (1984, Autumn). CBI research and development centers—Computer-based Education Research Laboratory, University of Illinois. *Journal of Computer-Based Instruction,* **11** (4), 129-130.

Polya, G. (1957). *How to solve it: A new aspect of mathematical method.* New York: Doubleday.

Schoenfeld, A. H. (1988). Mathematics, technology, and higher-order thinking skills in the near and not-so-near future. In R. S. Nickerson (Ed.), *Technology in education in 2020: Thinking about the not-distant future.* Hillsdale, NJ: Lawrence Erlbaum Associates.

Seiler, B., & Weaver, C. (1976, June). *Description of PLATO whole number arithmetic lessons.* Urbana, IL: University of Illinois, Computer-based Education Research Laboratory, CERL Publications.

Slottow, G. (Ed.). (1977, March). *Final report—Demonstration of the PLATO IV Computer-Based Education System,* NSF Contract C-723. Urbana, IL: University of Illinois, Computer-based Education Research Laboratory.

Smith, S. G., & Sherwood, B. A. (1976). Educational uses of the PLATO computer system. *Science,* **192**, 344-352.

Stifle, J., Smith, S., & Andersen, D. (1979). Microprocessor delivery of PLATO courseware. *Proceedings of the Annual Convention of the Association for the Development of Computer-Based Instructional Systems,* Volume III.

Swinton, S. (1978, March). *Outcomes of the PLATO elementary demonstration.* Paper presented at the 1978 American Educational Research Association Conference, Toronto, Canada.

Usiskin, Z. (1980, September). What should not be in the algebra and geometry curricula of average college-bound students? *The Mathematics Teacher,* **73** (6).

Whitney, H. (1986, August). Coming alive in school math and beyond. *The Journal of Mathematical Behavior,* **5** (2), 129-140.

2 From Syntax to Semantics in Foreign Language CAI

Gerald R. Culley
Department of Foreign Languages and Literature
University of Delaware

It was in 1975 that the University of Delaware began using the PLATO[1] system. A small beginning—two terminals—soon grew into a major commitment, with more than two hundred student terminals and participation by more than thirty academic departments. Somewhere early in this process I began to explore the system's potential for supporting instruction in Latin. That dalliance eventually led to six programs—close to a hundred hours of instruction in the aggregate.

Incorporated into the Latin curriculum as a supplement, the programs fill a role analogous to the language laboratories that are often part of modern language courses. Students spend from one to one and one-half hours per week at the computer, honing their skills in morphology, sentence translation, and the parsing of words in Latin sentence context. The department enrolls about one hundred new Latin students each year, most of whom use the computer materials regularly through the first year. Some of these students in fact follow a self-paced, variable-credit, individualized program for the first year's study which the computer materials have made possible (Culley, 1979, 1980). The flexibility of that self-paced program, which has no formal classroom component, has made Latin accessible and appealing to more students, as increased overall enrollments show.

---

[1]The PLATO system, originally developed at the University of Illinois at Urbana-Champaign, consists of a mainframe machine supporting hundreds of terminals which have high-resolution graphics, animation, and touch capability. Many semester-length courses in many disciplines were developed and delivered on PLATO systems. PLATO® is a registered trade mark of The Roach Organization, Inc.

SYNTAX: GENERATIVE COMPUTER ASSISTED INSTRUCTION

The programs are a mixed bag, but the process of developing and programming them was an education. The first thing I learned was the value of *generative* CAI. By this term I mean the technique of incorporating into CAI routines which can generate an essentially unlimited number of exercises of a particular kind.

In the case of Latin, generative routines can construct appropriate inflected forms of the various parts of speech. Although pointless in a language like English, a routine for inflecting words makes eminently good sense in Latin, where one verb can assume 191 different forms. Mastering the morphology (i.e., the range of forms such a word may take on in varying usage) is a major element in learning the language. A generative CAI program can powerfully aid in this process. For example, a routine for conjugating Latin verbs uses a stem like *ama-* (for the verb to love) and a set of parameters (say, first person plural, imperfect passive subjunctive) and returns the inflected form (*amaremur*—we were loved). As implemented in our programs, this procedure works by treating the finite Latin verb as a construct of three elements: stem, tense/mood sign, and personal ending, each of which is represented by a variable. Commands assign the appropriate string of characters to each variable. The preceding example is implemented by the following commands:

1. Set STEM to stem #34:
   STEM ⇐ *ama*
2. Set TENSE_MOOD_SIGN to a string corresponding to tense 2 and mood 2:
   TENSE_MOOD_SIGN ⇐ *re*
3. Set PERSON_ENDING to a string corresponding to person 1, number 2, voice 2:
   PERSON_ENDING ⇐ *mur*
4. Show (STEM)(TENSE_MOOD_SIGN)(PERSON_ENDING):
   amaremur

Such a system has several advantages. First, the individual exercise items need not be stored—only word stems and grammatical data. Second, a relatively small database of stems yields large numbers of exercises; a lesson on noun-adjective phrases uses 80 adjective stems and 100 noun stems to make up to 8,000 possible phrases, each of which may take one of ten forms (five cases, singular or plural) for a total of 80,000 potential drill items. A third advantage is that the same algorithm that produces forms can be used to analyze the forms typed by a student and to comment on them in terms of their form, for example, "The verb stem and tense/mood sign are ok, but the personal ending is wrong;" "That's the accusative plural of the noun, not the accusative singular;" "Third conjugation -io- verbs use -ie- before the -ba-."

Feedback

A very nice kind of corrective feedback can be done where students must identify a form, as in the screen shown in Figure 1. Perhaps a verb like *amabam*, I loved, is to be parsed. The screen shows:

"Identify: *amabam*"

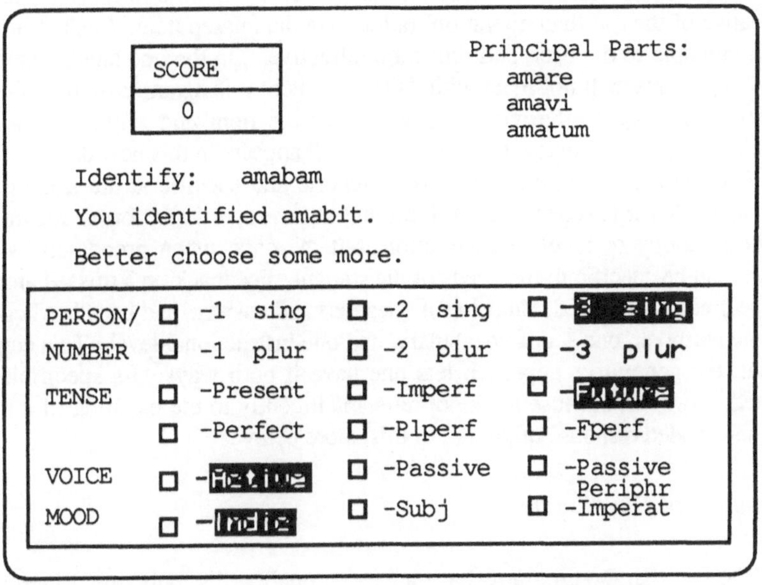

Figure 1: Feedback from a generative language program.

The student marks items on a grammatical chart to identify the form. Let's suppose, as in Figure 1, it is identified incorrectly: third person singular, future active indicative (rather than first person, and imperfect). The program then takes this input and uses it to inflect the verb stem again. The result is *amabit*, she will love. This is displayed for the student beside the target form:

"You identified *amabit*."

Each time the student inputs a set of parameters, their corresponding form is displayed. This feedback gives the student direct information on the form corresponding to the variables chosen and the basis for comparing this form with the desired form. In Figure 1, the comparison between *amabam* and *amabit* suggests that both the tense and the person are mis-identified.

"Invisible" Review

Another advantage of generative CAI is that "invisible" review is possible. By that I mean the capability to review missed forms by presenting, three or four items later, not the item that was missed, but a similar one. For example, a student misses *muniebat* in a drill. Three items later, by displaying *dormiebat*, the computer reviews the missed concept (third singular imperfect active indicative of the fourth conjugation) rather than the missed item. Such review is often invisible to the user, and thus more effective. On the one hand, a student prone to anxiety will not react with, "Oh no—there it is again!"; on the other, a student who might otherwise just remember the item and retype it without thinking is forced to review the concept when it appears in this new dress.

A generative program can be both generic and specific at the same time. That is, its driver is generic in that it produces the proper Latin forms, regardless of the textbook or level of instruction; but the data, when processed by the driver, can be specific to the needs of the student. Feedback on a missed answer can be precisely focused, almost as if questions and answers had been hard-coded for one textbook, one set of vocabulary, and one instructional level. To a certain extent, the generative approach lets one have it both ways. Its specificity is limited, however, because it cannot refer intelligently to the meaning of a form as a hard-coded response might do; of this, more below.

Efficiency of Development

The fact that the programs have a generic quality, that only one driver need be written for a broad range of uses, means a considerable saving in resources. It becomes possible to spend much more time on a single program when it is known that the program will produce many hours of instruction. For example, the program *Artifex Verborum*, which gives feedback on parsing of words in Latin sentences, devoured about a thousand hours of my time; but it yields about twenty hours of instruction for a given student. This translates into about fifty hours of development for each student hour, a quite acceptable ratio; but the dividend is that one can do a lot of rethinking, reworking, and polishing in that much time. The result is seen in higher quality overall. No secrets here: more time invested means more achieved.

But there is more to this saving of resources. That same program, *Artifex Verborum*, along with its editor, took about a thousand hours to develop, test, revise and polish. But that fifty-to-one ratio of development time to instructional time represents only the first database, the one made up of two hundred sentences specific to textbook number one in their vocabulary, grammar, syntax, and progressive complexity. The second such database, and the third, come much cheaper; only about thirty hours (and no programming, thanks to the editing facility) are needed to develop each new one. In fact there are now five databases for that program, one for each of five different textbooks. The net effect is a capacity to deliver a hundred hours of instruction—a ratio of only a little over ten development hours for each instructional hour.

This potential for multiple versions—and hence for wide dissemination—could best be exploited on inexpensive microcomputers rather than on PLATO. The University of Delaware accordingly funded the conversion of the programs to the Apple II series of machines. The six main Latin programs all eventually appeared in this format (Latin Skills, 1984 ff; Lector, 1988), as did the individualized course which utilizes them (Individualized Latin Curriculum, 1986). The series, in whole or in part, is in use at more than two hundred schools and colleges. A conversion to IBM microcomputers, accompanied by a major enhancement, is now in progress.

The Delaware Latin programs are six in number:

Verb Factory is a set of diagnostic exercises for verb morphology which includes an array of context-sensitive feedback.

Cursus Honorum gives remedial practice in four gaming formats tailored to the student's needs.

Mare Nostrum, conceptually similar to *Cursus Honorum*, builds skills with noun/adjective phrases.

Translat, the only program in the series which is not generative, offers practice in Latin sentence translation, with lexical, grammatical and syntactic helps available on every word and with diagnostic markups on the student's translation.

Artifex Verborum does parsing of words in Latin sentence context, with diagnostic feedback on wrong identifications. (Culley, 1984-5, pp. 38-42).

Lector, developed later to supplement the series, permits students to browse through a small database of Latin sentences in search of specific features of the language like instances of the genitive case, or of direct objects, or of indirect questions (Culley 1987).

Limitations

One can, however, hardly spend this long with a technique without seeing its disadvantages. Even if the developer could manage to avoid seeing them, colleagues will be glad to point them out.

The generative routines discussed here are designed to produce all of the forms of the Latin verb, noun, adjective, or pronoun—the parts of speech which undergo change of form. The trouble is, many Latin words occur in only some of the forms they could theoretically assume. For example, *decet*, "it is fitting," is an impersonal Latin verb; that is, it occurs only in the third person singular. Yet a student working with *Artifex Verborum* could identify the word as first person plural, producing the nonexistent form *decemus*, "we are fitting." One of the chief strengths of the generative approach, its ability to produce forms dynamically in response to student input and use those forms as corrective feedback, turns out to be downright dangerous. One might, for example, add flags to impersonal verbs to restrict them to the third person singular, but massive additions to the data structure would be needed to deal with all the idiosyncrasies individual verbs can display.

For all the flexibility of format and variety in application, the generative approach is simply a means of generating or recognizing different syntactic forms. If the pedagogical goal is something other than morphology, the generative technique can be stretched and bent to fit, but it feels the strain. A case in point is the program *Lector*, in which students study features of the language by drawing from a database of sentences which contain a selected feature. When the feature is a part of speech like a noun, or a grammatical element like the passive voice, the generative routines work well. But complex syntactic features, like indirect statements, require the program to identify and comment on the subject, verb, and object of the indirect statement and their modifiers, while also recognizing that the entire structure is itself the direct object of the verb of saying or thinking. For example, Figure 2, a screen from *Lector*, shows a complete Latin sentence, and asks the student to identify in the sentence a "Target" which is an indirect statement. The sentence reads, "Because he knew that the soldiers were few, he warned the general that it would be difficult to defeat the enemy." In Latin an indirect statement (here "that it would be difficult to defeat ...") employs an infinitive verb. Additionally the subject of this indirect statement is itself an infinitive (*superare*, to defeat.) Therefore this sentence has an infinitive as the subject of another infinitive.

The student here has just identified *superare*. The program must provide reinforcement by stating how the item found relates to the whole, here that the selected *superare* is an infinitive and the subject of an indirect statement. To infer such syntactic information from a data structure that was designed merely for inflecting discrete words is sometimes difficult, sometimes nearly impossible. The program must operate at the very limits of its capability.

Both of these problems, inability to distinguish sense from nonsense if the form is correct, and inability to work with complex syntax, arise because generative routines know nothing of meaning. The program treats (for example) all 1st conjugation verbs as identical. It does not know that *amare* refers to love, *portare* to carrying, and *laudare* to bestowing praise. Any appearance of such knowledge is only fancy footwork, and sooner or later that limitation makes itself felt. I have elsewhere (Culley, 1985) called lessons which use this approach "smart." That is their trouble: they are only "smart" when they need to be intelligent[2] .

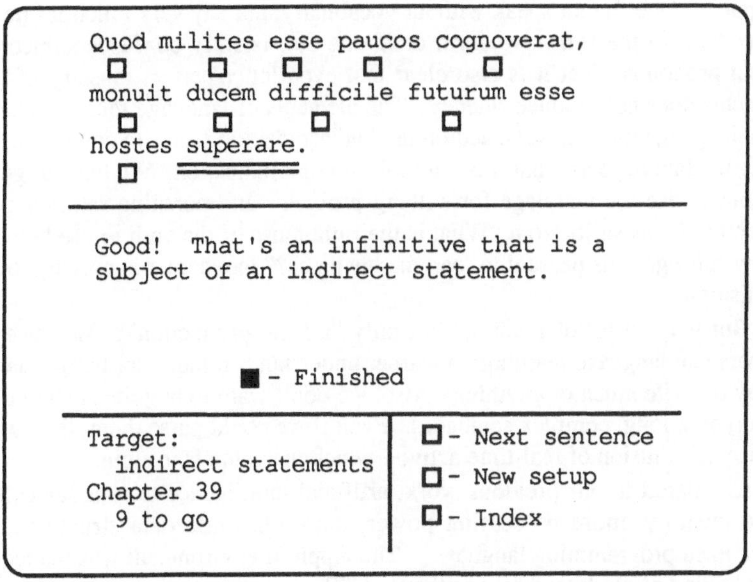

Figure 2: An exercise requiring interpretation of complex syntax.

[2] Editors' Note: Culley's experience parallels the general development of language parsers. Early parsers used only syntax. Soon it became clear that adequate parsing could be done only by a program having representation of the meaning of words, phrases, and sentences. Also note Reiser et. al. (this volume), trying to make a LISP tutor that is "intelligent" rather than "smart" about giving feedback.

SEMANTICS: INTERACTION WITH MEANING

Considerations like these led to our current project. In 1984, Dr. George Mulford and I proposed adapting the computer adventure game format and using artificial intelligence techniques to develop an instructional program in which the learner would use a foreign language in a communicative setting. We focussed on our own fields of French and Latin, and planned to produce an "adventure game" because of the interactive communication required by such a program.

In one sense, the whole program is an elaborate device to trick the student into a lot of reading and a little production. As every language teacher knows, the nuts and bolts must be mastered to some extent by anyone who learns a language. One cannot speak without vocabulary, nor say very much if one puts all verbs into the infinitive form or if one consistently confuses subject and object pronouns. Yet it is also clear that even letter-perfect mastery of these elements does not produce fluency. The elements of language must be learned, but a language itself must be acquired. And acquisition seems to come best from using the language as what it is—a tool for communication. We have to get the student to use the language for solving problems and pursuing rational goals. When the focus shifts from "What is the right tense of the verb to use here?" to "How can I get this peasant to loan me his horse?" the learner is moving toward acquisition.

But why "a lot of reading" but only "a little production"? Because that mirrors real language learning: a learner understands rather a lot before starting to say or write much of anything. Also, we don't want to bog the student down with typing long, complex sentences. Even if we could parse them, they would destroy the illusion of real-time activity which the game is to simulate.

Compared to our previous work, artificial intelligence techniques call for more memory, more processing power, more elaborate data structures, and specialized programming languages. The Apple II environment was inadequate for that kind of work, and so was the PLATO system.

The University of Delaware funded the project at first, and during the past two years we have had major assistance from the U.S. Department of Education. This level of support permitted us to assemble a highly talented project team, with two professional programmers in addition to Dr. Mulford and myself, plus two or three part-timers. For me, this team approach meant I had to learn to delegate—something I don't do well—and meant also that I had to try to keep up, at least in general terms, with what some very bright people were doing. It has been an exciting and challenging experience.

The Adventure Game Format

Computer adventure games create a miniature world and invite the player to explore it. The Latin adventure, for example, is set in the Teutoburg forest of northern Germany, where in early fall, AD 9, three Roman legions under Quintilius Varus were ambushed and destroyed by a coalition of German tribesmen led by the chieftain Arminius. The player is a survivor of that battle who must escape detection, find food and water, gather intelligence about the German plans and get back to safety west of the Rhine. This is a historical setting, and the program tries to simulate what a real survivor of that battle might have experienced—though computer adventures often are seasoned with touches of fantasy, and there is just a bit of magic in this forest. The player must deal with all of it—the hunger, the wolves, the German patrols, the ghost of the dead Roman commander. The player explores this world and faces its challenges by typing statements, such as "I go north," or "I open the chest," or "I read the inscription," or "I attack the ghost." The program responds to each statement either by carrying it out (that is, modifying the imaginary world) or by telling the player the statement was inappropriate or ineffective. The chest may be locked, the inscription too faint to read without a stronger light, or the ghost unimpressed by physical violence.

Computer adventure games generally follow this format. Our game, however, had to be instructional—not as a complete language curriculum, but as a legitimately useful supplement to an existing language course. Primary instruction in such things as vocabulary, grammar, and syntax would still be provided by textbook and teacher (and computer programs like those discussed earlier). The computer game would help the student acquire facility in using the language. An adventure game is well suited to this instructional goal because it can provide challenging and interesting exchanges in the foreign language; playing the game consists of communicative interaction. In the current state of the language teaching profession, where there is little agreement on how students in fact learn a second language (Larsen-Freeman, 1987), there is at least an emerging consensus that acquisition is facilitated when the learner uses the language in a communicative setting (Underwood, 1984; see especially his "Premises for CALL [Computer-Assisted Language Learning]," p. 52 ff.).

With communicative activity the central goal, we were able to list our priorities for learning in the game format: first, reading and all its subskills (vocabulary, idiom, grammar, syntax), then production of simple sentences, then culture (as embedded in the game script) and last, details of the plot (what shall I do about the wolves?).

Student input, then, will be relatively simple. A student will get no practice in typing the passé composé or subjunctive, or even third person plural forms. The parser can understand a vocabulary of perhaps six hundred words, but most students will get along by using a subset even of that number. No, the game is not a tool for teaching production.

One might then say, "Why parse anything? Just give multiple choices." But just to put A, B, C and D on the screen would be to abandon our key goal of plunging the student into a communicative exchange. We wanted to force the student to form an expression, even a modest one, and give us the chance to correct it for spelling, grammar, syntax, or idiom. And in the interest of verisimilitude, we wanted to keep the illusion that the student could do anything—"There's the prompt; be creative!" That is an illusion, of course; but important for the viability of a microworld which is itself illusory. If the artificial world of the game is to seem in any sense real, it must mimic the kind of world we know—in which at any moment I may inspect my surroundings, pick up some object, stroll into the next room, or decide to take a nap.

Placed in an exotic, perhaps dangerous, but inherently interesting environment, the player must master that environment to survive—and there is no choice but to use the language. The game strives to trick the student into using the language as a tool for communication. I use the word "trick" advisedly, because a student does not see the teacher's list of priorities, and the student's list is almost the reverse of the teacher's. The player wants to know, "What is going to happen to me?" and "How can I master this situation?"—in short, to know the plot. But the game won't reveal that. A player must draw, then, on knowledge of the culture: "Let's see...this is a forest in Germany. The battle was just yesterday. There will probably be patrols about."—and so on. But this sort of general knowledge won't get one very far without specifics. It is necessary to explore. Is there anything left in the Roman commander's tent? "*Intro in tentorium.*"—"I go into the tent." Production is forced on the player. And each new command expressed results in text on the screen which must be understood to know what to do next. The student wants most to know the plot, while the teacher wants most to encourage reading; in the end, both get what they want.

Instructional Features

But there are some specific ways in which a commercial adventure game, no matter how communicative it may be, fails to meet a teacher's needs. A truly instructional game needs the following features:

1. Spelling Correction. If a student types, "*Ineo in castra Gremanorum,*" "I enter the German camp," the program should echo a sentence with corrected spelling: "*...in castra Germanorum*?"

2. *Morphological Correction.* If a student types, "*Speculum Etruscus sumo,*" "I pick up the Etruscan mirror," with the word "Etruscan" in the wrong grammatical case, the program should echo, "*Speculum Etruscum*?"

3. *Sensible response to the Player's Foreign-Language Input.* When a student types, "*In tentorium imperatoris mei intro,*" "I enter my commander's tent," the program should know the name of the commander and respond, "*Nunc in tentorio Vari stas,*" "Now you are standing in the tent of Varus." This kind of sensible response requires "parsing" in the artificial intelligence sense—that is, determining the structure of the sentence, then extracting the meaning and responding in terms of the meaning. Sensible interaction also requires that the program draw inferences from the its own knowledge base. Given an input like, "*E scapha salio,*" "I jump out of the boat," the program should reply, "*Bene. In fluvio nunc natas,*" "Fine. Now you are swimming in the river."

4. *Natural Description of Actions.* Commercial adventure games tend to be dominated by compass directions. An instructional game should allow and encourage a variety of ways to express where one wants to go and what one wants to do. It should be possible to use not only compass directions, but handsides—"I run toward the right," or even goals—"I walk into the Roman camp" or "I return to the barbarian altar."

5. *Help in Understanding Text on the Screen.* The student should be able to move the mouse cursor to any word on the screen, click on it, and obtain lexical or morphological information. Thus, if the word *fecit* was selected, the program should offer the dictionary key ("*facio*"), the English meaning ("make, do"), a morphological analysis ("third singular perfect active indicative"), or a paradigm of the word in the perfect active indicative. An additional level of help might let one select some other paradigm of that verb for comparison. The student should be able to do this with any word on the screen, including those just typed.

6. *Help with Game Strategies.* If uncertain what to do next, the student should be able to click on a word that refers to some object in the game—say, a book—and get a list of the verbs useable with that object at that particular point in the game: *intueri* (examine it), *sumere* (pick it up), *aperire* (open it), *legere* (read it), *incendere* (burn it), and so on. But the verbs should only be the ones that apply in the present circumstance. That is, if the player is already holding the book, the program should not say it can be picked up; and so on.

7. *Rewards for Lexical and Syntactic Richness.* Players of adventure games, in their eagerness to move ahead, often slip into typing a kind of shorthand: "take goblet", "attack troll." A foreign language instructional game will have to discourage this, and in fact find ways to reward the use of language that is full and varied.

8. *Provision for Teachers to Design Their Own Scenarios.* Some of the most creative and committed teachers find it distasteful to use software which

they cannot modify to fit their individual needs. Adventure software would be much more useful if teachers could write their own scenarios and plug them into the game's parser and inferencing capabilities. Even better, they could include the class in a project to write a complete French or Latin game scenario, discussing each stage as it is implemented, and then running the completed game.

It was the need for features like these that got us into the project. As it turned out, we are getting some of them—though not all.

How Does the Program "Understand" the Student?

The program works by cycling through a series of actions and interactions with the player (Figure 3). The program begins in the INFORM stage when the student is presented with a situation, such as being beside a lake where there is a bush with red berries on it.

The student enters a sentence, such as "*Bacas rubras paucas de frutice capio*"—"I take a few red berries from the bush."

In the RECOGNIZE stage, the program analyzes the morphology of the words of the sentence to identify stems and endings, strips off the endings, and checks the stems against a dictionary. Spelling correction is done on the stems if needed. Then, using its knowledge of synonyms and modification, the program identifies the semantic entities referred to in the sentence.

In this example, the "few red berries" becomes "`baca-5`" (`baca` indicating a type of entity—berries—and `baca-5` being this particular instance of berries). `Baca-5` has a quantity of 3—three being "a few."

The entities, now identified, are next passed to the parser, which draws on its knowledge of semantics to establish relationships among them and thus parses the sentence in semantic terms:

`baca-5`, the patient, is to be taken from `frutex-2`, the source.

Next, this interpretation is checked (the VERIFY stage) by taking the stems of the words the player used (with spelling corrected) and generating a model sentence with semantic content matching the program's interpretation and with correct syntactic form.

If the generated sentence matches the student's original sentence, the program can proceed. If not, it displays the generated sentence (the CORRECT stage) and asks the student if that was the intent—in the process subtly correcting the error, as when a real respondent echoes a corrected version of one's badly-formed sentence. The student may not agree with the program's interpretation, in which case a new sentence can be entered, sending the process back to the RECOGNIZE stage.

At this point, there is a semantically unambiguous and syntactically correct sentence. The program now goes to the ACT stage, changing the state of the microworld as directed by the sentence—or attempting to do so and failing, if the instruction was an impossible one.

Finally the program proceeds to the INFORM stage, completing the cycle by generating a response in the foreign language describing the program's new internal state. This response is shaped in part by the program's rules for strategy of interaction: it may have allowed a student to say something syntactically correct but meaningless, like "I eat the rock," so as to point out now that rocks are inedible. In other instances, it will have used semantic contradiction as a device for correcting an ill-formed sentence: "I give the flower the girl"... "Do you mean, 'I give the girl the flower?'" This response becomes the next situation to which the student must respond. The description above gives an overview of the program's structure. We may turn now to a somewhat more detailed treatment of specific features of the program.

Recognition

Spelling Correction

There is something of a dilemma here. The program must check the words typed by a student against its dictionary, but any or all of these words may be misspelled. To resolve the dilemma, one has to make a few assumptions. First, no word of three or fewer letters is misspelled; attempts to correct such words lead to too many permutations because the remainder of the word is too short to be distinctive. If such short words are not accurately typed, they cannot be recognized. Second, for an inflected word, there is a difference between a misspelled stem and an incorrect ending. Endings are stripped off and the remainder of the word is checked against a list of stems. Error correction in a stem is limited to a missing letter, an extra letter, or transposed letters. Finally, errors in the ending of an inflected word are identified later in the process—what we have called the VERIFY stage.

Once the words are identified and corrected for misspellings, the program must identify the entities to which the words refer. Suppose the original sentence was a poorly formed one:

Bacam rubrem aliquid in fruticem capio.

Through several steps, the program works toward a reasonable understanding of this sentence.

Noun Phrase Modification

The first step would have identified the stems as *bac*, *rubr*, *aliquid*, *in*, *frutic*, and *cap*. The program, consulting the knowledge base, would establish that there are two kinds of berries in the game: red ones (*bacae rubrae*) and black ones

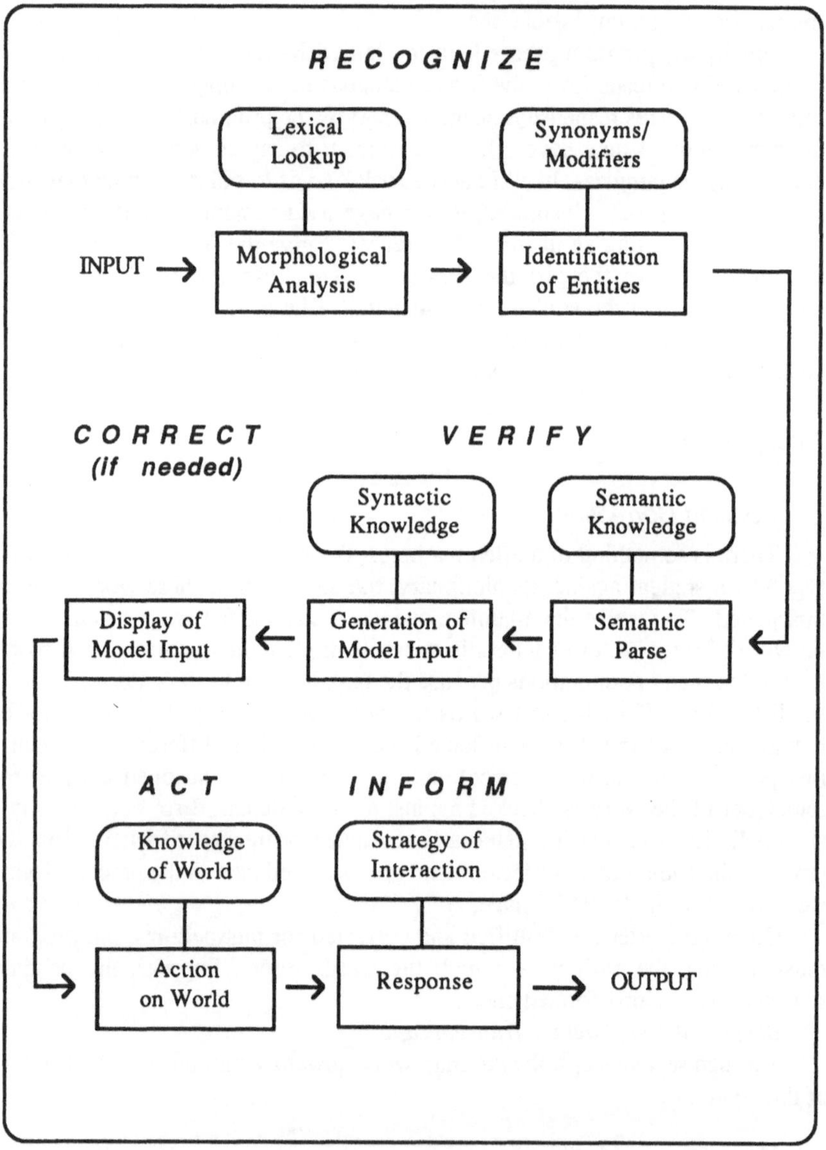

Figure 3. The cycle of processing of student input in the adventure game.

(*bacae nigrae*). Scanning the other words of the sentence, it would note that *aliquid* is a word that can only be applied to mass nouns like water or soup (*aliquid iuris* is "something of soup" or "some soup"), not to countable nouns like berries. It would conclude that *aliquid* is an error in usage—the proper expression being "*bacas rubras paucas*—a few red berries". Noting the number of red berries, it would fix the meaning of "a few red berries" at 3 and identify this as the entity `baca-5`, with quantity three. Incidentally, the noun phrase modification information for a given entity must allow for all reasonable means of describing the entity; for example, a black lead flask, *poculum nigrum plumbeum*, can equally be described as *poculum plumbeum*, *poculum nigrum*, or any of these phrases in any word order—since Latin word order is exceptionally free.

Proceeding to the next noun stem, *frutic*, the program would note that there are two bushes in the game, one with red berries and one with black ones. Using an immediacy hierarchy, it would conclude that the student is referring to the bush which has the red berries on it and would recognize that this is the entity it knows as `frutex-2`.

Verb Case Frame Assignment

For each verb known to the program, a case frame has been recorded to show the syntactic relationships it expects. For example, the English verb "to like" has a frame something like this:

<like> <patient/obj>.

That is, if the verb "like" appears in a sentence, we expect to see it followed by a noun or pronoun denoting the person or thing liked, the recipient (patient) of the act of liking. That patient will be in the objective case; one may say, "I like him," but not, "I like he." In the sample sentence,

Bacam rubrem aliquid in fruticem capio.

the verb *cap* (meaning take) has a frame specifying that: (a) the patient (the thing taken) must be in the Latin accusative case and (b) the source from which it comes, if specified, must be in the ablative case with a preposition such as *ab*, *de*, or *ex*. The program has identified two nouns in this sentence, *bac* (berries) and *frutic* (bush). Presumably they are a patient and a source. But does the student want to take the berries from the bush, or the bush from the berries? The knowledge base shows that the berries are "pickable" while the bush could only be removed with the help of some cutting instrument, so it determines that it is the berries that are wanted. The preposition *in*, however, does not fit this case frame at all; so it must be an error. Semantic information, then, has made it possible to assign the syntactic roles in the case frame as follows:

baca-5, quant3/patient *in*/unassignable frutex-2/source *cap*/take

Now the program thinks that the player wants to take three red berries from the bush.

Verification

To verify this interpretation, the program takes the stems of the words used by the student and inflects each of them according to the syntax called for by their roles in the case frame. If `baca-5` is really the patient, it should be in the accusative case with the verb *capio*, and so on. This stage generates a sentence as follows:

Bacas rubras paucas de frutice capio.

Since this sentence does not match the one the student typed (*Bacam rubrem aliquid in fruticem capio*), the program will present its version to the student. This simultaneously verifies whether this was the student's intent and provides a low-key correction of the errors in the input:

Volebasne scribere, Bacas rubras paucas de frutice capio?

The student will either verify that this was the intent, or will type some new input.

Spawning and Unspawning Entities

Identifying the entities requires a process to create or destroy entities as needed. An example may explain why this is necessary. Suppose that the player dips some water from the lake with a flask. In the game world, the water in the lake is the entity `aqua-1`. But what will the player take into the flask? Not `aqua-1`, surely; it would require a very large flask to drain a lake. In fact, the program arbitrarily treats all liquids as consisting of portions. Since this a lakeful of water, there are an infinite number of these portions: it is `aqua-1`, quantity infinite. When the player takes some water, the program spawns a new entity, `aqua-2`. The size of the flask determines that this entity will consist of six portions, that is, it will be `aqua-2`, quantity 6. If asked to describe the objects in the current room, the program can then say that there is a lake here, that the player is holding a flask, and that the flask contains some water.

Now suppose the player drinks "some water" from the flask. "Some" is defined as one-third of the quantity of an entity, rounded up to an integer (but no more than the capacity of the container into which the fluid is to be placed); a new entity, `aqua-3`, is spawned with quantity two; and this is what the player drinks. `Aqua-2`, in the flask, is now reduced by two to quantity four.

Now suppose that the player goes into another place where there is a stream and pours the water from the flask into the stream. The water in the flask is identical to that in the stream, so the program will unspawn the water from the flask (`aqua-2`) and merge it into `aqua-4`, which is the water of the stream.

Why? Consider: if this were not done, the next time the player came near this stream, the program would say that there is a stream of water here, and that there is some water here, on top of the stream. Unspawning is needed to get rid of entities whose continued presence would clutter up the game world and create confusion.

Spawning and unspawning are necessary not only for mass nouns like water, but for countables like berries. So then, when the player wanted to take some red berries from the bush, there was a bit more to it than I acknowledged earlier. In fact, the program spawned a new entity, `baca-5`, with quantity 3, and reduced the quantity of the original entity, `baca-1`, by three. Eventually, if the player picks enough berries, the bush will be empty.

Action

Calling an Operator: Preconditions

Now that the program knows what is wanted, it must change the state of the game world as required. The routines which do this we call operators. Operators include such actions as pick up, drop, offer, put on, examine, take off, attack, go, play tape, wait, and so on. There are about twenty of them in the game. In the example we have been following, the program calls the "pick up" operator for the patient `baca-5`, quantity 3, from the source `frutex-2`. But the action can only be performed if all preconditions are met. Here are the preconditions for the operator "pick up": You may pick up object X if:

X is not a body part;
X is not already being held by the player;
The current room is lit;
X is not hidden;
X is in the current room (X's "primary location");
The Source (X's "location," e.g., a table) is in the current room;
X is in or on the Source;
X is portable;
X is either inanimate, or animate and friendly.

Checking these items sometimes means just looking in the database ("Are berries a body part?"). Often, however, they involve drawing an inference. One determines portability by checking the object's weight and the player's strength, plus the aggregate weight of any objects already being carried. Determining whether the item is in the current room involves checking on where the player is, since "current room" means only "the room in which the player is currently located."

If all of the preconditions are satisfied, the action may be carried out. If any of them is not satisfied, an error message will be generated; such as, "There are no berries on the bush."

Note that the error message will be in French or Latin, not in English. It is necessary, then, to generate a message which will be in the correct form. The message for the situation above looks like this in the program:

"*Esse*/3rd/number *in* Source/ablative Patient/nominative *null*/nominative"

When the message is called, the variable elements are filled in. "*Esse*/`3rd person/num`" becomes "*Esse*/`3rd person/plural`" because the patient, berries, is plural; it will be inflected to *sunt*. The source, `frutex-2`, will be put into the ablative case and become *frutice*. The patient, `baca-5`, becomes nominative, *bacae*, as does the adjective, *nullae*. The sentence generated will then be *Sunt in frutice bacae nullae*, "There are no berries on the bush."

But there is more. The preconditions mentioned above are normal ones, that is, they must always be satisfied. But an action to be taken on a given entity may also depend on some special precondition; for example, maybe these are magic berries which can only be picked during the full moon. If so, the program will check for whether there is a full moon and, failing that, will tell the player, "For some reason, you are unable to detach the berries from the bush."

Note that the order in which preconditions are checked is important. If the player tried to pick berries from a bush which had no more berries on it, we would not want the program to reply that they were magically attached and would not come off. To avoid this sort of foolishness, normal preconditions are checked before eccentric preconditions.

Calling an Operator: Consequences

Once an action is performed, there are consequences. After the player picks the berries, they are no longer on the bush, but in hand. We want the program to say this: "You now have the berries." There may be other consequences as well: "The berries stain your fingers." Or even magical consequences: "The bush shrivels away before your eyes." We will want the ordinary consequences to be stated first, then any eccentric consequences: "You now have the berries. Being overripe and mushy, the berries stain your fingers."

Scheduling Consequences.

In the real world, not all events occur instantaneously. Some require a period of time. The reality of the simulation is enhanced if some events extend over more than one turn. For example, suppose that the player falls into the water. In the real world, such exposure could have ill effects if nothing is done about it, and the same thing occurs in the game. When the player gets wet, a potential event—pneumonia—is scheduled for four turns hence. A timer, which ticks once at each turn in the game, begins counting down to that event. At event-minus-three, the program prints a message: "You are wet and shivering." At event-minus-two, another message is printed: "You begin to sneeze; unless you can get dry, you will catch pneumonia." At event-minus-one, there is yet a third message: "You shiver uncontrollably." And when the count reaches zero, the player is informed that he has contracted pneumonia.

The potential event can be headed off, of course. Drying oneself at a fire will cancel the onset of pneumonia, as will changing into dry clothes.

At each turn, then, the program looks to see whether one or more events are on the scheduler. If the preconditions for continuing the countdown are still met, the program will print the message appropriate to that stage in the countdown and will reduce the counter by one. More than one event may be on the scheduler at a time, so that several imminent events may be announcing their approach simultaneously.

Scheduling Demons

In the real world, some things occur spontaneously, or through another's initiative. Storms arise; people drop by unexpectedly; dogs bite. The game world should include at least some of this kind of behavior. Not too much, or one would lose any chance of mastering the environment, but a limited amount will add excitement and verisimilitude. The mechanism that produces these spontaneous events is usually called a demon[3]. For example, in the Latin game, at any time one is out of doors there is a chance that wolves will attack. Nothing the player does brings on this attack; unlike the onset of pneumonia, which is a consequence of getting wet, the wolf attack is spontaneous. But, like the pneumonia, this event will be scheduled. When the random preconditions for a wolf attack are satisfied, the event is put on the scheduler and a countdown begins. Messages are printed in advance: "You hear a howling in the woods. Wolves!" If the player takes no action, such as fleeing or building a fire, the wolves will eventually attack— perhaps with fatal results.

Notice, then, that with each turn, the program checks to see whether there is a delayed consequence on the scheduler, or a demon that is waiting to fire. This procedure adds considerable overhead to the computing cycle, but it is invaluable for adding to the reality of the simulation.

To the player, it seems that a single source, "the game," is producing various kinds of messages. In reality, messages are being produced by many different parts of the program. Here is a sample exchange which illustrates the messages and their sources.

---

[3] Editors' Note: More generally a "demon" is a computer routine that can potentially execute at any time if its preconditions are satisfied. Here the preconditions include a random time parameter, as well as some fixed ones (e.g., being out of doors).

> *Induo glaeam.*	> I put on the helmat.
Volebasne scribere, Induo galeam?	Do you mean, I put on the helmet? (parser)
Ululatum in silvis audis. Lupi!	You hear a howling in the woods. Wolves! (demon schedules wolf attack)
> *Lupos neco.*	> I attack the wolves.
Tela nulla habes.	You have no weapon. (failed normal precondition)
Lupi circum te veniunt, in circulo qui umquam minor fit.	The wolves circle you, coming ever closer. (scheduled wolf attack)
> *Ramos incendo.*	>I build a fire.
Rami ardere incipiunt.	The branches begin to blaze. (natural consequence)
Lupi, territi igne, fugiunt.	The wolves, frightened by the fire, slink away. (eccentric consequence) (scheduled attack is cancelled)

Current State and Conclusion

With the aid of techniques like these, we hope to be able to provide an exciting, realistic experience for the student, who will be drawn into using the foreign language as a communications tool and so begin acquisition of the language.

But in the four years since the project began, many changes have occurred. We have not found it possible—and in some cases, not desirable—to implement every feature on our original agenda. Here is that same list of desiderata, with a report on what we have and have not implemented:

Correction of spelling and of morphological errors is working as described. So are the parser and the inferencing routines. Figure 4 shows two uneventful exchanges (*Sumo galeam*, "I pick up the helmet"...*Galeam tenes*, "You have the helmet"...*Induo galeam nitentem*, "I put on the shining helmet"...*Factum. Nunc galeam nitentem geris*, "Done. Now you are wearing the shining helmet."). Then comes a more interesting one: *Galdius in vaginam pono*, "I put the sword in the scabbard" (with sword both misspelled and in the wrong case, and scabbard also in the wrong case). The program echoes a sentence with all three errors corrected. Work continues on the parser and the inferencing routines, and it must be admitted that they commit occasional howlers; but they run, and they will get better.

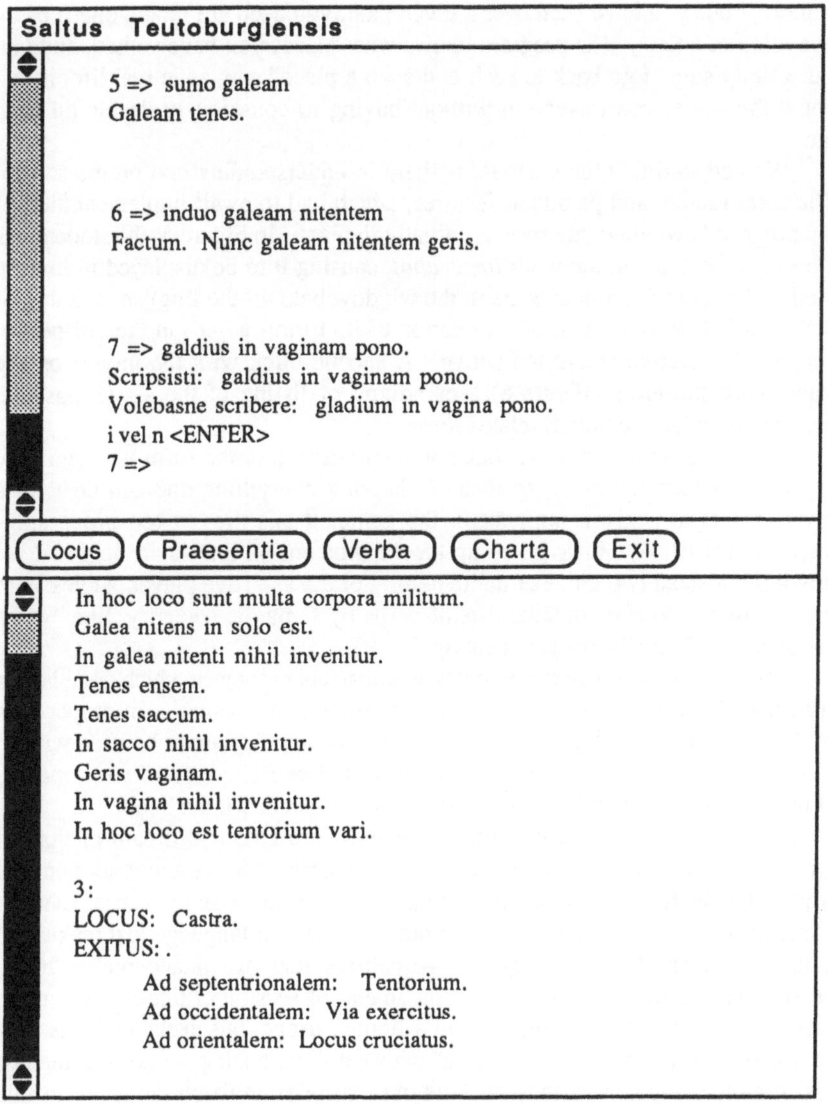

Figure 4: A screen from the Latin adventure game. The upper window shows a dialog between the player and the computer. The lower window shows information about the current situation.

Our determination to avoid the maze-solving syndrome has held up, and you can indeed move about using all of the different formats mentioned earlier. What is more, once you have been over a given path, you need not plod along it again one room at a time. The program knows what places you have visited, and you can simply say, "I go back to such-and-such a place" and, as in real life, if you know the route, you traverse it without having to consciously decide on each move.

We had said that there should be help in understanding text on the screen. The form lookup and paradigm features, which had to await implementation of the program's window interface, are finally in place. In Figure 5, the student has clicked the mouse on the word *imperabat*, causing it to be displayed in inverse mode. An identification appears in the window below: the English meaning of the word is followed by an identification of its form: a verb in the 3rd person singular imperative active indicative. A second click with the mouse on the same word produces (Figure 6) a paradigm, or listing of the six (3 possible persons, singular and plural) related forms.

Help with game strategies has not been feasible in the form we originally intended. Charming as is the idea of showing everything one can do with a given object at a given moment in the game, it has proven too processing-intensive for us. We have given up for the moment on this smart help and are providing instead two kinds of dumb help. For the assertive player, a click with the mouse on "*Verba*" obtains lists of verbs by semantic category, like "verbs about moving" and "verbs about eating."

For the confused player who types an unparsable sentence which nonetheless contains a legitimate verb, the program will offer some examples of proper uses of that verb, along with a list of any prepositions appropriate to be used with it. A sentence with *pono* in it would elicit models like *Pono ampullam in mensa,* "I put the flask on the table" and *Pono librum*, "I put down the book."

Rewards for lexical and syntactic richness are easier to dream of than to grant; this goal has been a real quagmire. The parser knows about six hundred words, but in fact any given player can get by with a small subset of that. Every trick we can think of to require more richness in language just makes the parser more rigid and unforgiving—qualities that are unacceptable in an instructional game. We are considering an end-of-session critique in which the program will comment on the student's limited usage, but in the end this may be less of a problem than we thought; two week-long testing sessions in the last two summers showed us that students used surprisingly rich language in this kind of game environment.

The editing facility to permit teachers to design their own scenarios is behind schedule, but we are committed to it. It will not be completed by the end of summer, when the federal grant ends, but we should have it within the next year.

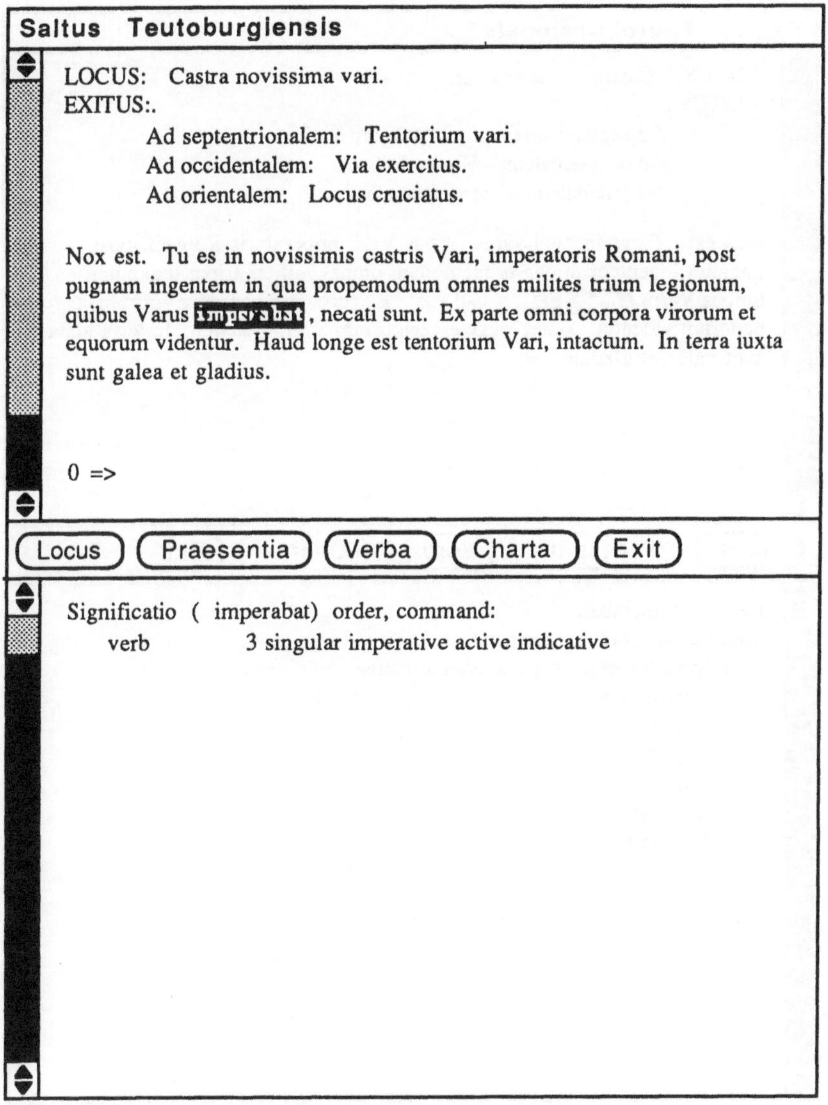

Figure 5: The student clicks on the word "imperabat" in the upper window. The first click provides its translation and form.

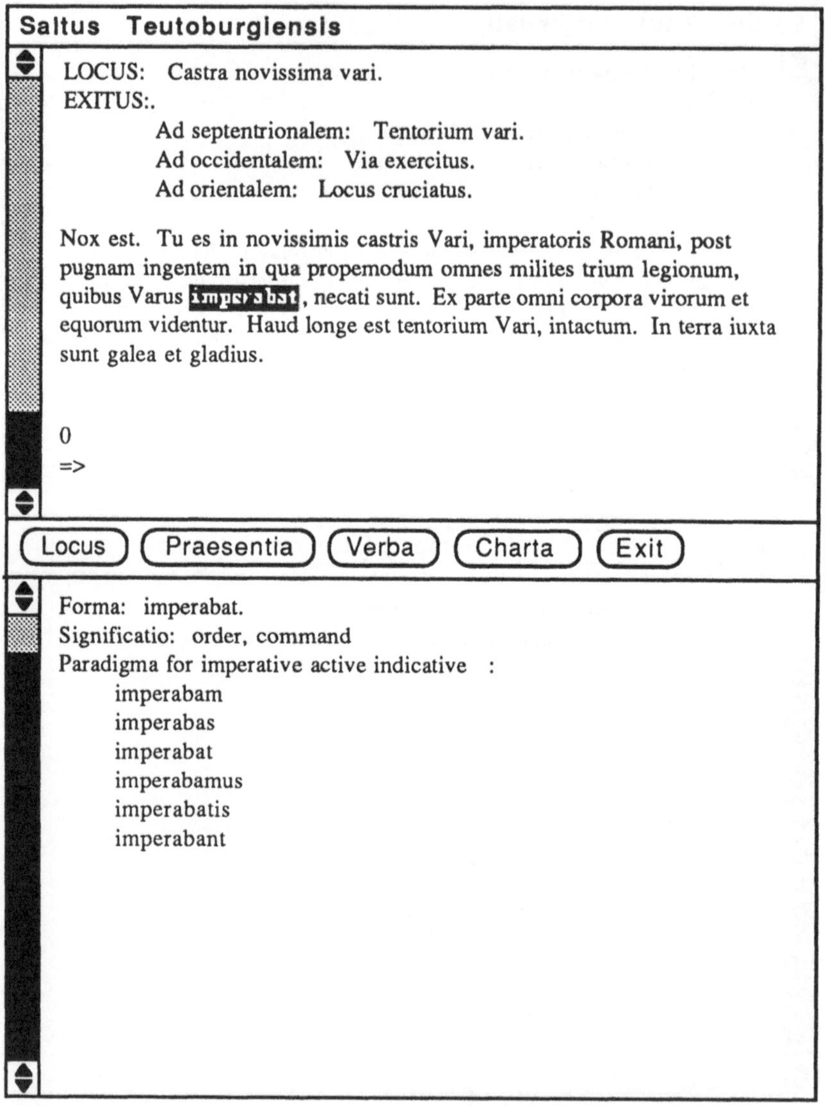

Figure 6: The second click on the word "imperabat" provides a paradigm of the verb.

As we approach the conclusion of this project, a look backward and ahead seem appropriate. It was the need to deal with the meaning of expressions that pulled us into the use of artificial intelligence techniques. The adventure game requires natural language parsing, the correction of both spelling and form, representation of world knowledge, and inferencing about semantics to achieve its goal of communicative exchange. It has not, however, required us to enter the world of intelligent tutoring systems. The game constructs no model of student behavior, much less one of student understanding. Perhaps one day it will, but there are other goals, more proximate and more pressing. The game editor needs to be completed. The game must be ported to the IBM-PC/AT family of machines. Other scenarios are coming. Our Roman soldier is not the only one who is not out of the woods yet.

ACKNOWLEDGEMENTS

The Foreign Language Adventure Game described in this paper has been developed with the aid of grants from the Office of Instructional Technology, University of Delaware (1984-1986) and the United States Department of Education, International Studies Branch (1986-1988). The author wishes to acknowledge their generous support.

REFERENCES

Culley, G. R. (1979). A computer supplement to individualize the Latin course. *Proceedings of the First National Conference on Individualized Instruction in Foreign Languages*, pp. 121-124. Columbus, OH: The Ohio State University.

Culley, G. R.(1980). Individualized Latin at Delaware: a progress report. *Proceedings of the 2nd National Conference on Individualized Instruction in Foreign Languages*, pp. 75-79. Columbus, OH: The Ohio State University.

Culley, G. R. (1984-5). The Delaware Latin Skills project. *The Classical Outlook*, **62**, 38-42.

Culley, G. R. (1984, 1985, 1986). *Latin skills, Five-diskette series for Apple II+, IIe and IIc microcomputers*. Newark, DE: Office of Computer-Based Instruction, University of Delaware.

(1984). Version keyed to Frederic M. Wheelock's Latin: an introductory course, 3rd ed. (Harper and Row, 1963).

(1984). Version keyed to Ullman, Latin for Americans, first book and second book (Macmillan Publishing, 1981).

(1985). Version keyed to Jenney & Scudder, First-year Latin and second-year Latin (Allyn & Bacon, 1984).

(1985). Version keyed to Goldman and Nyenhuis, Latin via Ovid, 2nd ed. (Wayne State Univ. Press, 1977).

(1986). Version keyed to Ecce Romani, North American ed. (Longman, Inc., 1985, 1986).

Culley, G. R. (1985). Developing 'smart' lessons: in S. Williams (Ed.), *Humans and Machines: Proceedings of the Fourth Delaware Symposium on Language and Linguistics* (pp. 268-272). Norwood, NJ: Ablex Publishing Corp

Culley, G. R. (1986). Individualized Latin curriculum (self-paced program consisting of syllabus, test-generating diskette [for Apple II] and six audio tapes to accompany Latin skills). Newark, DE: Office of Computer-Based Instruction, University of Delaware.

Culley, G. R. (1987). Blending database with CAI. In Bernard Frischer (Ed.) *Papers of the UCLA Conference on Classics and Computing*, Los Angeles, July 19-20, 1986 (pp. 81-90). Favonius Supplementary Volume I.

Culley, G. R. (1988). *Lector: a tool for Latin sentence analysis (computer software for Apple II series).* Newark, DE: Office of Instructional Technology, University of Delaware.

Larsen-Freeman, D (1987). Recent innovations in language teaching methodology. *Annals of the AAPSS*, **490**, 51-69.

Underwood, J. H. (1984). *Linguistics, computers and the language teacher: a communicative approach.* Rowley, MA: Newbury House Publishers.

3 LISP Intelligent Tutoring System: Research in Skill Acquisition

Albert T. Corbett and John R. Anderson
Advanced Computer Tutoring Project, Carnegie Mellon University

The LISP Intelligent Tutoring System (LISPITS) is an instructional program that helps students learn to program in the computer language LISP. Specifically, the tutor helps students with homework exercises. In each exercise the student is given a written description of a short program to write and, as the student types the program at the terminal, the tutor monitors the student's performance and provides assistance when errors are made. The tutor currently covers the first twelve chapters of an introductory LISP text (Anderson, Corbett & Reiser, 1987) and includes approximately 240 exercises.

LISPITS is dubbed "intelligent" because it is capable of generating correct solutions to the exercises and of assisting students based on this capability. The decision to build the tutor was inspired in large part by the collection of papers in *Intelligent Tutoring Systems* (Sleeman & Brown,1982) describing several tutors that embody the general approach described below. The tutor was developed for two major purposes:

- To automate some of the advantages of a personal tutor, thereby making them more widely available
- To test the real-world applicability of a psychological theory of skill acquisition, called ACT* (Anderson, 1983) and described below.

LISPITS was first tested in the summer of 1983 and has been used since then as a research tool. It has also been used in teaching a LISP course in the psychology department at Carnegie Mellon University each term since the fall of 1984.

The principal goal of the tutor is to allow students to practice programming. The tutor is constructed to be used in conjunction with an introductory LISP text *Essential LISP* (Anderson, et al. 1987) which describes the LISP language. After every major section in the text (roughly every two or three pages) there are coding exercises which require the students to write brief programs. Although these exercises can be done with LISPITS, they can also be done with paper and pencil or on a computer in the conventional mode of typing, executing and debugging solutions. The goal in developing LISPITS has been to optimize the time spent in doing these coding exercises. Given this goal, LISPITS does not do several things a human tutor might do. LISPITS doesn't try to provide any initial exposition of LISP, it doesn't make any provision for the students to ask general questions about LISP, and it doesn't try to assess the student's understanding of LISP (except in the context of doing exercises). Rather, the tutor provides an environment, similar to an editor, in which the student can do the exercises. But unlike an editor, it ensures that the student's final solutions are correct. More specifically, the tutor provides feedback when the student makes a mistake and, if the student appears to be floundering, will provide the next correct step in the solution. Thus, exchanges between the student and tutor are in the context of doing exercises and arise only if the student is having difficulties. Although in principle a student might complete all the exercises without knowing the tutor is in the background, in actuality, even if the student makes no mistakes, the tutor occasionally presents a menu in order to clarify the student's responses.

In this chapter we discuss assessment studies of the tutor and our experiences with it in the classroom. We then present the central assumptions of the ACT* theory and how these assumptions motivate the tutor's design and implementation. We then describe the research we have conducted with the tutor. To provide context, however, we precede the main part of the chapter with a brief discussion of LISP and a picture of the student's interaction with the tutor.

LISP AND AN ILLUSTRATIVE INTERACTION WITH LISPITS

At this point we first give a brief description of the language LISP and then run through a hypothetical interaction with LISPITS to give some idea what it is like to use the tutor.

Brief Description of LISP

LISP is an interpretive language, which means it is not necessary to compile LISP code before running it. Instead it is possible to "enter a LISP environment" on the computer, that is, run a program called a LISP interpreter and just type LISP code. The interpreter will "evaluate" (execute) the code and return an answer. For example, in the following interaction, the LISP interpreter has put a prompt (=>) on the screen. The user has typed a line of code, indicating the addition of three numbers. The LISP interpreter executes the line of code and returns the answer, `12`.

```
=> (+ 3 4 5)
12
```

Function calls

Functions in LISP are generally designed to accept one or more "arguments" (input values) and return an answer. The expression `(+ 3 4 5)` in the example above is a function call. The function + is applied to three arguments, and an answer is returned. There are two important points to recognize concerning the structure of function calls:

1. LISP uses prefix notation: the operator precedes all the argument values on which it operates.
2. A function call takes the form of a list: the operator, followed by its arguments, are all enclosed in a set of parentheses.

In evaluating a function call, LISP first evaluates each of the arguments and then applies the operator to them. For example, consider the following function call:

```
=> (+ 4 (* 10 5))
54
```

The user has called the function + with two arguments, but the second argument is itself a function call (* 10 5). Before LISP can apply +, it must evaluate this function call. The operator * performs multiplication, so (* 10 5) returns 50, and the call to + returns 54.

In the preceding example, LISP evaluates the numbers (4, 10, 5), returning their own values. LISP can also evaluate variables. For example, suppose the symbol `sym` has the value 5. Then, as above,

```
=> (+ 4 (* 10 sym))
54
```

because LISP evaluates `sym` as 5. If one wants LISP to evaluate a symbol literally rather than as a variable, then the symbol is preceded by a single quotation mark (e.g., `'sym`).

Function definitions

Programming in LISP largely consists of defining new functions. New functions can be defined in LISP by means of the built-in function `defun`.

This function takes three arguments: 1. The name of the function, 2. A list of variables called "parameters," 3. The body of the function describing what the function does.

Interacting with LISPITS to Solve a Problem

We now turn to the tutor LISPITS and how a student might work with it to define a LISP function.

A sample problem

Consider the following problem description:

> Define a function called `pal` that takes a single list as an argument and returns a palindrome that is twice as long. A palindrome is a list that reads the same forward and backward. For example, `(pal '(a b c))` returns `(a b c c b a)`.

Note that the argument of `pal` begins with a single quote, meaning that LISP should not evaluate the symbol `(a b c)` before applying `pal` to it.

The student is being asked to define a function which, when provided a list, creates a new list with a specific structure. The student must use the existing function `defun` to define a new function `pal`. As described above, `defun` requires three arguments. The following solution satisfies the problem description:

```
(defun pal (origlist)
   (append origlist (reverse origlist)))
```

The first symbol following `defun` (its first argument) specifies the name of the new function, `pal`. The second symbol `(origlist)` is a list containing a single parameter `origlist`. This parameter is a variable; when `pal` is subsequently executed and given a list, such as `(a b c)`, the list will automatically be assigned to the variable `origlist`. The final argument of `defun`, `(append origlist (reverse origlist))`, is the "body" of the function definition. To code the body of the function the student must code `(reverse origlist)` to generate a list which is a mirror-image reversal of the original list, then merge the original list and this reversal into a new list, with the function `append`.

Interaction with LISPITS

Let's trace the process by which a student might generate this code. The following snapshot shows the terminal screen shortly after the student has begun the exercise.

Tutor Window

```
Define a function called pal that takes a single list as
an argument and returns a palindrome that is twice as
long.  A palindrome is a list that reads the same forward
and backward.  For example, (pal '(a b c)) returns
(a b c c b a).
```

Code Window

```
    (defun <name> <parameters>
        <body>)
```

When students are working on an exercise, the terminal screen is divided in two, with a tutor window at the top of the screen and a code window at the bottom. The tutor communicates with the student by means of the tutor window; the problem description appears in this window at the beginning of an exercise and remains there except when the student makes a mistake. The code the student types appears in the code window.

In the preceding snapshot, the student has already typed a left parenthesis and `defun` and LISPITS has responded by putting up a template for the student. Specifically, it has provided a matching right parenthesis and put three goal symbols on the screen in angle-brackets. These angle-bracket symbols are not themselves LISP code, but stand for the three arguments for `defun` that the student needs to fill in. They represent remaining goals to be satisfied. LISPITS highlights the goal symbol which the student must work on next. LISPITS constrains the student to type the function definition from left-to-right and top-down, so the next symbol the student must replace with code is `<name>`.

As the student works on an exercise the tutor monitors the student's input on a symbol-by-symbol basis. LISPITS is intended to recognize any reasonable solution that conforms to both the problem specification and the stylistic guidelines specified in the text. In many exercises there are several possible solutions and in some cases LISPITS recognizes literally hundreds of acceptable variations. As long as the student remains on any reasonable solution path, the interactions with LISPITS are very similar to working with a programming editor. As the student types, the tutor replaces the goal symbols with the student's correct entries, and advances the cursor to the goal symbol that is to be expanded next.

After the student types `defun` and LISPITS has put up the three-part function-definition template, the tutor then highlights each of the three goal symbols in succession, for the student to fill in. The student would type `pal` over the first symbol `<name>`. Then the student would replace the symbol `<parameters>` with a list (i.e., parentheses enclosing a set of symbols for function parameters). As we have seen, the function `pal` takes a single argument, so only one parameter is required, and the student should type a list containing a single symbol here. There are many errors that students make at this point as they are first learning to code functions. One interesting error would be to type the parameter list `(list)`. Technically, this is is a correct step; in LISP the student can legally create a parameter called `list`. However, LISPITS would object to this step for two reasons. The following snapshot shows what the student's code would look like at this juncture and how LISPITS would respond.

Tutor Window

```
Remember that you are trying to get the parameter list of
the function here.  You should not be calling the
function list.  If you were thinking of using list as a
parameter name, it is a bad idea because you might get
confused between the function and the parameter.
```

Code Window

```
(defun pal (list)
    <process>)
```

Whenever the student makes a mistake, the tutor immediately provides feedback and, if the tutor can diagnose the nature of the error, it provides an explanation. After the student presses the return key, the erroneously typed symbol is erased and the student is given a chance to type a correct symbol. The student then types a new symbol. If this response is correct, the problem description reappears. If the response is again erroneous, another feedback message appears. If the student repeatedly makes errors at a particular step that the tutor cannot diagnose or, if the student is repeating the same type of diagnosed error, the tutor will intervene to prevent floundering and provide the student with a correct next step along with an explanation, then allow the student to proceed.

The message in the preceding sample tutor display is typical of the general framework for providing feedback on errors. It reminds the student of the current goal and tries to explain why the student's code does not accomplish the goal. As the feedback suggests, LISPITS does not just point out syntactic or algorithmic errors, but also enforces certain stylistic constraints. While `list` can be used as a parameter, it is not good style to do so since it is also the name of a function in LISP, which can cause confusion. The other interesting point about this error is that there is another interpretation. The student may have intended to call `list` as a function here, perhaps because he/she forgot the parameter list and began work on the body of the function. Since there are two explanations of the student's behavior and LISPITS cannot distinguish between them, it says something about both interpretations.

In the next snapshot, we assume that the student has typed the parameter list correctly, with a single parameter `origlist`. This parameter represents the list to be given to the function `pal`. The student now makes a mistake in beginning the body of the function. The Tutor Window shows LISPITS' response.

Tutor Window

```
Yes, you will need to use the function REVERSE, but not
yet. Remember that you need to make a new list that
combines the original list with its reverse, so first you
will need a list combining function.
```

Code Window

```
(defun pal (origlist)
    (reverse)
```

As the feedback suggests, the current goal is to code a function that will build a list, but the student's code, `reverse` will not accomplish that goal. However, LISPITS recognizes that `reverse` does accomplish a subgoal of the current goal. It tells the student that it is premature to be working on that subgoal and tries to explain what the current goal is.

In the next snapshot the student seems to be working on the correct goal, but has called the wrong function to accomplish it:

Tutor Window

```
You will need to make a list, but LIST is the wrong
combining function. If you LIST (a b c) with its
reverse, you will get ((a b c) (c b a)) instead of
(a b c c b a).
```

Code Window

```
(defun pal (origlist)
    (list)
```

In this message, LISPITS confirms that the student is working on the correct goal, but tries to show, by means of the example in the problem description, why the student's code won't satisfy the goal.

In the following cycle the student has the right idea, but has made a typing error. LISPITS has a simple spelling corrector which detects the likely error and queries the student.

Tutor Window

```
Define a function called pal that takes a single list as
an argument and returns a palindrome that is twice as
long.  A palindrome is a list that reads the same forward
and backward.  For example, (pal '(a b c)) returns
(a b c c b a).
```

Code Window

```
    (defun pal (origlist)
        (append orglist <list2>))

    Did you mean origlist?
```

In the next snapshot the cursor is on the symbol `<list2>` and the student has asked for an explanation of what to do next. LISPITS tells the student what the correct next step is and will put the correct symbol into the code for the student.

Tutor Window

```
Here we can see that the argument list needs to be
reversed.  REVERSE will flip around the order of the
elements in a list.  For example, if we apply REVERSE to
(a b c) we get (c b a).
```

Code Window

```
    (defun pal (origlist)
        (append origlist <list2>))
```

Finally, in the next snapshot the student has completed the code correctly.

Tutor Window

```
Define a function called pal that takes a single list as
an argument and returns a palindrome that is twice as
long.  A palindrome is a list that reads the same forward
and backward.  For example, (pal '(a b c)) returns
(a b c c b a)
```

Code Window

```
    (defun pal (origlist)
        (append origlist (reverse origlist)))
```

After completing each exercise the students have an opportunity to try out the code they just wrote. When students complete an exercise, they enter a LISP window that gives them access to the LISP Interpreter. Students can experiment in the LISP window as they choose; the only constraint is that they successfully call the function they have just defined at least once. The following snapshot shows the result of successfully calling the newly defined function `pal` on the list `'(d e f)`.

LISP Window

```
=> (pal '(d e f))
(d e f f e d)
```

LISPITS: ASSESSMENT AND CURRENT USE

Two studies of LISPITS were conducted early in its development to assess its effectiveness (Anderson, Boyle, & Reiser, 1985; Anderson & Reiser, 1985). The first study compared three groups of students, all novice programmers, who learned LISP by reading a text and doing a standard set of exercises. One group performed this task with the assistance of a human tutor, a second group used LISPITS to do the exercises, and the third group performed the task on their own, doing the exercises entirely in the LISP window. There were no differences among the three groups on a post-test, but there were substantial differences in how quickly they worked through the exercises. The students working with a human tutor completed the task in approximately 12 hours, those working with LISPITS finished in about 15 hours, while those working entirely on their own required approximately 28 hours.

The second study assessed LISPITS in the context of a class. The students in this study had taken a prior programming class (in Pascal). These students attended lectures on LISP and performed the same set of exercises. Half the students did the exercises with LISPITS, while the other half did the exercises on their own in the LISP window. The students working with LISPITS took 30% less time to complete the exercises and scored 43% higher on a posttest. Thus, while LISPITS is not as effective as a human tutor, it leads to strong performance gains in comparison with students doing exercises on their own.

Currently LISPITS is used to teach a self-paced course in LISP offered each term in the Psychology Department at Carnegie Mellon. Most of the work in the course involves completing LISPITS' twelve lessons. Two mechanisms are built into the program to ensure that students are learning the material. First,

LISPITS assesses students' performance as they complete exercises and provides additional exercises to students who are having difficulties (this mechanism is described in more detail below). Second, after every other lesson LISPITS gives an on-line quiz, in which students are asked to perform four programming exercises without tutoring assistance. Students must pass this quiz before they can move on. If they flunk a given quiz twice, LISPITS has them repeat the material in the two preceding lessons. If they flunk the quiz two more times, students are required to see the instructor before proceding. In addition to these internal mechanisms, there are external mechanisms to ensure that students are able to function in LISP without the assistance of LISPITS. First, they are asked to do a handful of exercises entirely outside the tutoring program with a standard LISP interpreter and a typical screen editor. These non-tutor assignments culminate in a final project that typically involves writing a program that employs artificial intelligence search techniques to perform a problem solving task. In addition, students typically take paper-and-pencil midterm and final exams involving programming exercises.

THEORETICAL PRINCIPLES UNDERLYING LISPITS

The goal of this research project has been to develop a programming tutor on the basis of principles derived from the ACT* theory of cognition (Anderson, 1983). ACT* is a general theory of cognitive processing and, as such, is necessarily complex, but only some of its assumptions are directly relevant to the tutor. Table 1 contains a summary of the relevant assumptions from the ACT* theory, with corresponding tutoring principles derived from these assumptions (Anderson, Boyle, Farrell, & Reiser, 1987).

These principles generally governed the development of LISPITS and other programming and mathematics tutors developed by Anderson's group (cf. Anderson, Boyle, & Yost, 1985; Lewis, Milson, & Anderson, 1987; Anderson, Boyle, Corbett, & Lewis, 1990). In this section we will elaborate the assumptions of the model and the tutoring principles from Table 1.

Behavior is Goal-Driven (Principle 1)

Like most theories of problem solving, ACT* assumes that behavior is goal driven (Miller, Galanter, & Pribram, 1960; Newell, Shaw, & Simon, 1958). Problem solving requires that the goal specified in the problem description (e.g., writing a program) be decomposed into subgoals which can either be satisfied directly or, in turn, decomposed. Thus, to a first approximation, acquiring a skill such as LISP coding requires the student to learn both (1) operations that can accomplish specific goals and (2) how to decompose high-level goals into subgoals that can be satisfied by known operations.

Table 1:
ACT* assumptions and related principles for a computer-implemented tutor.

	ACT* Assumptions	Corresponding Tutoring Principles
1.	Problem-solving behavior is goal driven.	Communicate the goal structure underlying the problem-solving task.
2.	Declarative and procedural knowledge are separate. The units of procedural knowledge are IF-THEN rules called productions.	Represent the student's knowledge as a production set.
3.	Initial performance of a task is accomplished by applying weak (general) procedures to declarative knowledge structures.	Provide instruction in the problem-solving context; let student's knowledge develop through successive approximations to the target skill.
	Task-specific productions arise by applying weaker productions to declarative knowledge. These task-specific productions underlie more efficient performance.	Provide immediate feedback on errors.
4.	As a result of additional practice, productions can be chained together into larger-scale productions.	Adjust the step size of instruction as learning progresses.
5.	The student maintains the current state of the problem in a limited-capacity working memory.	Minimize working memory load.

Declarative vs. Procedural Knowledge (Principle 2)

A second fundamental assumption, again shared by many cognitive theories, is that a distinction must be drawn between declarative and procedural knowledge. Students are assumed to acquire declarative knowledge of programming by reading or listening to lectures. Declarative knowledge can be readily learned but, in isolation, does not lead to behavior. Instead, performance requires procedural knowledge. It is assumed in ACT*, as in many other psychological models, that this knowledge is represented in the form of IF-THEN rules called productions. When a production is triggered (by the satisfaction of its IF clause), behavior results (through the execution of its THEN clause).

For example, one of the first declarative facts a student learns about LISP might be rendered in English as: *The function + takes one or more numbers as arguments and returns the sum of those numbers.* This declarative knowledge could be employed in different types of tasks, for example:

A code generation task:

Write a function call that will add the numbers 10, 20, 30 and 40.

A code evaluation task:

Compute the answer LISP would return if given the expression `(+ 3 4 5)`.

The assumption of the ACT* theory is that the declarative knowledge alone is not sufficient to perform either of these tasks. Instead, procedural knowledge is required; productions must execute (or "fire") to lead to any behavior such as writing code or evaluating code. In terms of the ACT* model, the ultimate goal in learning a programming language is to acquire productions that can be employed to perform these operations, for example:

A code generation production:

IF the goal is to add together a set of numbers
THEN code a call to + and set goals to code the arguments.

A code evaluation production:

IF the goal is to evaluate a function call of the form
`(+ <arg1> ... <argn>)`
THEN evaluate each of the n arguments and generate the sum
of the resulting numbers.

Note that each of these rules refers to the student's current goal and what to do to satisfy the goal. It is an important assumption of the theory that a production will lead to behavior only in the context of a particular goal. If the current goal is to write code, the second production cannot execute, while if the current goal is to evaluate a LISP expression, the first production cannot execute.

Acquiring Procedural Knowledge (Principles 3 and 4)

When the student first codes a call to +, it is not by firing a production like the one described above. Instead, the student executes a more general production for coding function names that refers to declarative knowledge structures, for example:

IF the goal is to perform an operation and the appropriate function name is in declarative memory
THEN code a call to that function and set a goal to code its arguments.

It is only as a result of successful applications of such general productions to specific declarative knowledge that the more specific coding production for + is acquired.

Once goal-specific productions have been formed, additional practice leads to two additional types of learning. First, productions are strengthened with additional practice. That is, with practice, they come to execute more quickly and reliably. Second, with practice, sequences of productions can be composed into larger-scale productions. One of the first obvious candidates for this composition process that arises in learning LISP concerns the operation of returning the second element of a list. LISP provides a function, `car`, which returns the first element of a list, e.g., `(car '(a b c))` returns `a`. LISP also provides a complementary function, `cdr`, which takes a list as an argument and removes the first item, e.g., `(cdr '(a b c))` returns `(b c)`. In order to return the second item in a list, it is necessary to remove the first item, by applying `cdr` to the list and then to return the first element of the resulting list with `car`. Thus, `(car (cdr '(a b c)))` returns `b`. When students first solve this problem (in Lesson 1) presumably they trigger two separate productions that code `car` and `cdr`. However, with experience, they are assumed to develop knowledge characterized by the following composed production:

IF the goal is to code a function call that returns the second element of a list,
THEN code a call to `car` on the result of a call to `cdr` and set a goal to code the argument to `cdr`.

Working Memory (Principle 5)

According to ACT*, the current state of a problem is stored in a limited capacity working memory. It is the current state information that can satisfy the IF clause of a production and so cause it to execute. Implementing the THEN clause of a production ordinarily causes a change in working memory so that some new productions are satisfied.

In the early phases of learning, before efficient productions have been built, relatively large amounts of information must be stored in working memory over relatively long periods of time. As more efficient productions are built, the load on working memory decreases.

Tutoring Principles

These fundamental assumptions give rise to the tutoring principles summarized in Table 1 and govern the general nature of LISPITS. The text enables the student to encode declarative knowledge structures and, as Tutoring Principle 3 suggests, the tutor concentrates on giving the student the opportunity to practice the skill and build productions. It is certainly likely that the student will not, by studying the text, completely and correctly encode the necessary declarative knowledge to complete the exercises in the tutor. In fact, empirical estimates of the probability that the student will correctly encode the declarative knowledge to construct various production rules ranges from 15% to 90% with a mean of about 60%. However, the assumptions underlying the tutor suggest that the most efficient course of action is to give students the opportunity to write code, and to repair declarative knowledge as the need arises in the course of coding.

Of course, within this general framework, it is necessary to make various decisions about the specifics of the interface. Again, theoretical assumptions suggest goals to strive for (although not necessarily how to obtain them). For example, in problem-solving, the process of recognizing which productions will satisfy the current goal relies heavily on working memory. This is particularly true in the early stages of problem solving, when larger declarative knowledge structures must be maintained in working memory to allow more general productions to execute. As a result, it should be optimal to reduce the load of non-essential information in working memory. Indeed, research by Anderson & Jeffries (1985) suggests that many errors made by novices learning to program are slips that result from the loss of information from their working memory. This research examined a simple code generation task (among other tasks) involving list operations and found that when more complicated arguments were involved, students were more likely to make errors in selecting the correct function to accomplish a goal. The fact that subjects were making errors inconsistently, i.e., making errors in some situations and not in others, suggests that the errors were slips rather than systematic misconceptions. The fact that errors occurred more often in more complex exercises suggests that the slips may have resulted from working memory overload. The tutor reduces working memory load largely by providing templates for function calls. By providing balancing right parentheses these templates reduce the burden of syntactic considerations in coding. By providing angle-bracket symbols for arguments these templates also provide external cues concerning pending goals (and simultaneously satisfy Principle 2 in Table 1).

One of the tutoring principles in Table 1 has proven quite controversial and deserves special discussion. This is the principle of immediate feedback. This principle is derived from both theoretical and practical considerations. Theoretically, it is assumed that procedural learning is based on a memory trace of the student's practice. If a student makes an error while coding a function and must go back and self-correct then, first, the memory trace is more complicated and, second, it reflects error repair rather than correct generation. These two factors combine to decrease the potential for successful learning. First, it is less likely that a correct production will be formed from the more complicated trace. Second, even if the correct production is formed, it is less likely that the student will recognize its goal at the next opportunity without going through the same error and repair process.

There are two practical reasons for preferring very immediate feedback over more delayed feedback. First, if feedback is to lead to a useful production, it is necessary that it be provided in the context of the appropriate active goal and working memory state. If feedback is delayed it may be less likely that the appropriate context will be reinstated, rendering the feedback less useful. Lewis and Anderson (1985) have provided some evidence of a weaker effect of delayed feedback in an adventure game which is formally equivalent to solving equations. A second reason for providing immediate feedback is that once a student has branched onto an erroneous path, the error can be compounded by additional errors and the student can spend a lot of time and become quite distressed trying to recover. Since the tutor is unable to follow a student once he/she has diverged from a successful path, the simplest solution to this problem is to immediately bring the student back to a correct path. The adequacy of the immediate feedback principle is an open issue, and we will return to it in the final experiment discussed in this chapter.

Of course, if the tutor provides feedback on an error, the consequence can only be to repair declarative knowledge and not to encode a production for doing it correctly in the first place. However, the student is given the opportunity to try again at the point of the error, so the possibility remains of generating the correct symbol and perhaps encoding the corresponding production. If the tutor tells the student what code to generate, for example, "code a call to + here," the production a student is likely to form is:

IF the goal is to code what the tutor tells me to and
the tutor says to code "+"
THEN code +.

This production is not likely to be generally useful so, in responding to errors, the goal of feedback in the tutor is to provide a reminder of the current goal and why the student's code does not achieve the goal. It is not to tell the student what the correct code is. The tutor only gives the student the correct code when the evidence is that the student is lost.

MODEL TRACING: IMPLEMENTING LISPITS

To construct a tutor that performs according to the specifications in the preceding section, it is necessary to have at all times a pattern against which the student's behavior can be measured. That is, as the student generates a LISP program step-by-step, the tutor must have information that allows it to recognize whether each successive step is on the path to a successful solution. One way to accomplish this task is to provide the tutor with a catalog of possible solutions for each exercise. This approach would allow it to recognize whether each symbol of code does or does not match a known solution. It could recognize correct steps, could have relatively simple rules for deciding if a mistake was close to, or far from, being correct, and could readily tell the student steps that would work. The difficulty arises in trying to explain steps to students, in terms of underlying goals and constructs. A given function always performs the same operation, so it is possible to describe to the student *what* the next step in the algorithm is but, with this approach, it is not possible to say *why* that step is appropriate. This difficulty with a solution catalog might be surmounted, e.g., by providing hand-coded explanations for each solution or, perhaps, by providing the tutor with a description of each exercise and with rules for inferring, in relation to the description, the purpose of each symbol of code. However, we have taken a different approach with LISPITS. Instead of providing LISPITS with a set of solutions for each exercise, we provide LISPITS with rules that allow it to generate solutions.

In this approach LISPITS is provided a set of general rules for writing LISP code and a specification of each exercise. From these, it attempts to model the steps that a student might take in solving a problem. Thus, while the student is working, the tutor in lock-step simulates the steps that a knowledgeable student could take in writing the code. In addition, it models errors that students make at each step on the basis of known misconceptions. By comparing the students' response to the set of possible legal actions and the set of known erroneous actions, the tutor is able to recognize whether the student is on a correct solution path, appears to be suffering from a known misconception, or has typed something unrecognizable. This set of correct and incorrect rules for writing LISP programs is referred to as the student model and is described in more detail in the following section. We refer to this process of comparing the student's steps in writing a program to the steps generated by the student model as model tracing.

The Student Model

The student model that underlies the LISP tutor is partly descriptive and partly prescriptive. That is, it is derived in part from observations of students learning LISP (Anderson, Farrell, & Sauers, 1984; Pirolli & Anderson, 1985) and in part from analysis of requisite knowledge for LISP programming and considerations of good programming style. As described earlier, procedural knowledge of how to write LISP code is modelled by a set of productions. Each production is essentially an IF-THEN rule. An English translation of a typical production rule that students learn in Lesson 1 would be:

IF the goal is to form a list by inserting an item at the beginning of an existing list
THEN code a call to the function `cons` and set subgoals to code the item and the list.

A more complex rule that is encountered in a later lesson is:

IF the goal is to code a function that takes a list and the function must access every atom in the list structure and the list structure can be arbitrarily complex
THEN code `cond` to implement car-cdr recursion and set subgoals to code terminating cases and to code recursive cases.

The complete set of correct rules for writing code is referred to as the ideal student model and represents the instructional objectives of the text and tutor. The student model also includes a set of incorrect rules that reflect known misconceptions and are collectively referred to as the bug catalog, or the set of student model buggy rules.

In actually modelling student behavior, the production system is given a specification of the LISP program to be written and a goal is set to write the program. The problem description, which is analogous to the English description provided the student, is loaded into the production system's working memory. At each step in generating a program, the production system examines its correct and buggy rules and decides which ones could execute according to the IF clauses satisfied by the current problem state, i.e., by the current goal and the current contents of working memory. This set of eligible rules is termed the conflict set and will always contain one or more correct rules and will generally contain one or more buggy rules. Only one of these eligible rules in the conflict set can actually be triggered, and the next step is to decide which one best describes the action taken by the student. LISPITS does this by comparing the symbol the student types to the symbol that would be generated by each of the rules in the conflict set.

If the student's input matches the symbol generated by a correct rule, then that rule is triggered. As a result, the student's symbol is added to the permanent problem solution, one or more new goals may be set, and information may be added to working memory. At that point, a new goal is activated (drawn from the list of unsatisfied goals) and the cycle is repeated. If the student's input matches the symbol that would be generated by one of the buggy rules, or does not match any rule in the conflict set, then no rule is triggered. Instead, the tutor provides a feedback message and gives the student another chance. If the student then types a correct symbol, a correct rule is then triggered as described above. If the student repeatedly types symbols that either do not match any rule in the conflict set or match the same buggy rule, then the tutor intervenes to prevent floundering. This is done by triggering one of the correct rules in the conflict set and providing an explanation of why that rule is appropriate to accomplish the current goal.

This cycle of activating goals, generating conflict sets, and matching the student's inputs continues until the exercise is completed.

Why Model Tracing?

As suggested earlier, given our goal of providing assistance to students as they work on programming exercises, it is necessary to provide the tutoring program with either a set of exercise solutions or a mechanism for generating solutions. In model tracing, we provide LISPITS with a mechanism for generating solutions; more specifically, we provide a mechanism that is intended to model the student's thought processes in completing the exercises.

As mentioned earlier, the chief reason that model tracing is useful in tutoring is that there can be different underlying reasons for employing a given LISP function in different contexts. For example, the function `setq` always has the effect of assigning a value to a variable, but there are different underlying goals that can be achieved by performing this action. One distinction concerns the type of variable being assigned a value: we could be assigning a value to a global variable so that it is available to any function we define, or we could be updating a local variable that is only needed within a specific function. The reason for the assignment can also vary: we could be storing intermediate results within a loop, or we could be storing the result of a complex operation to avoid having to repeat it.

In the student model different production rules govern the coding of a given symbol (such as `setq`) for different purposes. As a practical matter, this allows LISPITS to generate contextually appropriate explanations, since we can associate a contextually appropriate explanation with each production. When the student model is running through an exercise, contextually appropriate rules will be available at each goal and, if an explanation is required, a contextually appropriate one is automatically produced.

The student model is intended to be more than a convenient formalism for generating explanations, however. It is intended to be a psychological model of the knowledge the student is acquiring. Indeed, examination of the log files of the students' interactions with LISPITS supports the hypothesis that different rules generate the same symbol in different contexts (Anderson, 1990; Conrad & Anderson, 1988). As described in the following section, LISPITS maintains a model of how well each student understands how to program in LISP. To the extent that different rules govern the coding of a single symbol in different contexts, it is important to represent and track the rules separately to maintain an accurate model of the student's knowledge. Again, the student model allows us to do this. It provides us with a list of the rules to track and, as the student model is running, ensures that the student's responses at each goal are associated with the appropriate production rules.

In addition, student modelling also allows us to automate the initial stage of data analysis. When students interact with LISPITS it maintains a time-stamped log file of the student's inputs and LISPITS' responses. Since LISPITS is modelling the student's behavior, it can conveniently identify and store the underlying rules which theoretically give rise to each of the student's responses.

Finally, there is at least one beneficial side effect of model tracing. Development of the student model is a useful aid in curriculum development, since it forces us to think in specific terms about what a student needs to learn.

Model Tracing and Mastery Learning

When the tutor was first used in teaching LISP to programming novices, it became clear in posttests that an appreciable minority of the students were not learning LISP well enough. In a rare case or two, it turned out the student was just asking the tutor for an explanation at each step and having the tutor generate the code. In most cases, however, even though students were doing most of the work themselves in getting through the exercises, they had trouble doing exercises on their own.

The current configuration of the course, as described in an earlier section, in large part reflects this observation. We instituted a handful of non-tutor exercises and frequent quizzes to provide the students as well as the instructor a measure of the student's understanding. Moreover, quiz results are used to implement a mastery learning paradigm: students cannot proceed to later lessons until they have passed each quiz.

In addition to these revisions in the course structure, we introduced a degree of mastery learning within LISPITS itself. We modified LISPITS so that it monitors the student's performance in completing exercises and tailors the exercise sequence to accommodate the student's rate of progress. Specifically, the tutor maintains a model of the student's knowledge state in the course of proceeding through the twelve lessons. The model of each student is essentially an overlay model that consists of a list of the production rules in the ideal student model. For each rule LISPITS maintains an estimate of the probability that the student has learned the rule. By examining log files of students who have used LISPITS to see what percentage of them use a given rule correctly the first time, we can compute an estimate of the average probability that students will learn that rule just from reading the text. These estimates are initially assigned to the production rules when an overlay model is first created for an individual student. Then the probability estimate for a rule is updated when the student has the opportunity to employ the rule. The new estimate of whether the student has learned the rule depends on whether the student responds correctly or makes an error and is computed according to a simple two-state learning theory[1] and Bayesian statistics.

Of course, once these probabilities are computed, it is a separate issue how to use them. As previously mentioned, we have opted for a mastery-based system of learning. We have adopted a probability value of 0.95 as the criterion for concluding that the student knows a rule. Each time a new set of rules is introduced in the text and the student is ready to do exercises, the tutor presents a set of required exercises that draw on the new rules. After the student has completed the required exercises, the tutor reviews all the rules in the student's knowledge model to see if any fall below the 0.95 criterion. If so, the tutor selects the best exercise to practice the rule(s). An optimal practice exercise is defined as one in which the student knows 90% of the rules required to write the code but needs to learn the remaining 10% of the rules, and LISPITS selects an exercise that comes closest to this ratio. Only after the student has brought all rules above the 95% criterion does the tutor allow the student to move on to the next section in the text.

We refer to this process of monitoring and remediating the student's knowledge as *knowledge tracing*. As a final fail-safe measure in knowledge tracing, if the student completes many exercises in a lesson (operationally defined as twice the number of required exercises) without completing the lesson, the tutor requires the student to see the instructor before proceeding. This allows us to deal with the rare student who has fundamental misconceptions. A later section describes assessment of this knowledge tracing.

---

[1] A two-state model assumes that a production rule can be in exactly one of two states in memory; either the student has learned it or not. ACT* is not a two-state model, and there are ample learning data that support either multi-state or continuous-strength memory models. However, the estimates of all such models are highly correlated and the data generated by the tutor is not sufficiently powerful to distinguish among them. Thus, we have opted for the computationally simplest model.

SKILL ACQUISITION RESEARCH WITH LISPITS

At this point we would like to describe some research we have conducted with LISPITS. An earlier section provided a comparison of students using LISPITS with students who used only a standard LISP programming environment to do exercises. The results do indicate that LISPITS lets students learn at least as much LISP in a considerably shorter time. The following studies address more detailed questions about what features of LISPITS are useful, and what might be eliminated or changed.

The first study examines whether practice in evaluating sample programs transfers to skill in writing programs. The outcome of this study has practical pedagogical implications and is of theoretical interest, since it investigates the possible transfer between two types of procedural skill based on common declarative knowledge structures. The remaining studies examine two aspects of feedback: content and control. In the first two of these studies, we examine the effectiveness of the explanations LISPITS provides by comparing the standard tutor with a version that notifies students of errors but does not try to explain them. In the final section, we address some practical issues that arise in implementing the tutor and describe some preliminary results obtained with a version of LISPITS in which the student controls the timing of feedback.

Does Practice in Code Evaluation Improve Code Generation?

The first pedagogical issue we addressed with the tutor concerns the assumption that time should be concentrated on practice in writing programs rather than in other activities. In particular, we examined whether better performance in *writing* programs can be produced by practice in *evaluating* programs (i.e., executing them in the mind to predict their results). Textbooks and instructors ordinarily assume that an effective way to introduce new programming constructs is to show sample code and to explain how the code is executed, i.e., to evaluate the code. An interesting question is whether such practice in evaluating code contributes substantially to skill in generating programs. ACT* would suggest that practicing evaluation would provide relatively little benefit in learning to generate code. At least three studies have confirmed this prediction over two restricted areas of LISP, basic LISP functions (McKendree & Anderson, 1987; Kessler, 1988) and recursive functions (Pirolli, 1985).

We used the tutor to investigate the issue systematically across the eleven lessons that existed in the fall of 1985. In this experiment, all students went through the tutor and took a paper and pencil test after the sixth lesson and after the final lesson. Half the students received practice in evaluating sample functions in addition to performing the tutor's programming exercises.

Specifically, before starting each section of code generation exercises, the tutor presented students one or two code evaluation exercises. In each evaluation exercise the students were presented with a function definition and a sample call to the function. By pressing special keys the student indicated how LISP would sequentially evaluate the function definition in the course of executing the sample call. To solve an evaluation exercise, students indicated not only the order in which the expressions were evaluated, but also the result of each evaluation step. Students continued through this evaluation process until a final result was obtained. As the students worked, the tutor provided immediate feedback on errors concerning both evaluation sequence and results.

Table 2:

Transfer from code evaluation to programming.

	With Practice on Evaluation	With No Practice on Evaluation
LISPITS programming exercises:		
Average time for one production execution	12.5 sec	12.0 sec
Percent correct on posttest		
Coding	60 %	62 %
Evaluation	66 %	56 %
Debugging	61 %	65 %

Table 2 presents the results of this experiment. This table contains one measure of performance from the tutor exercises and one posttest performance measure. The measure of performance in completing the LISPITS exercises is average production execution time for goals at which the student's first response is correct. The operational definition of execution time is the average time it takes students to respond to each of the angle-bracket goal symbols in defining functions. Each such step the student takes corresponds to executing a production in the student model, so this measure is theoretically a measure of the time for a student to make an inference corresponding to the execution of one production. As can be seen, evaluation practice had no impact on coding time for the tutor exercises. Average production execution time is essentially the same for the two conditions.

The posttest score is percent correct across the midterm and cumulative final exam. As indicated in the table there were three types of exercises on the exams: coding exercises in which the student wrote function definitions, evaluation exercises similar to the ones administered by the evaluation tutor, and debugging exercises in which students were asked to repair buggy programs. As can be seen, students in the two groups obtained virtually the same score on the coding exercises; if anything, the students who used the evaluation tutor scored slightly lower in these exercises. Students who practiced evaluation exercises did perform slightly better on the posttest evaluation exercises, 66% vs 56%. Thus, the data suggests that students who practiced evaluating code were acquiring some knowledge that was not acquired by the students who did not practice evaluation. However, there is no indication that this knowledge transferred to writing code, nor to debugging code. While there is common declarative knowledge underlying coding, evaluation and debugging, this result supports the assumption that employing that knowledge in the pursuit of one type of goal will have minimal impact on the pursuit of different goals.

Effects of Explanatory Feedback and Remedial Practice

In a pair of studies conducted over the past year we evaluated the effectiveness of the tutor's feedback and the tutor's ability to provide remedial practice based on knowledge tracing. In the case of feedback, we were interested in whether LISPITS' explanations are helpful, or whether students might benefit from generating their own explanations when the tutor has identified an error. To evaluate the effectiveness of explanations, we simply shut them off for half the students. The tutor continued to interrupt as usual if an error occurred and continued to provide correct answers under the standard rules when the student appeared to be floundering. However, the tutor no longer attempted to explain the nature of errors nor to explain correct answers it provided. That is, if the student made an error, the tutor interrupted immediately but just responded, "That doesn't seem to be correct." When the tutor provided a correct answer, it simply told the student what code to write, but not why, e.g., "You need to call the function APPEND here."

To assess the effectiveness of knowledge tracing, and its individually tailored remedial practice, we shut it off for half the subjects. These students completed just the required exercises in each section. While the tutor continued to update estimates of the student's understanding, it did not provide any additional practice exercises with the aim of remediating weaknesses in the student's knowledge. The manipulation of explanations and remediation were crossed in these studies, yielding a two-by-two between subjects design. By crossing the manipulations we can observe whether the presence of either explanations or remediation alone compensates for the absence of the other.

We ran two replications of this experiment: Study 1 in the spring of 1987 covered Lessons 1-3, 5, and 6; Study 2 in the fall of 1987 covered all 12 lessons. Table 3 presents the results of both experiments.

Table 3 presents, for Study 1, two measures of performance in completing the LISPITS programming exercises: average production execution time for goals at which the student's first response is correct and average number of errors in responding at each goal. These LISPITS performance measures are derived from the required exercises, which are common to all groups. The posttest score is percent correct on a cumulative final exam. As can be seen, there is virtually no effect of either manipulation on posttest performance. An analysis of variance confirmed that the two main effects and interaction were non-significant.

Table 3:
Performance based on combinations of error explanation and use of knowledge tracing with its remedial practice.

Exercises: production firing time (sec) and errors per goal

		Study 1		Study 2	
		Explanations:		Explanations:	
		Yes	No	Yes	No
Remedial Practice:	Yes	14.9 sec 0.23 errors	13.6 sec 0.28 errors	10.4 sec 0.13 errors	11.1 sec 0.18 errors
	No	15.5 sec 0.15 errors	22.8 sec 0.38 errors	12.4 sec 0.18 errors	10.6 sec 0.26 errors

Posttest performance (percent correct)

		Study 1		Study 2	
		Explanations:		Explanations:	
		Yes	No	Yes	No
Remedial Practice:	Yes	80%	79%	95%(quizzes) 87%(exam)	94%(quizzes) 82%(exam)
	No	85%	85%	86%(quizzes) 65%(exam)	88%(quizzes) 79%(exam)

The manipulations of explanations and remediation did have measurable effects on students' performance with LISPITS, however. Averaging over subjects who did and did not receive remediation, subjects who received explanations made fewer errors per goal than subjects in the other group, 0.19 errors/goal vs. 0.33 errors/goal. This effect of explanations was significant in an analysis of variance $F(1,21) = 6.58$, $p < .05$. Neither the main effect of remediation on this measure of accuracy nor the interaction of explanations and remediation were significant. Thus, students who received explanations from LISPITS made fewer errors in completing the tutor exercises.

Knowledge tracing remediation did influence production execution time, however. Students who received remedial exercises responded more quickly at each goal, 14.3 seconds/production vs. 19.2 seconds/production. This difference was significant in an analysis of variance, $F(1,21) = 7.97$, $p < .05$. Production execution times were also faster for subjects who received explanations, 15.2 seconds/production vs. 18.2 seconds/production, although this effect was only marginally significant, $F(1,21) = 3.11$, $p < .10$. Finally, the interaction of explanations and remediation was significant in this analysis, $F(1,21) = 6.16$, $p < .05$. As can be seen, students who received neither explanations nor remediation were particularly slow in responding.

The pattern of effects on performance with the tutor is understandable. First, if the explanations are useful, then we would expect students to make fewer second and third errors at a goal after having received an explanation on the first error. In that case, we would expect fewer errors per goal as observed. Second, students in the remediation condition performed more total exercises with LISPITS than did students in the non-remediation condition. This fact is likely to influence response speed, even though the measure is based just on the required exercises common to all groups. Once the first few required exercises have been encountered, students in the remediation condition will begin doing remedial exercises with the result that, when any subsequent required problem is encountered, students in the remedial groups will have performed more prior exercises. Since performance speed generally decreases with time on task, it follows that students in the remedial condition would on average perform the required exercises more quickly.

Two other results concerning the measures of performance with LISPITS are perhaps less predictable. Consider first the interaction of explanations and remediation on production execution time. Apparently the presence of explanations roughly compensates for the extra practice received in the remediation condition. Reduced practice only leads to reduced speed of production execution when explanations are shut off. Perhaps the most surprising result, however, is that while the explanation and remediation manipulations affected tutor performance, there were no long-term effects on posttest performance. Students' performance on the posttest was independent of the version of LISPITS used.

The results for Study 2, also presented in Table 3, are slightly different. There are again two measures of performance with LISPITS: production execution time for goals at which the student's first response is correct and average number of errors per goal. (These analyses were performed just on the five lessons that also appeared in the Study 1). The table also contains two posttest performance measures. One is percent correct across a midterm exam and a cumulative final exam, both paper-and-pencil tests. The other measure is percent correct across six on-line quizzes presented by the tutor.

As can be seen in Table 3, the manipulation of explanations had little impact on either posttest score. In this experiment, unlike the previous one, there was an effect of knowledge tracing on posttest measures. When knowledge tracing was shut off, students scored lower on both the quizzes, 87% vs. 95%, and on the tests, 72% vs. 85%. The effect of remediation on quiz scores was significant, $F(1,29) = 6.48$, $p < .05$, while the effect on final exam scores was marginally significant, $F(1,29) = 2.97$, $p < .10$. The main effect of explanations was non-significant in the analyses of both the quizzes and final exams, although the interaction of explanations and remediation was marginally significant in the final exam analysis, $F(1,29) = 3.18$, $p < .10$. Examination of Table 3 indicates that there may be less effect of the remediation manipulation in the No-Explanation condition.

The two manipulations had weaker effects on the measures of performance with LISPITS than in the previous experiment. The explanation manipulation had no reliable effect on production execution speed and only a marginal effect on the number of errors. Subjects who received explanations made fewer errors per goal than those who did not receive explanations, 0.16 vs. 0.22, $F(1,29) = 3.08$, $p < .10$. The manipulation of remediation also had no reliable effect on production execution speed, but it had a marginal effect on errors per goal. Students made fewer errors in the remediation condition, 0.16/goal vs. 0.22/goal, $F(1,29) = 2.99$, $p < .10$. Finally, the interaction of the two manipulations was non-significant in both analyses.

In summary, there is no indication in either study that explanations are having an effect on degree of learning as measured by posttest scores. There is evidence that knowledge tracing has an impact on posttest scores in the second experiment; students seem to learn the material better when knowledge tracing is turned on. This effect is not obtained in the first experiment, but this inconsistency is not entirely surprising. So far, no research limited to the first part of the LISPITS curriculum has led to posttest performance differences. In particular, the first assessment study of LISPITS described earlier, which covered just the first eight lessons, led to total time differences but no posttest differences among students in the three conditions. In the second assessment study, differences in posttest performance did not appear on the midterm, but only appeared on the cumulative final exam.

Concerning measures of performance with LISPITS, again the pattern is not entirely consistent across the two studies. The explanation manipulation did have an impact on accuracy in both studies, although the effect is marginal in the second one. Knowledge tracing chiefly affects performance time in the first study but affects accuracy in the second study.

The absence of an explanation effect on the posttest and the marginal effect on tutor performance in the second study is interesting. It may suggest that most of the effectiveness of LISPITS is obtained just by interrupting students immediately after an error and simply providing the correct next step when students are floundering. The tutor's efforts to provide explanations in those situations may not be helpful. One possible explanation of the small effect of shutting off explanations is that students simply aren't reading the explanations when they are presented. One way to investigate this issue is to ask: If a student makes a mistake that LISPITS can diagnose and explain to the student, what is the probability that the student will get the answer correct on the next attempt? If the explanations were effective, we would expect that students who received the explanations would be less likely to make another mistake at the same goal. Table 4 provides evidence on this point for Lessons 1-3, 5, and 6 in the Study 2.

Table 4:

Effect of explanation on probability of immediate correction of an error.

Probability of immediate error correction (LISPITS exercise in Study 2)			
		Explanations	
		Yes	No
Remedial	Yes	0.88	0.65
Practice:	No	0.70	0.62

This table displays the probability that students take a correct step at a goal immediately after making a diagnosed error at the goal (i.e., a mistake for which the tutor could provide an explanation, but does so for only half the students). As can be seen, students who received explanations are more likely to make a correct response immediately after an error. Thus, there is some internal evidence that the students are reading the explanations. However, there is little evidence of a long-term effect of this feedback.

MODEL TRACING AND STUDENT-CONTROLLED FEEDBACK

As described earlier, LISPITS constrains students to type in their code in a strict top-down, left-to-right order and provides error feedback on a symbol-by-symbol basis. The first characteristic may appear to be a superficial property of the program's interface, and the second characteristic may appear to be purely a tutoring principle. However, these characteristics are closely tied to two characteristics of the student model. The input-order constraints are tied to assumptions built into the production system concerning active goals. While there is generally more than one unsatisfied goal pending at any point during problem solving, only one goal can be active at each step in problem solving[2]. Additional assumptions concerning which of the pending goals will be selected at each step give rise to strict top-down, left-to-right behavior in the student model, which in turn governs the tutor's interface (see Corbett, Anderson, & Patterson, 1988 for more details). Symbol-by-symbol feedback is tied to the grain-size of the productions in the student model. The student's knowledge of LISP is modelled at the finest grain-size that has meaning in LISP—roughly the level of individual symbols. Any finer grain-size would begin to model typing

[2] This theoretical assumption has been relaxed since work on the tutor was initiated. A new production system, in which all pending goals are active in each cycle, reflects this modification in the theory.

skill. The immediate feedback principle specifies that feedback should be presented right after an erroneous production is triggered, but it is the grain-size of the tutor which dictates the symbol-by-symbol feedback presented by the tutor.

Given this relationship between the student model and the tutor's behavior, modifications in coding order or feedback units would require modifications in the student model and not just in the interface and tutorial components of the program. This is an important point since the student model is fairly large, consisting of approximately 1200 rules. Fortunately, model tracing can be implemented by means of a technique called problem compilation that facilitates such modifications. This technique is described in the next section.

Model Tracing and Problem Compilation

We originally adopted problem compilation as a means to speed up the tutor. Running a production system, such as the student model, imposes high computational demands on the computer because of the large amount of pattern matching required in determining the conflict set at each goal. As a result, the tutor in its initial form had trouble keeping up with students as they worked through an exercise. Fortunately, model tracing does not actually require execution of the production system student model on-line with the tutor. The reason is that the dynamic behavior of the student model in writing a program can be captured in a data structure which contains all the information required for tutoring. For example, consider a function called `insert-two` that takes three arguments, the third of which must be a list, and inserts the first two arguments at the beginning of the third. For example, given the arguments `'x`, `'(y z)`, and `'(a b c d)`, `insert-two` would return `(x (y z) a b c d)`. Two possible definitions of the function are:

```
(defun insert-two (item1 item2 alist)
     (cons item1 (cons item2 alist)))
(defun insert-two (item1 item2 alist)
    (append (list item1 item2) alist))
```

Figure 1 displays a tree structure that represents the possible steps the student model would take in coding this function. Each node (ellipse) in this tree represents a goal that is set in writing the code. The link descending from each node represents a production execution and ends at the symbol the production generates, e.g., `defun` is the symbol generated from the goal "code function." Links descending from the code symbol represent goals set by the production. The top goal in the tree represents the initial goal of defining the function `insert-two`. The link leading from that goal represents a production that generates the symbol `defun` and sets three goals: to code the function name, the parameter list, and the body of the function. All three of these goals must be satisfied. The first two of these goals are satisfied by productions that code the name insert-two and parameter list (item1 item2 alist) respectively and do not set any subgoals. As indicated by the arc labeled "OR", the third goal, coding the function body, can be satisfied by either of two productions. One of these productions generates the symbol cons and sets two subgoals. The other production generates the code symbol append and also sets two subgoals. Each of these subgoals is satisfied by additional productions and so on.

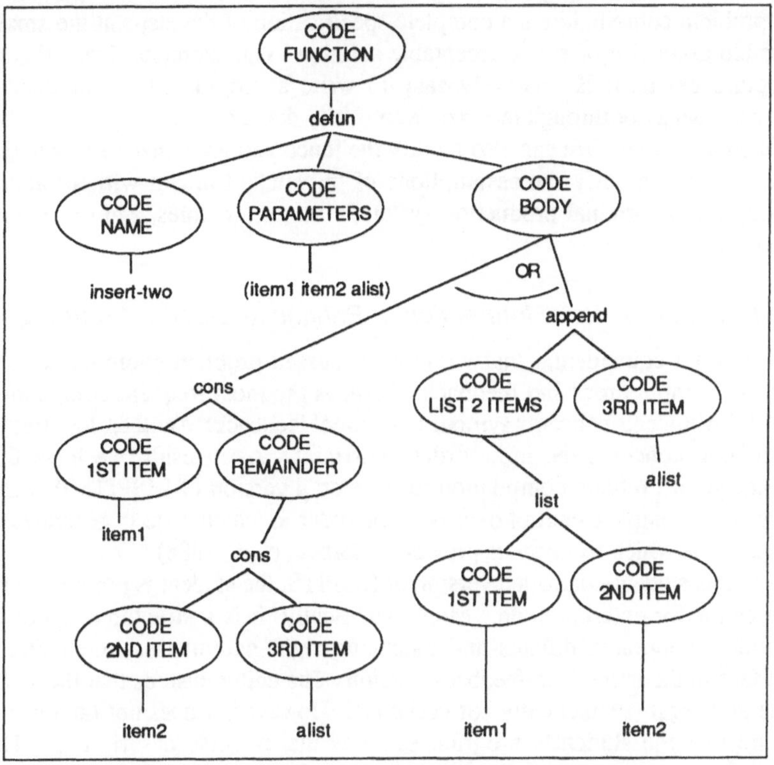

Figure 1: The hierarchical goal structure underlying the definition of `insert-two`. Each elliptical node represents a goal. The link descending from each goal represents a production execution. Each production link leads to the code symbol it generates, then to any additional goals that are set by the production.

In essence this data structure contains the information we need to know in order to tutor: the goal that is set at each step in a solution and the production(s) that satisfy the goal (including the buggy productions not depicted in the figure). We can provide LISPITS a data structure analogous to the hierarchical goal tree in Figure 1 by running the student model through the exercise ahead of time, allowing it to pursue every path it can find that leads to a correct solution, and saving the relevant information. Thus the high computational demands of recognizing appropriate productions at each step in problem solving are met in advance and the results of the process are stored in a structure that can be processed quickly. (See Sleeman, 1983, for a description of a similar process.)

While problem compilation was initiated to speed LISPITS' performance, it also has a beneficial side effect: it allows us to conveniently modify the tutor's behavior without actually rewriting the production rules. Note that the result of the problem compilation is a complete specification of the steps at the smallest possible grain size of every acceptable solution to an exercise. Once this data structure exists, it is relatively easy to write a program that can track the students' behavior through the tree, even if they deviate from a top-down left-to-right coding order. We can also modify the functional grain-size of productions. Thus, we can modify the assumptions of the student model without actually modifying the original production system, writing new rules, and regenerating solutions.

Modifying the Tutorial Interaction: Enhanced Student Control

It is not coincidental that we have discussed problem compilation in the context of input order and feedback. Perhaps the most frequent complaint we hear from students concerns symbol-by-symbol feedback. Another, less frequent complaint, concerns the input-order constraint. As a result, we have taken advantage of problem compilation to develop a version of LISPITS that gives the student complete control over both the order in which code is generated and the points at which feedback is provided (Corbett, et al., 1988).

In this student-controlled version of LISPITS, the student is provided with a true editor for entering code. More specifically, it is a structured editor that provides function templates and balancing right parentheses much like the interface in the immediate-feedback version. The editor ensures that the student generates legal (syntactically correct) code. However, it does not (and cannot) ensure that the student's program satisfies the exercise description. Thus, students can generate code in any order, including right-to-left and bottom-up. Unlike the immediate-feedback version, students can also modify parts of the code they have already completed. While the student is working with the editor, the model tracing/tutoring component of the program is disengaged and never interrupts. However, the student is provided with three commands to request tutoring. One of these commands asks the tutor to check over the entire solution as it currently stands. When the student selects this command, the tutor checks the code in the same top-down left-to-right order as it ordinarily would in the immediate feedback version. If the code is correct and complete, the tutor recognizes that the student is done. If the existing code is correct but is not a complete solution, the tutor tells the student that the code is correct so far and returns editing control to the student. However, if an error is detected, the tutor stops and gives the same error feedback as in the immediate-feedback version and deletes the incorrect symbol from the code. Any code which follows the error remains unanalyzed and is moved from the code window to a separate buffer on the screen to emphasize to the student that that code has not been checked. (This code can readily be transferred back to the code window as the student sees fit.) After performing these actions, the program returns editing control to the student.

The two other tutoring commands allow the student to request either a goal hint or the correct code symbol at any goal, just as in the immediate feedback version. If one of these commands is selected, the tutor begins by checking over any code in the student's solution that precedes the goal in question. If an error is found, the program provides feedback on that error (to avoid discussing the goal specified by the student in an erroneous context). Otherwise, the tutor provides the same information on the requested goal as it would in the immediate feedback version.

Testing Student-Controlled Feedback

Our study with the student-controlled tutor covered the first two lessons. Half the students completed the two lessons with the new student-controlled version, while the other half used the standard immediate-feedback version. Knowledge tracing was shut off, so all students completed the same set of exercises across the two lessons. After completing the lessons, the students took a cumulative quiz.

Assessment Measures

Two measures of student performance are of interest for pedagogical as well as theoretical reasons: posttest performance and total time to complete the exercises. This control manipulation had no effect on posttest scores; both groups scored 83% correct on the quiz. However, the manipulation did affect the time required to complete the exercises. Students using the immediate feedback version required an average of 2.9 minutes to complete each exercise, while students using the student-controlled version required an average of 4.3 minutes. This difference is significant, $t(30) = 3.9$, $p < .001$.

Processing Measures

The total-time difference in completing the exercises may in part reflect the fact that the editor in the student-controlled condition is intrinsically more difficult to use than the constrained interface in the immediate feedback condition. In examining the log files, there are indeed occasions in which the student seemed to struggle with the interface. However, examination of the log files also suggests a second reason that students may be taking longer in the student-controlled condition. Specifically, in the student-controlled condition the tutor is detecting an average of 0.83 errors per exercise per student, while in the immediate-feedback condition the tutor is detecting 1.15 errors. This difference is reliable ($t(30) = 2.48$, $p < .05$) and suggests that, in the student-controlled condition, students are detecting and correcting their own errors, which also may contribute to total processing time.

Error Detection and Code Revision

There is an alternative explanation of this difference in error detection rate: subjects could be more cautious and simply make fewer errors in the student-controlled condition. To obtain firmer data on this point, we performed a detailed analysis of the editor actions performed in Lesson 2 by subjects in the student-controlled condition. The results of this analysis are summarized in Table 5.

Table 5:

Student-controlled feedback: Error detection and code revision.

	Total tutor-detected errors	165
	Total student-initiated revisions to erroneous code	86
Changes of erroneous code		
	To correct code	49
	To other erroneous code	37
Changes of correct code		
	To other correct code	9
	To erroneous code	12

This table shows the total number of errors detected by the tutor across the sixteen subjects in the student-controlled condition for the seven exercises in Lesson 2. It also shows the total number of code revisions made by these sixteen subjects across those seven exercises. As indicated, students detected and revised a total of 86 errors, while the tutor detected 165. Of the errors detected and revised by students, 57% are corrected (49 out of 86) while the remaining 43% are changed to a different error. In addition, students went back and changed correct symbols in the code 21 times. Forty-three percent of these changes resulted in alternative correct code, while the remaining 57% of the modifications introduced errors. Thus, students do rethink and revise code when given an opportunity that is not afforded them by the immediate feedback tutor. However, only about half (44%) of the revisions are constructive, that is, move toward a correct solution. The remaining non-constructive modifications are inefficient in the sense that they take time without yielding any progress to a successful solution. We don't know if there is a cognitive benefit of such non-constructive changes, although the posttest results don't suggest that subjects in the student-controlled condition learned the material more effectively.

A final code-revision issue we addressed concerns the relative position in the code of the revisions students make. Specifically, when a revision occurred, we looked at the structural relation between the goal the student had been working on prior to the revision and the goal at which the revision was made. Gray and Anderson (1990) investigated the code revisions students made in writing fairly complex iterative LISP functions and found that students are likely to make revisions only at the goal they are working on (or have just completed) or at a superordinate goal in the tree structure. To exemplify this result, consider the function insert-two. Suppose a student has just satisfied the goal "CODE 2ND ITEM" at the lower left in Figure 1 by typing the symbol item2 in the body of the function. At this point the code window would look like this:

```
(defun insert-two (item1 item2 alist)
   (cons item1 (cons item2 <list2>)))
```

The symbol <list2> denotes the pending goal of coding some list as the second argument of cons.

Gray and Anderson's results suggest that the symbol the student is most likely to change at this point is item2, which has just been typed. The only other symbols the student would be likely to immediately change are defun and the two instances of cons, since these symbols were generated at the goals CODE FUNCTION, CODE BODY, and CODE REMAINDER, which are superordinate to CODE 2ND ITEM in the tree diagram. In Gray and Anderson's analysis the student is much less likely to revise the function name, parameter list or reference to item1 in the body of the function since these symbols were generated at goals that are not superordinates of CODE 2ND ITEM.

Table 6:
Position of code revisions with student-controlled feedback.

Structural relation of revised goal to current goal	Number of revisions	Probability that revision corrects error
Same	61	0.51
Superordinate	31	0.42
Other	15	0.33

An inspection of the Lesson 2 log files in this study confirmed this prediction, as shown in Table 6. Of the 107 revisions students made, 57% were at the current goal, 29% were at superordinate goals and only 14% were at other goals. Analysis also indicated that the probability a revision is productive (i.e., corrects an error) varies with the relative position of the revision. Of the revisions at the current goal, 51% corrected an error, whereas only 42% of the revisions at superordinate goals and 33% of revisions at other goals corrected errors.

Immediate Feedback and Input Order

Examination of the log files in the student-controlled condition also allows us to evaluate students' complaints concerning input order and immediate feedback. For example, concerning feedback, students asked LISPITS to check over their solutions 661 times across the two lessons. Only 15 of these requests came when the student had a partial solution. In the other 646 cases the student had complete, though not necessarily correct, code. Students also asked for goal hints or explanations a total of 72 times. Necessarily the student's code is incomplete when such requests are made but, even when these 72 requests are included, students are asking for help with partial code only 12% of the time. Thus, students' behavior in this experiment is consistent with previous complaints about step-by-step immediate feedback. When students are in control they not only do not request immediate feedback, they seldom ask for feedback until they are done. Moreover, when their code is not channeled into a correct solution path by the tutor, students do take advantage of the opportunity to rethink and revise their answers. The pattern of results concerning feedback on partial solutions may change in later lessons as exercises become more complex. However, the present results indicate that students would be happy with a tutor that only provides feedback on complete code, as in the case of PROUST (Johnson & Soloway, 1985; Sack & Soloway, this volume).

Finally, we examined the editor interactions in Lesson 2 to evaluate student complaints concerning input order. Across all students and exercises in Lesson 2 there were about 400 goals that could have been solved in a bottom-up rather than top-down order. (That is, there were about 400 non-terminal goals which entailed subgoals.) Among those 400 opportunities, there were only 5 occasions in which students coded bottom-up rather than top-down. In addition, there were about 450 occasions in which students could have generated code in a right-to-left fashion, rather than left-to-right. On only one occasion did a student take advantage of this opportunity. Thus, despite student complaints concerning coding order (which actually occur frequently in the context of Lesson 2 exercises), students took little advantage of the opportunity to deviate from top-down and left-to-right coding.

CONCLUSION

The goal of the LISPITS project is to create an environment in which students can practice LISP programming productively. More specifically, our goal has been to monitor students' performance in programming exercises, to recognize errors as they occur, and to provide feedback on these errors. The project has adopted a student-modelling approach to this task that is based on a cognitive model of (1) the programming knowledge we want the students to acquire and (2) misconceptions that may arise. By applying this model of ideal and buggy programming knowledge to the exercises that the students perform, we can generate a dynamic model of correct and incorrect steps to solve the exercises and we can use this dynamic model to assess the students' behavior and provide feedback.

This general approach has proven quite successful. In the assessment research to date, students using LISPITS complete the coding exercises substantially more rapidly than those working on their own, although not as fast as students working with a human tutor. Furthermore, students using LISPITS perform as well or better on posttests.

Current research focuses on the control and timing of feedback and the effectiveness of explanations. Much of LISPITS' effectiveness apparently can be attributed to the immediate feedback it provides on errors. When students are given control of feedback timing (and input order) exercise completion times increase by 50%. Moreover, research on LISPITS' feedback suggests that the explanations it provides have no impact on posttest scores and relatively little consistent impact on performance in completing the exercises. This suggests that it is the immediate noting of errors and the immediate provision of correct answers when the student shows signs of floundering that are critical in LISPITS' success. Nevertheless, students' most frequent complaint concerns immediate feedback. As a result, much of our current research involves resolving this conflict between the efficiency that is gained with immediate feedback and the students' desire for greater control.

Simultaneously we are examining other factors that govern the effectiveness of explanations. Some of these factors are internal to LISPITS, e.g., the tutor's ability to determine what instruction the student needs and how to present it clearly. Other important factors, however, may be external to LISPITS. For example, the components of the overall curriculum, including the quality of the text and non-tutor programming experience, may have a strong impact on the usefulness of explanations the tutor provides. Finally, the student's perception of control over the tutoring interaction may also have a strong bearing on the effectiveness of explanations the tutor attempts to provide.

ACKNOWLEDGEMENT

This research was supported by the Office of Naval Research contract N00014-87-K-0103.

REFERENCES

Anderson, J. R. (1983). *The architecture of cognition.* Cambridge, MA: Harvard University Press.

Anderson, J. R. (1990). Analysis of student performance with the LISP tutor. In N. Fredericksen, R. Glaser, A. Lesgold & M. Shafto (Eds.), *Diagnostic monitoring of skill and knowledge acquisition.* Hillsdale, NJ: Erlbaum, 27-50.

Anderson, J. R., Boyle, C. F., Corbett, A. T., & Lewis, M. W. (1990). Cognitive modelling and intelligent tutoring. *Artificial Intelligence*, 42, 7-49.

Anderson, J. R., Boyle, C. F., Farrell, R., & Reiser, B. J. (1987). Cognitive principles in the design of computer tutors. In P. Morris (Ed.), *Modelling cognition.* New York, NY: Wiley.

Anderson, J. R., Boyle, C. F., & Reiser, B. J. (1985). Intelligent tutoring systems. *Science, 228*, 456-462.

Anderson, J. R., Boyle, C. F., & Yost, G. (1985). The geometry tutor. *Proceedings of the Ninth International Joint Conference on Artificial Intelligence*, 1-7. Los Angeles, CA.

Anderson, J. R., Corbett, A. T., & Reiser, B. J. (1987). *Essential LISP.* Reading, MA: Addison-Wesley.

Anderson, J. R., Farrell, R., & Sauers, R. (1984). Learning to program in LISP. *Cognitive Science, 8*, 87-129.

Anderson, J. R., & Jeffries, R. (1985). Novice LISP errors: Undetected losses of information from working memory. *Human-Computer Interaction, 22*, 403-423.

Anderson, J. R., & Reiser, B. J. (1985, April). The LISP Tutor. *Byte, 10* (4), 159-175.

Conrad, F. G, & Anderson, J. R. (1988). The process of learning LISP. *Proceedings of the 10th Annual Conference of the Cognitive Science Society*, 454-460. Montreal.

Corbett, A. T., Anderson, J. R., & Patterson, E. G. (1988). Problem compilation and tutoring flexibility in the LISP tutor. *Proceedings of ITS-88: The International Conference on Intelligent Tutoring Systems* (pp. 423-429). Montreal.

Gray, W., & Anderson, J. R. (1987). Change-episodes in coding: When and how do programmers change their code? *Proceedings of the Second Conference on the Experimental Study of Programming*, NJ: Ablex, 185-197.

Johnson, W. L., & Soloway, E. (1987). PROUST: An automatic debugger for Pascal programs. In G. Kearsley (Ed.), *Artificial intelligence and instruction: Applications and methods. Reading, MA: Addison-Wesley.* (Originally published in 1985 in *Byte, 10*, (4), 179-190).

Kessler, C. (1988). *Transfer of programming skills in novice LISP learners.* Ph.D. Dissertation, Carnegie-Mellon University.

Lewis, M. W., & Anderson, J. R. (1985). Discrimination of operator schemata in problem solving: Learning from examples. *Cognitive Psychology, 17*, 26-65.

Lewis, M. W., Milson, R., & Anderson, J. R. (1987). The TEACHERS APPRENTICE: Designing an intelligent authoring system for high school mathematics. In G. Kearsley (Ed.), *Artificial intelligence and instruction: Applications and methods*. Reading, MA: Addison-Wesley.

McKendree, J., & Anderson, J. R. (1987). Effect of practice on knowledge and use of basic LISP. In J. M. Carroll (Ed.), *Interfacing thought*. Cambridge, MA: MIT Press.

Miller, G. A., Galanter, E., & Pribram, K. H. (1960). *Plans and the structure of behavior*. New York, NY: Holt, Rinehart & Winston.

Newell, A., Shaw, J. C., & Simon, H. A. (1958). Elements of a theory of human problem solving. *Psychological Review, 65*, 151-166.

Pirolli, P. L. (1985). *Problem solving by analogy and skill acquisition in the domain of programming*. Ph.D. dissertation, Carnegie-Mellon University.

Pirolli, P. L., & Anderson, J. R. (1985). The role of learning from examples in the acquisition of recursive programming skill. *Canadian Journal of Psychology, 39*, 240-272.

Sleeman, D. H. (1983). Inferring student models for intelligent tutor-aided instruction. In R. Michalski, J. Carbonell, & T. Mitchell (Eds.), *Machine learning*. Palo Alto, CA: Tioga.

Sleeman, D. H., & Brown J. S. (1982). *Intelligent tutoring systems*. New York, NY: Academic Press.

4 Knowledge Representation and Explanation in GIL, An Intelligent Tutor for Programming

Brian J. Reiser, Daniel Y. Kimberg, Marsha C. Lovett, Michael Ranney
Princeton University

PROBLEM SOLVING KNOWLEDGE IN INTELLIGENT TUTORS

A central issue in designing intelligent tutoring systems is the nature of the knowledge of the target domain. In problem solving domains such as mathematics, computer programming, and the physical sciences, a tutor needs to be able to solve the problems presented to students, step by step, following any reasonable path to a solution. The system must be able to trace the student's reasoning so that it can offer suggestions or criticisms on individual steps, rather than being limited to advice on a complete solution attempt. By inferring the student's reasoning the tutor can respond to the underlying misconceptions that motivated the actions rather than being restricted to comments concerning the surface form of the solution (Anderson, 1988). For a student's actions to be interpretable to the tutoring system, each student action should correspond to a step in the system's problem solver. Hence, it is particularly important that steps in the tutor's problem solver be represented at an appropriate grain size so students are not forced to specify their intentions in smaller steps than desired nor prevented from entering intermediate or partial products in a solution. Furthermore, the tutor's domain knowledge must provide sufficient coverage that the tutor can follow any path to a solution, inferring the student's plan and recognizing when a step diverges from a valid path to a solution.

A frequently used strategy is the representation of domain knowledge as a set of problem solving rules. Each rule contains a description of a particular problem situation and a step to take in that situation (Anderson, Boyle, & Reiser, 1985; Clancey, 1987). A tutor based on rules tracks a student's solution by matching each student step against the actions of the rules in its problem solving model. A similar strategy for representing domain knowledge in a tutor makes use of plans as the basic unit (Bonar & Cunningham, 1988; Johnson, 1986; Johnson & Soloway, 1984, 1987; Sack & Soloway, this volume). Each plan specifies how to achieve a goal, either by decomposing the goal into several subgoals or by achieving the goal directly through a sequence of actions. As in rule-based systems, a tutor built upon a knowledge base of plans compares each student's step in a solution to those steps suggested by its plan-driven decomposition of the problem.

There have been a number of recent demonstrations that knowledge representations such as rules and plans can be effectively used to track and provide assistance for a student's problem solving in mathematics (Anderson, Boyle, & Yost, 1985; Burton, 1982; Lewis, Milson, & Anderson, 1987; Sleeman, 1982), computer programming (Anderson & Reiser, 1985; Bonar & Cunningham, 1988; Corbett, Anderson, & Patterson, 1988; Johnson, 1986; Johnson & Soloway, 1984, 1987; Reiser, Anderson, & Farrell, 1985), and medical reasoning (Clancey, 1982, 1987, 1988). In these systems, the knowledge base is used to analyze the components of a solution and to determine which steps are correct, which are incorrect, and which reveal poor strategies, so that appropriate instruction can be provided.

In this chapter, we explore the issues involved in using rule-based problem solving models not only to analyze the student's actions but also as a knowledge base from which to generate advice and feedback. We will describe GIL, an intelligent tutoring system for programming that generates explanations directly from its problem solving knowledge rather than relying on prestored text associated with that knowledge.

The Domain of Computer Programming

The research on rule-based problem solving systems has focused on well-structured problem domains for which it is possible to construct systems of rules to solve a variety of problems. In order for an intelligent tutor to offer advice and correct student errors, its problem solver must be able to solve the problems given to the student. Computer programming is an interesting domain for research on intelligent tutoring, because it is constrained enough to be tractable, yet rich enough to present a real modeling challenge. The domain is well structured enough that it is possible to determine whether an answer is correct or not, in contrast with "ill-structured" domains such as economics and political science (Simon, 1973). Indeed, a functional model of computer programming, including goals, problem states, and problem solving operators can be specified precisely in computer simulations that mirror the reasoning of human subjects (Anderson, Farrell, & Sauers, 1984; Anderson, Pirolli, & Farrell, 1988; Klahr & Carver, 1988).

Programming is richer than many mathematics domains in that there is typically a variety of correct answers for a programming problem. The student can often choose the type of algorithm, data structure, and implementation to achieve the goals of the programming problem. In an intelligent tutor for programming, the problem solver must know about the variety of algorithms and the goals that each algorithm achieves. The problem solving rules must encode the constraints that govern the use of the algorithms, the data structures required for an algorithm, and the techniques for storing and manipulating different types of data. It is not sufficient for the rules to be able to solve the problem. The model should solve the problems as students solve them, using a psychologically accurate simulation of the knowledge representations and procedures actually used by students. Thus, the rules must contain information about how to break a higher level goal into simpler subgoals and about plans for achieving each subgoal. Learning the constructs of a programming language is only the beginning—the most important task in learning to program is learning the plans that use those constructs (Anderson, et al., 1984; Ehrlich & Soloway, 1984; Rich & Shrobe, 1978; Soloway, 1985; Soloway & Ehrlich, 1984; Soloway, Ehrlich, Bonar, & Greenspan, 1982; Waters, 1985).

Another important type of knowledge required concerns the combination of plans that handle the various subgoals. For example, writing a computer program may require a plan for reading in the data, a plan for guarding against improper data, a plan for calculating an average, and a plan for printing out the result. Indeed, novice programmers frequently have difficulty, not with the syntax or semantics of the individual programming constructs, but with the process of assembling the solutions to the individual subproblems into a program and avoiding unintended interactions between the components (du Boulay, 1986; Spohrer & Soloway, 1986; Spohrer, Soloway, & Pope, 1986).

Therefore, students face a number of challenges in learning to program. First, they must learn the syntax and semantics for the available programming constructs. Difficulties may arise with inappropriate analogies to the natural language usage of programming words (e.g., *until*, *when*, *if*) or from ascribing too much intelligence to the computer and hence assuming that it will figure out what the programmer intended (Bonar & Soloway, 1985; Pea, 1986; Putnam, Sleeman, Baxter, & Kuspa, 1986; Sleeman, Putnam, Baxter, & Kuspa, 1986). Students need to acquire a mental model of how the computer executes programs in general, in addition to how it implements individual programming statements, so that they can reason through a program's execution (du Boulay, 1986; du Boulay, O'Shea, & Monk, 1981). In order to provide helpful guidance and feedback for students writing computer programs, an intelligent tutoring system will need to understand and be able to explain each of these aspects of the problem solving process.

Model Tracing Using Rule-Based Systems

Anderson and his colleagues have argued that the problem solving skills acquired when students learn to program can be represented as a production system, in which steps to plan and implement a computer program are encoded as rules called "productions" (Anderson, 1983, 1987; Anderson, et al., 1984; Anderson, et al., 1988; Pirolli, 1986; Reiser, et al., 1985). The general form of the production system architecture, and the learning mechanisms used to acquire rules through instruction and modify them through problem solving experience, are described in Anderson's ACT* model of human problem solving (Anderson, 1983, 1987). In this model, students first acquire the primitive operators or steps that can be invoked to construct a solution, and then learn to compose several steps together to form larger plan units. Knowledge is represented as a set of production rules, each containing a *condition* that recognizes a particular configuration of goals and problem features, as well as an *action* that specifies how the problem state should be updated. The actions include inferences about the problem, partial results, and additions to the solution. For example, the condition of a rule might recognize that the solution requires extracting the last element of a list; the action of that rule would initiate a plan of flipping the list around and then extracting the first element. An important characteristic of the ACT* production system architecture is that production rules are organized by goals. The condition or test for each rule contains a description of the particular goal that the associated action can achieve. A sequence of rules that combine to achieve a subgoal can be "chunked" together to form a plan. Learning effective sequences to achieve a goal is an important characteristic of production system models of results in human learning (Anderson, 1983, 1987; Laird, Rosenbloom, & Newell, 1986).

Production rules of this sort have been used as the problem solving component of the CMU LISP Intelligent Tutoring System (abbreviated LISPITS and discussed in Ch. 4 of this volume). LISPITS is an intelligent tutor that teaches students to program in LISP (Anderson & Reiser, 1985; Corbett, et al., 1988; Reiser, et al., 1985). The design of this tutor is motivated by a set of pedagogical principles derived from the ACT* theory of problem solving (Anderson, Boyle, Farrell, & Reiser, 1987; Anderson, Boyle, & Reiser, 1985). The tutor provides instruction in the context of problem solving by monitoring a student's solution and providing feedback when the student needs guidance or demonstrates a misconception. The tutor provides immediate feedback upon errors to obviate the deleterious consequences of a student's floundering when recovering from a costly error. However, the tutor is also designed to enable the student to generate as much of the solution as possible. Enough guidance must be provided to limit the student's floundering and facilitate a successful solution to the problem without leading the student more than necessary.

LISPITS uses the technique of model tracing to understand the student's reasoning as each step is taken (Anderson, et al., 1987; Anderson, Boyle, & Reiser, 1985). The tutor analyzes each step of the student's solution to determine whether it is on the path toward a solution or indicates a misconception. The student's step is analyzed by comparing it with the rules currently considered by the tutor's problem solving model, called the ideal student model. If the student's action is one that would be produced by executing one of the rules considered by the ideal student model at that point in the problem, the model applies that rule, thus following the student's path through the problem. Following such a correct step, the tutor is silent and permits the student to continue. Alternatively, if the student's action does not correspond to a correct step, the tutor considers its catalog of buggy rules, which represent general patterns of errors encoded also as production rules (Brown & Burton, 1978; Burton, 1982; Sleeman, 1982). Errors are diagnosed when the student's step matches the action of a buggy rule, whereupon the tutor interrupts with the advice associated with the rule. Buggy rules may represent incorrect syntax, semantic confusions, or planning errors. In this way the tutor understands each step the student takes to build a program and stays in the background when the student is following a path leading to a correct solution, but upon request or an erroneous step it provides a hint or the next step in the solution, enabling the student to continue. This model tracing methodology has also been used for intelligent tutors that teach students to construct proofs in geometry (Anderson, Boyle, & Yost, 1985) and solve algebraic equations (Lewis, et al., 1987).

A Brief Overview of LISP Programming

In order to discuss LISPITS and our own work on a programming tutor, we begin with a brief overview of the task domain—elementary LISP programming.

The programming language LISP has the following advantages as a language for introducing students to programming. It is an interactive language, like LOGO or BASIC. The student types in a LISP expression and the interpreter responds by evaluating that expression. Each LISP expression consists of a function call composed of a function and its arguments, enclosed in parentheses. The arguments for LISP expressions can be atoms (single words or numbers) or lists. Lists are ordered collections of elements, each of which itself may be a list or an atom. Like function calls, lists are enclosed in parentheses:

`(dog cat horse)`	a list
`(first '(dog cat horse))`	a function call

The function call `(first '(dog cat horse))` operates the function `first` on the list `(dog cat horse)` and returns `dog`, the first element. Since `dog` is not a list, it is not enclosed in parentheses.

Function calls can be embedded so that one function operates on the result of another function call. Thus, the single quotation mark in the previous example tells LISP that the list `(dog cat horse)` should be considered literally as a list rather than as an attempt to call the function `dog` on the arguments `cat` and `horse`. Contrast that example with the expression:

```
(first (rest '(a b c d))).
```

This expression calls the function `first` on the result of taking the `rest` of the list `(a b c d)`, thus returning `b`, the second element of the original list.

The embedded function call works as follows. The function `rest` returns a list, enclosed in parentheses, that contains the "rest" of the original list after its first element has been removed:

```
(rest '(a b c d)) returns the list (b c d).
```

Then `first` returns the first element from the list given to it:

```
(first '(b c d)) returns the element b.
```

The LISP language is designed to manipulate data contained in lists to achieve a particular set of constraints. Therefore, most LISP problems require the student to write a LISP program that does such manipulation. The central means of constructing a program involves using the `defun` construct, which defines a LISP function. A function definition consists of writing `defun`, followed by: (1) the name of the function, (2) a list of variables, and (3) the body of the function, which specifies what the function should do. For example, one could define a function called `getends` to take any list and construct a new list that contains just the first and last elements from the original list. It could use the following functions that are normally a part of LISP:

- `cons` takes two arguments, an element and a list, and returns a new list that includes the element inserted into the front of the original list;
- `first` takes one argument, a list, and returns the first element from the given list; and
- `last` takes one argument, a list, and returns the list that consists of the last element from the given list.

Using the variable `lis` to represent the list that would be used as input, the definition of `getends` would be:

```
(defun getends (lis)
   (cons (first lis) (last lis)))
```

Then `getends`, applied to a list such as `(a b c d)`, would apply `first` to `(a b c d)`, returning `a`, apply `last` to `(a b c d)`, returning `(d)`, and then apply `cons` to `a` and `(d)`, returning `(a d)`.

The beginning LISP curriculum involves learning the syntax for defining functions, the syntax for referring to function parameters, the semantics of the functions that extract items from lists and construct lists, the embedding of function calls so that the result of one operation will be applied to the result of another operation, and the use of plans or algorithms to chain together primitive operators in order to achieve a desired goal. Later topics in the curriculum include predicates (for testing properties of data), conditional expressions, iterative expressions, recursive methods, and additional data structures.

Empirical Studies of LISPITS

LISPITS helps students learn to write LISP programs by providing feedback as students compose a program to solve a problem. The system monitors each word a student enters in a function definition, matching the step taken by the student against the possible next steps suggested by the tutor's problem solver, providing immediate feedback when an error is diagnosed as well as hints concerning overall strategies and possible next steps when requested by the student. Evaluation studies have demonstrated the effectiveness of this system for college students learning LISP. The system has been tested with both students who had already learned a previous programming language and students who were learning LISP as their first introduction to programming. On average, students working with this tutor learn the material more quickly and achieve a higher level of proficiency than students working with the same textbook and problems in the standard learning environment, namely, an interactive LISP environment and an editor (Corbett & Anderson, this volume; Reiser, et al., 1985).

Although this tutor is generally quite successful, the computer tutor alone is not always sufficient for all students in these courses. Some students go through each lesson making a large number of errors, finally getting through each problem, but without seeming to understand the solutions to which they were led by the tutor. These students eventually learn the material, though they often require a good deal of individualized help from teaching assistants. It is important to characterize the type of assistance these human tutors can provide that is absent from the instruction in this computerized tutor.

LISPITS is designed to teach the construction of computer programs, hence the rules in the ideal model concern planning programs and implementing the resulting algorithms in code. Analyses of students having difficulty suggest that a lack of ability to *reason causally* about these programs interferes with the successful construction of a working program (Reiser, 1987). This causal reasoning knowledge is only implicit in the rules in LISPITS. The ideal model rules are essentially *action-oriented*, in that they associate an action to take with a particular problem situation. However, the ideal model lacks causal knowledge about how these rules work. Essentially, the ideal model always knows *what* action to take at any point in the solution but not *why* that particular action would be effective. This additional knowledge is needed to reason about the conditions that allow an operator or a plan to be used, the goal achieved by a plan, its effects on the data objects involved, and possible interactions with other plans. Confusion concerning this underlying knowledge can lead novices into trouble.

For example, one student had difficulty with the chapter on conditional expressions. The conditional function, `cond`, in LISP takes as its argument a list of pairs called "cases". LISP evaluates these cases sequentially. If the first item, the test, of the current pair is true, then LISP evaluates the second item, and exits from the `cond` structure. If the test in the case is false, then LISP proceeds directly to the next case in the list.

In tutoring this student on using `cond`, LISPITS had pointed out errors on several problems in which she had tried to construct a conditional with the cases in the wrong order. The following is a portion of a program written by this student to classify data based on its type. The program is supposed to take an argument `item` and indicate whether it is a non-numerical "atom," a number, a list, or an empty list. What is shown below is the first element of each case in the `cond` construction. The property tested is shown after the semicolon, which indicates a comment in LISP.

```
(defun classify (item)
  (cond ((listp item) ...)     ;a list?
        ((atom item) ...)      ;an atom?
        ((numberp item) ...) ;a numeric atom?
        ((null item) ...)      ;an empty list?
    ...))
```

If the argument `item` is a list, then `(listp item)` is true, and the function `classify` executes the first line of code and stops. If the argument `item` is an atom, then the first test fails and it proceeds to the second case, in which the test succeeds, the action is returned, and the program stops. But, if `item` is a number, then `classify` will never get to the third case. The reason is that in LISP, numbers are atoms, and so `(atom item)` is true. Worse, suppose `item` is an empty list. Then `(listp item)` is true, and `classify` executes the first line and quits, never getting to the fourth line, which would have identified `item` as an empty list.

This student understood the syntax for conditional expressions and had correctly learned the LISP functions (e.g., `atom, listp, numberp`) to test properties of data. However, the ordering of the clauses in the conditional expression in this program will not satisfy the goals of the problem. Unsure why the tutor was forcing a seemingly arbitrary ordering of these clauses, she brought her original solution which the tutor had rejected to the teaching assistant to ask for help. In the discussion of her program it became clear that she had a sophisticated but incorrect model of how conditionals in LISP were treated. She apparently assumed that LISP would find the "best" test rather than the first test in the expression that was satisfied. In fact, LISP simply processes the tests in a conditional expression in sequential order and executes the action associated with the first test that is successful. Therefore, it is essential to put more specific tests before a more general version of the same test. This student had not understood that a program must test for an empty list before testing for a list, assuming LISP would be "smart enough" to find the matching empty list test in the program, even though it might be after a list test that would also be satisfied.

Discovering the source of this student's consistent errors on conditional programs would be a difficult diagnosis problem even for human tutors, but it illustrates a general point. Within the architecture of LISPITS, it would be possible to add a bug detector to recognize the case in which students began to code a clause in a conditional structure that was more general than another needed test. The tutor could then respond with an explanation as to why specific tests must come before more general tests. However, this explanation draws on knowledge not contained in the tutor's problem solving model. The knowledge that recognizes that one test is more general than another and then selects the most specific test to code first is not the same as the knowledge as to why this rule is needed. Explanations need not only to point out a relevant discrimination but also to explain why the discrimination is necessary to achieve the goals of the problem. In this case, for example, it would be useful to explain that if the more general test appeared earlier in the function, inputs satisfying the more specific test would also match the general test and hence LISP would never reach the appropriate clause later in the conditional. In other words an action-oriented rule, such as the ones used in LISPITS, can recognize that it must put a more specific test first. However, such rules cannot be used to reason through the logic required to explain why it is necessary or to predict what would go wrong if the rule were violated.

Knowledge for Problem Solving and Explanation

Model tracing tutors are effective in analyzing student solutions to problems. However, in many cases, the explanations provided by these tutors refer to knowledge that is not explicitly contained in the problem solving model. Each rule in the model specifies a set of conditions under which a particular action should be taken, but it does not contain the information as to *why* that action is effective. Action-oriented rules do not specify what results from the application of a given operator, or how that result is closer to the goal. For example, consider the following typical action-oriented rule to write LISP code.

IF the current goal is to extract the *second* element of a list,

THEN use a function to extract the first element of the list's "tail" (a list that contains all but the first element) and set a goal to construct this tail.

This rule does specify what to do to begin to get the second element. What is not represented in this rule is the following reasoning behind the general algorithm: by taking successive tails of the list, the target element is moved closer to the front, until finally it can be extracted by the LISP function `first`. This general reasoning works not only for the second element, but for any desired element in a list.

A similar problem exists for rules in the bug catalog used to provide feedback on student errors. These rules capture the nature of the incorrect action and the conditions under which it occurs but, as in the case of correct rules, not the faulty reasoning behind it. For example, a LISPITS "buggy" rule recognizes an attempt to use successive tails of a list in order to extract the *last* item in a list. If this buggy rule corresponds to a student's action, LISPITS responds with a message describing why taking successive tails is not a good strategy since the function must work for a list of any length. The advice offered the student by LISPITS is constructed in advance by the system designers, and not drawn directly from the tutor's problem solving knowledge. The tutor does not contain the knowledge required to reason about the student's solution and understand why it would not work.

It is commonly assumed that a major pedagogical contribution of an intelligent tutoring system is its error diagnosis and planning assistance. Presumably the success of LISPITS lies in the usefulness of the explanations associated with the correct and buggy rules. To the extent that the task analysis in the problem solving model is a good representation of the reasoning students use, an explanation can be provided in the particular context in which it is relevant. Thus, by matching each student step against its correct and buggy rules, the model tracing tutor is very successful in tracking a student's reasoning, discovering when the student diverges from a correct solution path, and categorizing the type of misconception that most likely underlies the error. Explanations associated with correct rules selected by the ideal model can be provided as hints to suggest a strategy or step to take next, and explanations associated with buggy rules can be provided in response to errors to point out why a student's step is wrong. The model tracing technique, based on a running simulation of the student's reasoning, enables tracking student behavior in fine enough detail that errors can be detected immediately and corresponding explanations presented. However, these explanations are constructed from "canned" templates that draw on knowledge *not* represented in the problem solving rules. The tutor relies on the problem solving model to determine when an explanation is needed and which subskill in the domain needs instruction, but the instruction then conveys knowledge that is not contained in its domain model and was instead hand-crafted for each situation.

We suggest that a more complete simulation of the student's reasoning makes possible an alternative approach in which explanations can be constructed directly from the content of the rules themselves. In such a system, whatever information was required to solve the problem could in principle be conveyed to the student. The knowledge used to explain an action would be the same knowledge used to reason about it, providing a more robust pedagogical tool than one in which explanations were individually prepared for each situation. More effective explanations could be constructed to help students reason about the conditions that enable an operator or plan to be used, the effects of executing the operator, and the way in which an operator achieves or brings the student closer to a goal. In general, the tutor would contain a "mental" model of how programs are executed, which could be used to help students acquire such knowledge. This mental model enables understanding the flow of a complex program similar to the qualitative simulations used in recent work on the intelligent tutoring of understanding electronic circuits (White & Frederiksen, in press). Learning such models can facilitate the process of learning to solve problems involving complex systems (Hollan, Hutchins, & Weitzman, 1984; Kieras, 1988; Kieras & Bovair, 1984).

Constructing a tutor with the ability to explain its reasoning would have additional advantages. Explanations could be dynamically constructed in response to errors rather than relying on a bug catalog that contains specific recognizers for each error situation. Instead, the tutor could compare the student's step with the steps considered in the ideal model and describe the way in which the student's step results in less desirable consequences. In addition, explanations could be tailored to the particular student's current knowledge state. More or less detail could be given, contingent upon information in the student model.

In order to enable these explanations to be constructed from the rules, it is necessary to augment action-oriented rules such as those in LISPITS with knowledge for reasoning about intermediate products and underlying justifications of these rules. In LISPITS, intermediate products computed by an operation are not explicitly represented; instead each rule simply sets a goal for the next target object. Furthermore, causal relations between the various parts of a plan are not represented. In general, these rules only prescribe what step to take in a given context, while the knowledge used to reason about the effects of a particular operator and thus why it is useful in a given context has been "compiled out" of the rule. This information is crucial for providing good explanations for novices, since their knowledge is not yet well proceduralized. Novices may be forced to fall back upon weak problem solving methods, which rely upon an evaluation of the situation that results from applying an operator (Anderson, 1983; Newell & Simon, 1972). Yet novices lack a rich model of the domain, so they may not be able to predict reliably the results of applying an operator, and may not be able to recognize that a resultant state is closer to the goal. Novices may have difficulty, therefore, in reasoning effectively about what is possible in the domain. The tutor must be able to provide feedback that addresses these issues, rather than merely reminding the student what step would be appropriate at a given point.

Clancey (1983) has argued that it is essential to associate justifications with diagnostic rules in order to provide good explanations as to why a particular medical symptom is associated with a disease. We suggest that justifications are even more important for a synthesis domain such as programming, in which a solution involves constructing something from a set of components, than they are for a diagnosis domain, in which a solution involves a classification. A student may accept the tutor's assertion that a symptom is strong evidence for a particular disease even without understanding the causal model underlying the association; indeed in some areas of medical diagnosis, the causal mechanism underlying an association between a symptom and disease may not even be known. In a synthesis domain, however, the student must construct a solution from components. If the student does not understand what effects a particular step will entail, it will be difficult to proceed with the solution using that step in combination with other components. In addition, the student must come to understand why a particular step is appropriate in order to recognize the other situations in which the same principle could be applied.

GIL: A PROGRAMMING TUTOR THAT CONSTRUCTS ITS OWN EXPLANATIONS

GIL, an acronym for Graphical Instruction in LISP, is an intelligent tutor for programming that begins to address these knowledge representation issues (Reiser, Friedmann, Gevins, et al., 1988; Reiser, Friedmann, Kimberg, & Ranney, 1988). GIL follows the model tracing method used in LISPITS, but it contains a different type of problem solving model, designed to make explicit the causal knowledge about programming operations, and an explanation component that constructs hints and error feedback directly from the content of its problem solving knowledge.

As each student step is generated, GIL processes it and relates it to its problem solving knowledge. A step in GIL consists of selecting a LISP function and specifying the function's input and output. GIL consists of four main modules: a graphical interface, a response manager, a problem solver, and an explainer. The graphical interface is a graphical environment in which students construct LISP programs. The response manager processes each step taken by the student and determines whether it is on the path toward a solution or whether it is an error. The analysis is performed by comparing the student step with the steps suggested by the problem solver. If an error is found, the explainer analyzes the discrepancies between the student's step and the closest matching correct rule and offers suggestions to the student about how to improve the step. Explanations may draw upon the problem solving rule, general knowledge about the operator being used, and the higher-level plan of which the step is a part. Figure 1 shows the four modules (shaded) and the knowledge bases that these modules draw upon and modify. The rounded boxes are the knowledge bases that GIL uses to understand and explain solutions; the ellipses are data structures constructed by GIL as it tutors. We will discuss each of the GIL modules in turn.

The GIL Graphical Interface

The GIL tutor is embedded in a graphical programming environment (Reiser, Friedmann, Gevins, et al., 1988). Students build a program by connecting together objects representing program constructs into a "graph"—a set of connected visual icons each representing a portion of LISP code. This visual programming replaces defining LISP functions in their traditional text form. Such a graphical interface seems a promising environment in which to provide programming instruction. Proponents of graphical programming languages have argued that such environments enable students to learn to program with less focus on the syntactic details of a language (e.g., Cunniff & Taylor, 1987; Wight, Feurzeig, & Richards, 1989). We anticipate that a graphical programming environment will help the student understand the causal structure of programs and will therefore be a good context in which to provide explanations of the type GIL constructs.

There are several reasons to experiment with graphical representations. First, a graph is a better representation of the structure of the planning needed for a solution. Each branch of a graph corresponds to a chain of reasoning that achieves a subgoal of the overall plan. In contrast the syntax of the text form of a LISP program does not make its structure easily interpretable. Furthermore, students can work both forward from given data and backward from goal states. For example, a student trying to write the `getends` program described earlier (to construct a list containing the first and last elements of its argument) could work out the algorithm using a specific example, such as obtaining the list `(a d)` from the original list `(a b c d)`. One might work backward from the goal by determining what input data would be necessary to construct the goal list `(a d)`. Alternatively, one might work forward from the given data `(a b c d)` in an attempt to transform it to be closer to the goal state, for example, by trying various operations to see what can be extracted from this list.

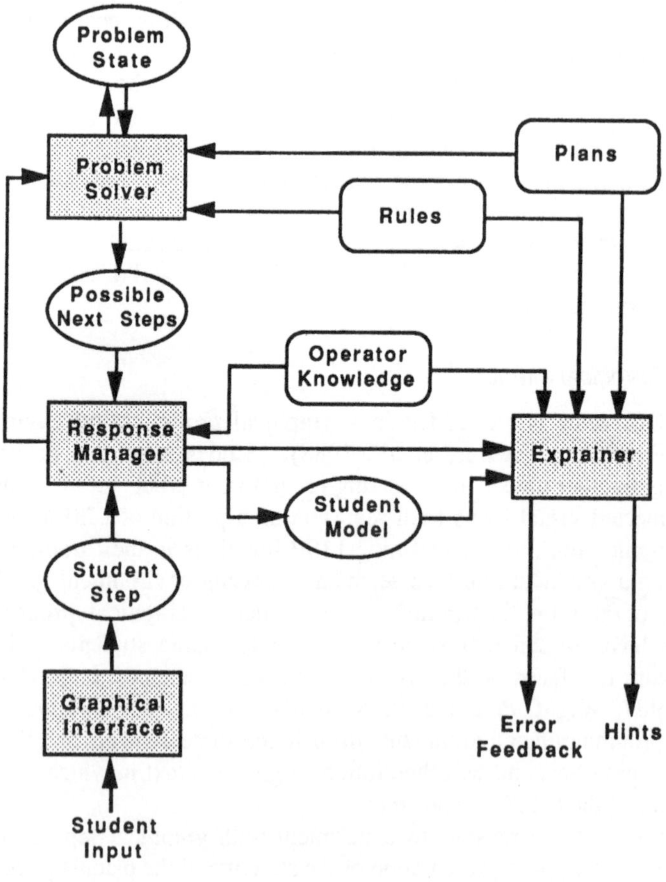

Figure 1: The architecture of the GIL programming tutor.

A second advantage of the graphical interface is that it provides a representation more congruent with the student's reasoning. It is important to note that the embedded nature of LISP requires the surface form of the solution to be a top-down ("backward") description of the way LISP interprets the given data. For example, the LISP code

```
(cons (first lis) (last lis))
```

specifies "insert the first element of the list into a list consisting only of the last element," rather than "get the first element, get a list of the last element, then combine the two together." Thus, a student forced to work within the surface LISP code, particularly if forced to work a solution in the top-down left-to-right order in which the final code appears, may be forced to reason in terms of the final solution rather than the planning necessary to construct the solution. In contrast, providing a graphical interface to LISP enables students to work in a medium that more closely corresponds to their planning operations. As we will describe in the next section, the GIL graphical interface enables students to combine forward and backward reasoning to solve a problem. In this way GIL exhibits an important advantage of computerized tutors that provide a spatial representation useful for characterizing the process of constructing a solution, rather than requiring students to work with the surface form of a solution (Brown, 1985; Collins & Brown, 1988). Although expert programmers often write LISP programs top-down and left to right (Anderson, et al. 1984), novice reasoners typically require more search as they fall back on weak methods (Anderson, 1987; Chi, Feltovich, & Glaser, 1981; Larkin, McDermott, Simon, & Simon, 1980). A tutor that can facilitate this search with an interface that supports these steps will be more helpful than a tutor that forces the student to plan a solution first, independent of the tutor, before submitting the solution attempt. Again, model tracing will be most effective if the interface makes it possible for students to make their reasoning explicit through interaction with the tutor whenever possible.

A third advantage of the graphical interface is the use of diagrams. Diagrams are useful in many problem solving tasks in that they efficiently represent information that may be difficult to keep current in working memory, and suggest appropriate inferences that may not be apparent in other representations (Larkin & Simon, 1987). In programming, graphical representations are better illustrations of the structure of the object being created than a simple stream of text. In particular, graphical representations are well suited for demonstrating causal relations, control flow, and data flow. Evaluations of a graphical representation for Pascal suggests that using these diagrams better enables students to reason about the flow of control in a program (Cunniff & Taylor, 1987). Bonar and his colleagues have successfully used visual representations as a transitional medium between natural language descriptions and the final text form of the program (Bonar & Cunningham, 1988). Visual representations have also been successfully used to help students construct proofs in geometry (Anderson, Boyle, & Yost, 1985), view medical reasoning during a consultation (Clancey, 1988; Richer & Clancey, 1985), and construct medical treatment plans (Musen, Fagan, & Shortliffe, 1987).

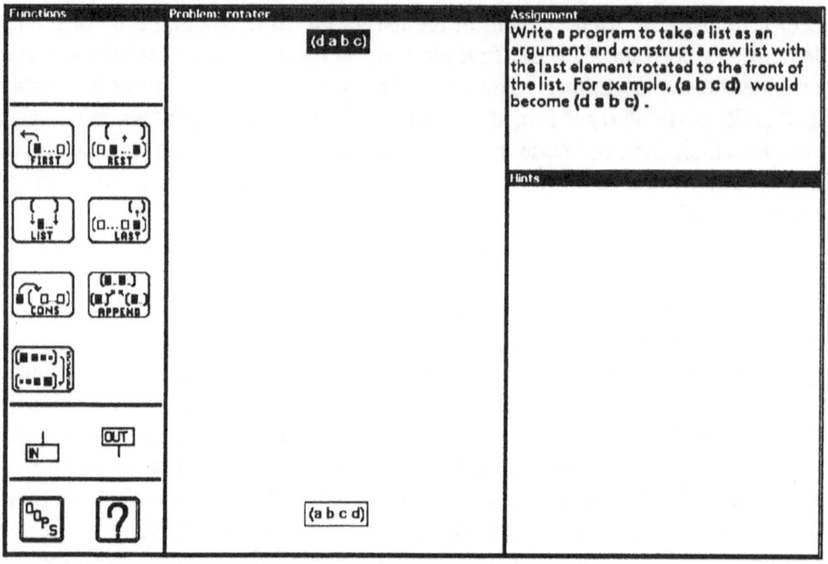

Figure 2: The initial state of a GIL problem.

In each problem with GIL, the student attempts to construct a graph of a program that meets the problem's specifications. The tutor monitors the student's problem solving, providing guidance upon request and feedback upon student errors. Figure 2 shows the initial GIL screen at the start of a problem. The Problem window (labeled with the name, "`rotater`," of the function to be written) contains nodes representing inputs at the bottom and the output to be computed by the function at the top. The statement of the problem is shown in the Assignment window. The goal is to define a LISP function by constructing a graph of connected icons so that the chained operations transform the given inputs into the target output. Each icon represents a LISP programming operation or function and has one or more input nodes below the icon, and one output node above it. The icons are contained in the functions menu on the left. The input nodes are the data operated on by the particular LISP operation; the output node is the result of that operation. In each step, the student selects a programming icon from a menu, drags it into the program window, and specifies its inputs and outputs. A mouse click can be used to connect a data node on the screen as an input or the output of the icon. New intermediate data nodes are entered using the input and output data icons; the data for the nodes are typed in from the keyboard.

By assembling a chain of LISP functions to connect the given data to the goal data, students build a general LISP program to achieve the specifications of the problem. In this way, students see the result and preconditions for each step as they reason through the program. Our attempt in designing the interface has been to provide a direct manipulation interface in which the effects of the students' actions are immediately visible and in which students manipulate data directly rather than by describing the desired effects (Hutchins, Hollan, & Norman, 1986; Miller, 1988; Shneiderman, 1983).

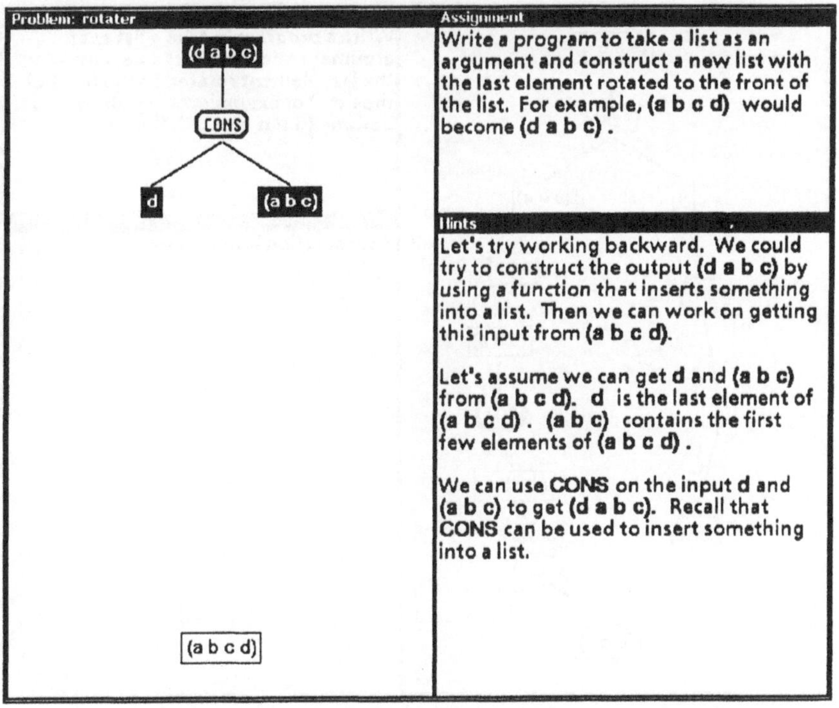

Figure 3: A backward-working step to decompose the rotater problem into two simpler goals. The Hints window shows GIL's suggestions on how to begin the problem.

A student working with GIL can use forward or backward chaining steps in any combination. A forward chaining step consists of applying an operation to one or more given nodes to produce a new given node; this intermediate product is a step forward toward the goal. In the graph, this corresponds to building up from the bottom. Students can also apply an operation whose output is a goal node, thus chaining backward toward the givens. This corresponds to working down from the top. The input to that operation then becomes a new goal node. Goal nodes are distinguished graphically from given nodes by appearing in darkened boxes. In Figure 3, the student has worked backward from the goal, reasoning that if the atom `d` and the list `(a b c)` were available, they could be combined to produce the goal list `(d a b c)`. The prior hints, requested by the student that suggested the backward decomposition, are shown in the Hints window.

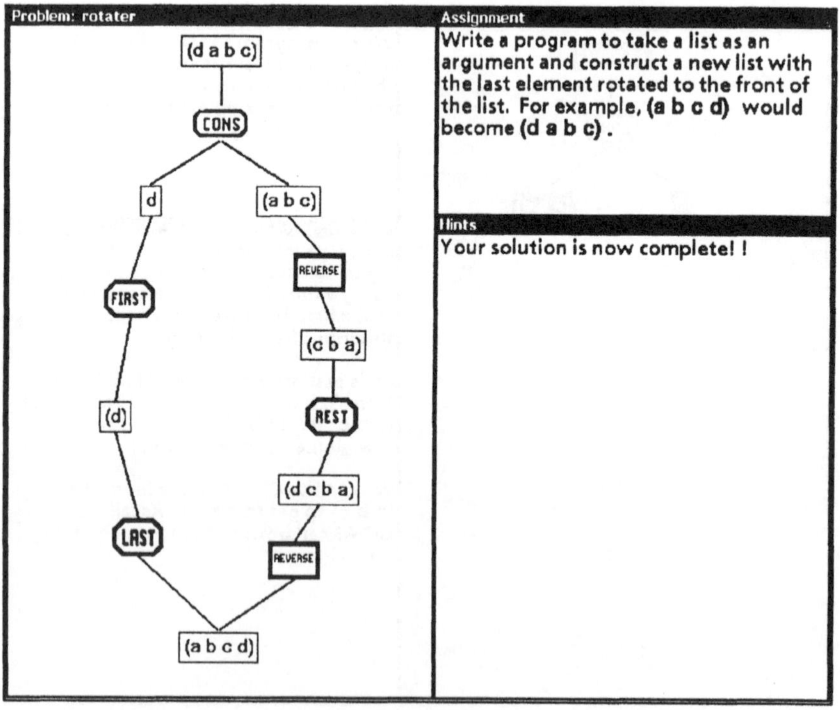

Figure 4: A completed graph for the rotater problem.

The algorithm design process is complete when the graph connects the inputs and the goal (Figure 4).

The GIL Problem Solver

The GIL problem solver consists of a set of reasoning rules and high-level plans. We will describe two features of this problem solver that are designed to facilitate the construction of explanations. First, the knowledge base includes rules to reason from the givens as well as rules to reason backward from the goal. Second, each rule contains an explicit representation of the properties of the input and output data objects. Rules that create intermediate products describe the characteristics of these new objects. These descriptions can be used to explain why a step is strategic or to explain why a student's step is in error.

A difficulty in learning to write computer programs is that in functional languages such as LISP, the order of functions in the surface code may not correspond to the order in which the student plans the operations. For example, one way to extract the second element of a list, `lis`, is the program `(first (rest lis))`. This code instructs LISP to return the first element of the rest of the original list. The goal decomposition required to produce this code, if constrained by the order in which it appears in the solution, is to decide initially to take the first element of some list, *then* to consider the goal of constructing a list such that the target element is in the first position. Consider, however, a student who has not yet learned this particular plan for extracting the second element, and must construct it. This student might not realize that `first` would be useful until *after* realizing that taking the `rest` of the original list would move the target item into the first position.

In order to conduct a dialogue with students to devise this plan, it may be necessary to help them reason through the algorithm in the order in which the data are manipulated. To model this reasoning, the GIL problem solver contains many forward reasoning steps, in which an operator is applied to a given object to transform it to a new object. By using forward steps, students can work through a simulation of the algorithm in forward temporal order, rather than being forced to write their programs in the usual backward order of the surface code. At any point they may reason forward from given data or backward from the goal. The ability to reason forward allows explanations to be provided to guide students through a new plan. For example, suppose a student is stuck. Rather than being forced to construct a hint concerning `first`, the initial component of the surface code, the tutor can discuss how to manipulate the original list to construct a list that is closer to the goal.

The problem solver contains two types of forward reasoning rules: those that achieve an active goal (Achieve Rules) and those that create intermediate products (Enable Rules) on the path to a goal. Applying the operator `last` (which returns a list of the last element) to the `rotater` problem state shown in Figure 3 would construct an intermediate product, the list `(d)`. This step does not directly achieve a goal but is on the path to the goal `d`. By definition, every backward reasoning step creates intermediate products since it creates new data objects as goals. Thus, the backward step in Figure 3 creates two new intermediate products, the atom `d` and the list `(a b c)`.

The current problem solver contains approximately 180 rules and 15 plans that manipulate lists, construct lists, and extract items from lists. Approximately half of the rules represent goal decomposition or backward reasoning steps, and half represent forward reasoning steps. The rules are constructed so that the student can take any strategic step at any point in the problem. Following the step shown in Figure 3, for example, the student can work backward from either of the two goal nodes, `d` or `(a b c)`, or can work forward from the given node `(a b c d)`. Although the final solution contains only a relatively small number of LISP functions, there are many different paths that a student can take through the problem. For example, there are eight different solutions to the `rotater` problem, one of which is shown in Figure 4. There are a total of 650 different paths that a student working with GIL can take through this problem.

A second important characteristic of the GIL problem solver is that intermediate products are made explicit in the rules. Each rule contains a description of the properties of the intermediate products created by applying the operator. The tutor needs to understand how LISP transforms the data at each step so that it can guide the student in reasoning through a new plan. Thus, it is not sufficient for the rules to encode the knowledge that taking the `first` of a reversed list will return the last element; the rules must also represent the fact that this algorithm works because reversing the list results in the last element being moved into the first position, enabling the use of `first` to extract that element. To represent this knowledge, each rule describes the properties that are true of the intermediate product. When the rule is executed, these properties are added to the current problem state as new inferences about the problem. These properties then affect the selection of further steps involving the object because the conditions of other rules may depend on properties added by this rule. For example, the following forward reasoning rule reverses a list to enable extracting the last element. (The pattern matching variables of the rule are printed in capital letters.)

CONDITIONS	the goal is extract ELEM
	ELEM is the last element of GIVENLIST
	FST is the first element of GIVENLIST
DIRECTION	Forward-reasoning
RULE-TYPE	Enable
OPERATOR	reverse
INPUT	GIVENLIST
OUTPUT	FLIPPEDLIST
PROPERTIES	FLIPPEDLIST is a list
	ELEM is the first item in FLIPPEDLIST
	FST is the last item in FLIPPEDLIST
	FLIPPEDLIST is the reverse of GIVENLIST
NEW-GOAL	extract ELEM from FLIPPEDLIST

It is important to stress that the problem solver relies on these intermediate products—they are not attached to rules simply for the explainer to use. The rules add inferences about the intermediate properties, and rules that match later in the problem include such properties in their conditions. In this way, GIL solves problems using the rules to reason about how each step in the program affects the data, rather than relying on rules that merely associate an action with a context in which that action should be taken.

The interaction of students with the GIL interface is structured to take advantage of this additional knowledge. As described earlier, students take a step in GIL by selecting a function and specifying its inputs and outputs. Hence, all intermediate products are explicit in the program graph. This forces the student to predict correctly the behavior of the selected operation in order to complete a step. Rather than specifying only the sequence of operations, such as "take the `first` of the `rest` of `(a b c d)`," the student must indicate the input and output for each operation, e.g., "extract the element, `b`, by taking the `first` of `(b c d)`; get `(b c d)` by taking the `rest` of `(a b c d)`." The use of intermediate products makes the process of combining steps more explicit and enables tutoring on individual steps in the solution. This represents a more finely grained interaction than one in which students specify only the final surface form of the solution. The interaction also allows the tutor to monitor students more closely and provide more useful assistance as they learn to construct these plans. We expect that providing this type of interaction for students in GIL will lead to better understanding of the causality in programs. Our experiments with GIL should provide data that bear on this empirical issue.

The GIL Response Manager

The GIL response manager controls the model tracing. The response manager processes the step entered by the student and compares it with the possible next steps suggested by the problem solver. If necessary, it directs the explainer to provide error feedback or hints.

An interesting complication for the model tracing method as used in GIL lies in the problem of ambiguity. The model tracing method requires that the response manager match each student step against the action of a problem solving rule. In some cases, however, several rules considered by the problem solver would take the step just made by the student. In these cases, of course, GIL permits the step, but it is important for the response manager to notice the ambiguity, because the rules may add different inferences or set different goals, even though they have the same external behavior on the current step. For example, consider the forward step in the `getends` problem shown in figure 5-1. The strategy in this problem is to extract the first and last elements from the original list and put them into the target list. Two possible intentions underlie the step of reversing the given list to construct the list (d c b a). First, the student might intend to take the first of this list in order to get d. Alternatively, the student might intend to take the last of this list in order to get (a). Finally, the student might intend to use (d c b a) for both purposes. The tutor must consider all these possibilities but cannot resolve the ambiguity at this point without querying the student, which would violate our general guideline in model tracing: The student should be asked to specify information when it serves a pedagogical purpose (e.g., specifying intermediate products in the graphical programming language), otherwise the model tracing of the student's behavior should proceed as much as possible in the background, relying only on observation of the student's natural problem solving behavior. Therefore, the response manager notes the ambiguity internally by making inferences and setting the goals associated with all rules, and then later prunes

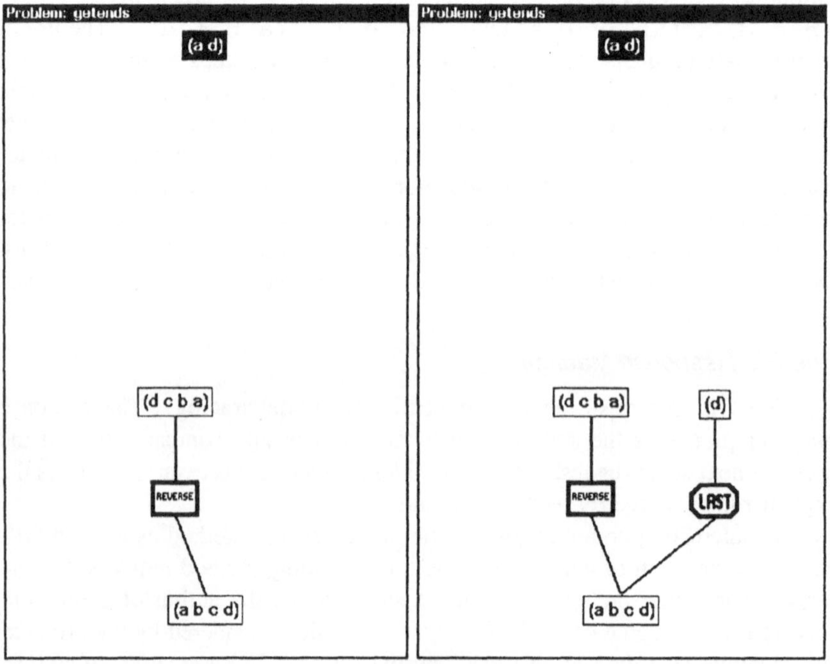

(1) (2)

Figure 5: (1) An ambiguous forward step in getends. The student may intend to use (d c b a) to extract d or to extract (a) or both. (2) A subsequent step that resolves the ambiguity. Since the student is getting (d) using last, GIL infers that the reverse is on a path to extract (a).

the goals when the ambiguity has been resolved. For example, in Figure 5-2, the student has taken the step of using `last` on the original list to get `(d)`. At this point the response manager infers that the purpose of the previous step must have been to get `(a)` rather than `d`, since getting the `(d)` using `last` is in service of the same goal that getting the `d` would have been.

It is important to consider why tracking this ambiguity is crucial for the tutoring strategies employed in GIL. In the model tracing method, students are given feedback when their steps demonstrate a misconception or poor strategy. GIL does not permit all legal LISP steps; it restricts the student to those that are possible steps toward a solution. If GIL does not understand the purpose of each step that is taken, it will not be able to follow the student's reasoning and will be unable to offer suggestions about how to continue the problem solving path if the student needs help, nor would GIL be able to explain why an incorrect step was in error. For this reason, GIL responds to each step as it is taken.

An interesting situation can arise when a student forgets a path that started earlier in the problem, or perhaps decides to achieve a goal using a different method from that begun earlier. This points to a pedagogical decision in GIL's design: the model tracing method requires that all steps accepted by the tutor be steps toward a solution. If students are permitted to achieve a plan using a different path, without deleting the part of the graph representing the plan previously initiated, then the program graph would have stranded paths, i.e., chains of steps that are not connected to the goals. Permitting such steps creates a difficult modeling problem, in that the problem solver would always have to be prepared to follow any alternative through the problem space, irrespective of the work that had been done up to that point. This would make it very difficult to select a step to suggest to the student or to provide error explanations. A more important issue, however, is that there is a pedagogical advantage in structuring the interaction so that the interface always accurately presents a record of the current problem state, rather than including potentially distracting information such as abandoned paths.

For these reasons, when students decide to follow a different plan from the one previously indicated, they must delete the steps in the plan being abandoned to "make room" for the new plan. Such a situation is shown in Figure 6. Here the student has taken the `first` of the original list to get `a`. Recall, however, that in the previous step GIL inferred that the student intended to use `(d c b a)` to get `(a)`, so if the student proceeded instead to use `first` to get `a`, the `reverse` step would become a stranded path. Thus, the tutor recognizes that this step was previously suggested by the problem solver but is no longer a current option, and it finds the plan initiated that replaced the use of this step. The explainer points out that using `first` at this point is redundant with the work the student has already done. If this step represents a confusion, and the student had not realized how `(d c b a)` could be used, then the feedback suggests how to proceed. If, on the other hand, the student has simply decided to use the `a` from `first` instead of `(a)` from the `last` of the `reverse` of `(a b c d)`, then previous steps can be deleted to make room for this new plan.

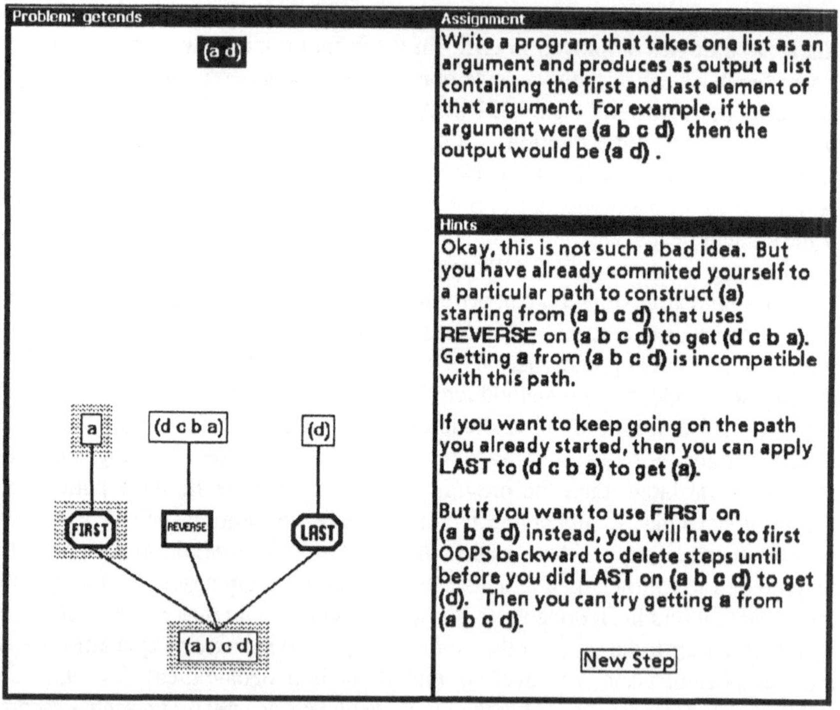

Figure 6: Feedback on a step redundant with a plan already initiated by the student.

The GIL Explainer

GIL constructs explanations in two types of situations. A student may request a hint at any point in the step. In addition, GIL constructs an explanation in response to a legal or strategic error to point out the part of the step that is in error. The GIL explainer draws upon the same knowledge base that the problem solver uses to construct solutions. This includes the problem solving rules, plans, and general knowledge about the operators.

Generating Hints

A student can ask for a hint at any point during a step by selecting the "?" button in the menu. If the student requests a hint at the beginning of a step (before selecting a function, inputs, or output), then GIL examines the possible next steps suggested by the problem solver to select one to recommend. Heuristics are typically necessary to decide which rule to recommend, because in most situations there are a number of rules whose conditions are applicable. For example, at the problem state shown in Figure 3, the set of matched rules contains two forward rules in service of the "extract `d`" goal, one forward rule in service of the "extract `(a b c)`" goal, and backward reasoning rules from each of these two goals. If the student has made an error on the step prior to requesting a hint, then GIL selects a rule involving the components selected by the student. If no error has been made on this step, the response manager considers, in order, the following categories of steps to suggest: (1) a step that achieves a goal, (2) a problem decomposition step, if none has yet been taken, (3) a forward step that continues the strategy of the student's last step. For example, in Figure 3, the tutor has suggested a backward reasoning step to decompose the problem into two subgoals: first, extracting `d` from `(a b c d)`, and, second, extracting `(a b c)` from `(a b c d)`.

The GIL explainer uses the information in the selected rule to construct a hint. The explainer uses a small number of general templates that guide the construction for each type of step: backward decomposition, forward enable, or a forward achieve step. These general templates indicate the parts of the goal and the rule that should be described, along with some general English to tie them together. For example, the hint provided in Figure 3 refers to the goal ("construct `(d a b c)`"), the function used in the rule (`cons`) and its purpose ("a function that inserts something into a list"), the current starting point (the list `(a b c d)`), the inputs for the step (the inputs `d` and `(a b c)`), and the relations between the inputs and the starting point. In backward decomposition hints, the explanation template organizes the information to be discussed, but again the information itself is extracted from the rule.

All hints and error messages have two levels of help. In this case, after receiving the hint shown in the first paragraph, the student again selected the "?" button and so received more explicit information, shown in the second and third paragraphs. In most hints and error feedback explanations, the second level of help suggests actual values for the input, function, or output. In this case GIL follows up the general strategy of inserting something into a list to construct `(d a b c)`, suggested in the first paragraph, with more specific suggestions about which input to use and why, and what function will accomplish this insertion.

When a hint is requested in the middle of a step, the response manager uses information about the student's partial step to select the most appropriate rule to use as the basis for the hint. For example, if the student has selected both the function and the input and then asks for a hint, GIL reassures the student that the step is on the right track so far and then describes the general properties of the output for the function, e.g., "`last` returns a list containing the last element of its argument." If more help is requested, GIL suggests the actual output for the step and uses information in the rule to describe the relation of the function's output to the input.

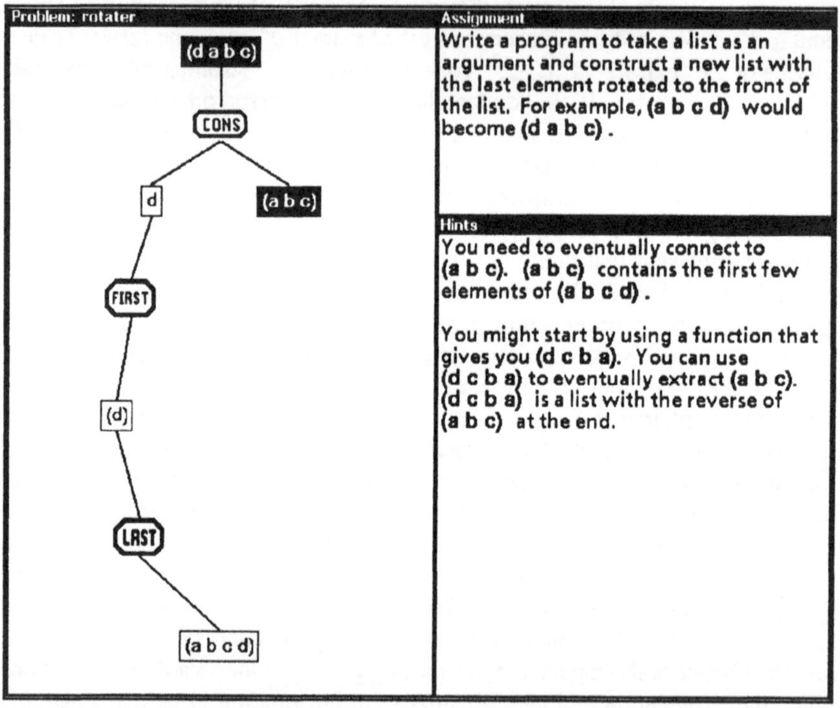

Figure 7: A hint in the `rotater` problem that suggests working forward from the input `(a b c d)` towards the goal `(a b c)`.

We expect the most useful type of hint to involve suggestions concerning the initiation of a plan to achieve a goal. Such a hint is shown in Figure 7. This hint occurs later in the `rotater` problem after the student has achieved one of the two subgoals set in Figure 3. The student asks for a hint, and GIL suggests a forward step that works toward the goal of extracting the sublist `(a b c)`. In this case, only the first level of help is shown (although it is generated in two paragraphs for clarity). GIL contains a simple natural language generator to translate into English the clauses from the predicate calculus representation used by the problem solver. To illustrate where the text of this hint is derived, the rule chosen by the Explainer from those suggested by the problem solver and the bindings for this particular match of the rule are shown here:

CONDITIONS	the goal is extract PART from GIVENLIST PART is a list PART is a beginning-sublist of GIVENLIST LSTEL is the last element of GIVENLIST
DIRECTION	Forward-reasoning
RULE-TYPE	Enable
OPERATOR	reverse
INPUT	GIVENLIST
OUTPUT	FLIPPED
PROPERTIES	FLIPPED is a list LSTEL is the first item in FLIPPED FLIPPED is composed of LSTEL and NEWPART NEWPART is the reverse of PART
NEW-GOAL	extract PART from FLIPPED
Bindings	PART = `(a b c)` GIVENLIST = `(a b c d)` LSTEL = `d` FLIPPED = `(d c b a)` NEWPART = `(c b a)`

In this hint, GIL begins by describing the goal and then finds the clause in the rule that connects the goal to the step's input. In this case the goal, `(a b c)`, is the beginning sublist of `(a b c d)`, which is expressed as the phrase "contains the first few elements of." GIL suggests applying a rule to construct a new list, `(d c b a)`, and explains the properties of this new list, namely, that it is composed of `d` and something that is the reverse of `(a b c)`. In general, Forward Enable hints suggest a target output that is a step toward the goal and then explain the properties of that target output that enable it to be used as input to further steps toward the goal. The construction of these hints would not be possible if the rules merely associated actions to take with particular problem situations. Instead, the rules in the GIL problem solver explicitly represent and track the properties of the intermediate products. In this way, the explainer can point out what properties result from each step and how these features feed into further steps toward the goal. The descriptions of the intermediate products provide the basis for the problem solver's further reasoning about these objects. As described earlier, the information is not added solely for the purpose of generating explanations; rather it represents the system's knowledge about these objects used by the problem solver.

Generating Error Feedback

The student is required to be explicit about the inputs and output for each selected programming operator, so the tutor has useful information for diagnosing errors in the student's intended plan. Because the rules contain a description of the input and output, the student's step can be compared with the information in the most similar matching rule and the discrepancies can be described. GIL handles two types of errors: legal errors, in which the chosen function and inputs do not return the indicated output, and strategic errors, in which the chosen step is a legal LISP operation but is not strategically useful. Responding to errors combines general knowledge about operators with specific knowledge from the rules and associated plans.

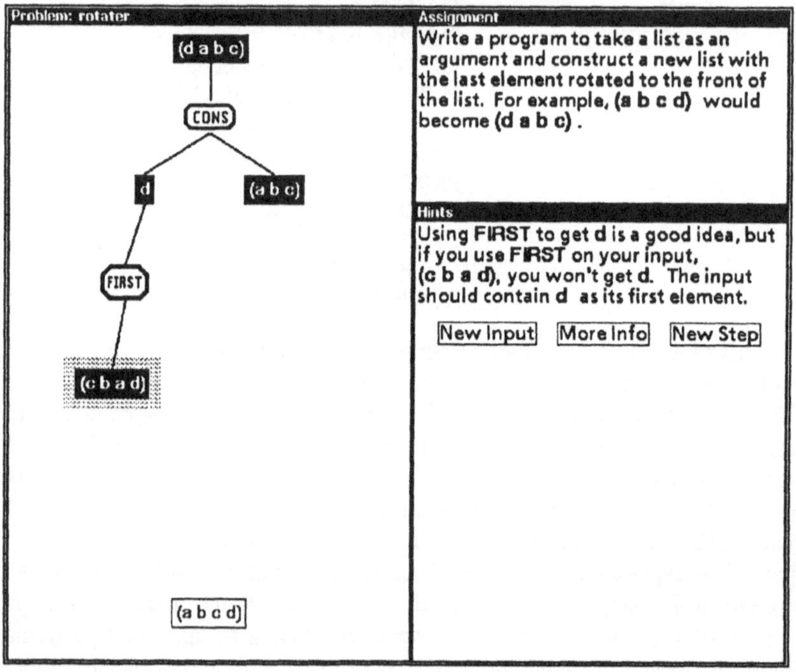

Figure 8: Error feedback on a step that violates the legal constraints of the operator.

The explainer is invoked when the response manager discerns that the student's step fails to match any of the possible next steps suggested by the problem solver. At that point, the response manager passes the student step and the possible next steps to the explainer. The explainer then attempts to discern the most likely source of the error. This analysis may also draw upon information about the solution history for this problem, contained in the student model (a model of the individual student's problem solving attempts so far). The response of the explainer to a student error first requires finding the closest matching rule. The simplest cases are those in which two of the three components of a step (inputs, function, and output) match those of a rule considered by the problem solver. GIL first describes what is good about the student's step and then points out the ways in which the step is in error or could be improved.

Consider the step shown in Figure 8. This somewhat confused step occurred following the initial backward step shown in Figure 3. In this case, the function and the output selected by the student match a rule considered by the problem solver, but the input provided by the student does not. This is a legal error, in that the function selected by the student, when applied to the input, does not produce the selected output. In this case, GIL describes the differences between the student's input, the list `(c b a d)`, and the input considered by the matched rule, `(d c b a)`. The properties of the input are found by consulting general operator knowledge about the function `first`. Associated with each operator are the characteristics of the input and the output and the relations between them. To construct a hint, the explainer uses this knowledge of inputs and outputs rather than knowledge in the specific rule. Operator knowledge is used because in the case of an illegal proposed step, the strategic constraints contained in the rule are less important than the legal constraints on applying the function. The operator knowledge for `first` contains the constraints that the input is a list, it contains at least one element, and the output consists of the first element of the input. In this case, the third constraint is violated, because the student input does not contain `d` as its first element. The tutor describes the violated constraint and gives the student the option of replacing the input, asking for more information, or redoing the entire step.

In the next example, shown in Figure 9, the student replaces the input and this time finds a list that satisfies the legal constraints. However, the student's step again fails to match any rule, so the explainer is invoked to find and explain the discrepancy. In this case, the error is a strategic one. The closest matching rule is again the `first` rule with `d` as output. The rule recognizes that a target element is the last element of a given list and proposes taking a backward step, applying the function `first` to a new list, such that the list is the reverse of the original list. The general form of the rule is shown here. In the case shown in Figure 9, the variable `NEWLIST` is bound to the value `(d c b a)`.

CONDITIONS	the goal is extract LSTEL
	LSTEL is the last element of GIVENLIST
	FSTEL is the first element of GIVENLIST
DIRECTION	Backward-reasoning
RULE-TYPE	Subgoal
OPERATOR	first
INPUT	NEWLIST
OUTPUT	LSTEL

PROPERTIES	NEWLIST is a list
	LSTEL is the first item in NEWLIST
	FSTEL is the last item in NEWLIST
	NEWLIST is the reverse of GIVENLIST
NEW-GOAL	extract NEWLIST from GIVENLIST

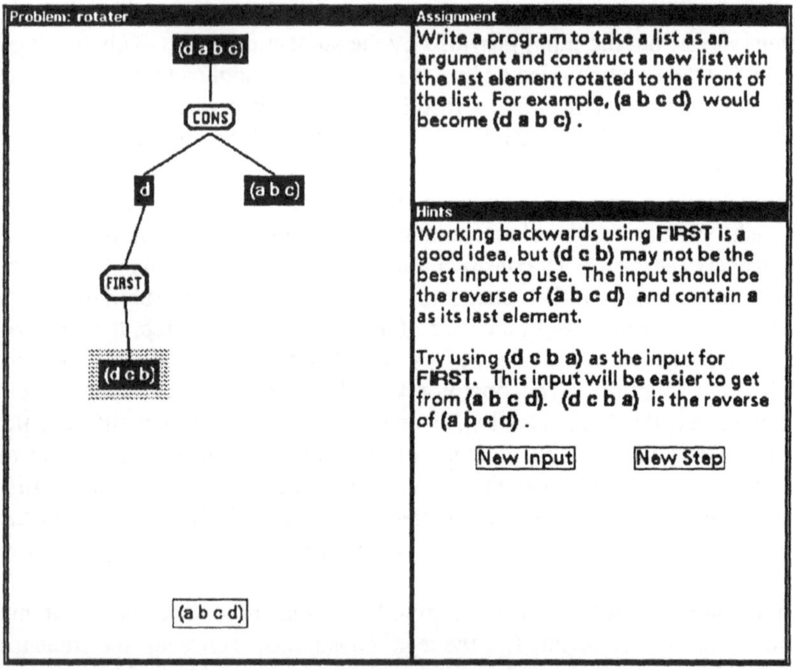

Figure 9: Error feedback on a step that violates the strategic constraints of the rule.

In the case of a strategic error, the explainer examines the clauses in the rule to find those that are violated by the student's step. In this case, the third and fourth properties are violated. The tutor describes these violated properties. In some cases the delineation of the discrepancies is sufficient for the student to infer what type of input to use. If still unsure, the student can request more information, whereupon the second level of help will describe the specific input indicated by the rule and suggest how to proceed. In this case, the tutor suggests the input `(d c b a)` because this input can be more easily extracted from the given list than that specified by the student. Both levels of help are shown in the figure.

The more difficult cases for the GIL explainer are those in which the step is legal and the problem solver has not considered a rule that involves that operator (unlike the case in Figure 9). Explaining these errors draws upon rule and plan knowledge. In some cases, such plan-based errors are cases of redundant effort, such as the error shown in Figure 6. In other cases, the student may be confused

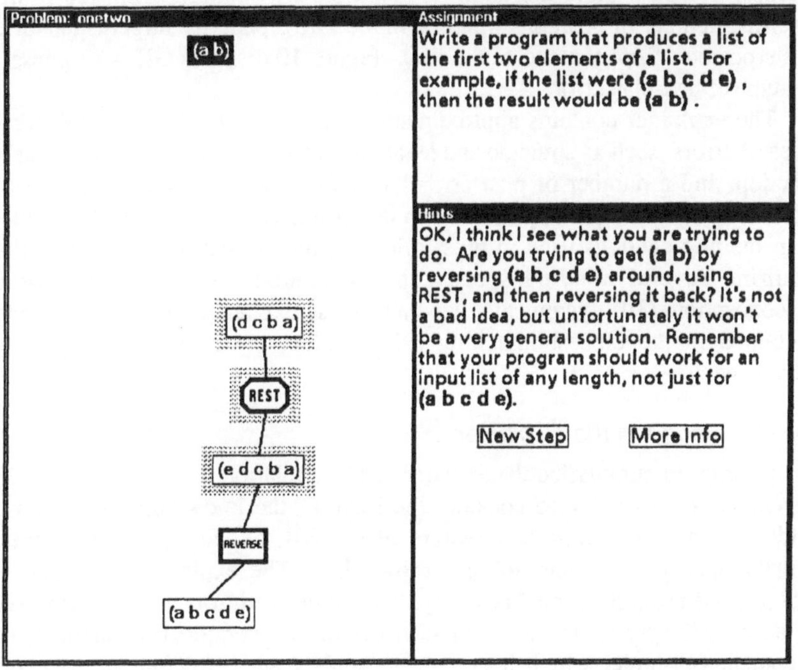

Figure 10: GIL's response to a bad-plan error.

about what plans are possible in the current situation. For example, a student may select the function `rest` as a step toward extracting the last element of a list. This represents a bad plan, because applying successive `rests` could be used only if the exact number of elements in the list is known in advance (or if the student uses recursion or iteration, which are not presented until later in the curriculum). The problem `rotater` requires writing a function that would work for a list of any length. In these cases, explaining why the step is not strategic requires comparing the effects of the nonstrategic step with the desired effects. This is a more difficult explanation problem than responding to the legal and strategic errors in Figures 8 and 9. In these cases, describing the discrepancies between the student's input and the rule's input provides a useful contrast. In the case of a bad-plan error, the differences in the immediate input or output are less informative. Ideally, the role of the step in the larger plan would be considered in the explanation. The explainer handles some of these cases by recognizing that the plans involved achieve similar goals (to extract an element that is not at the head of a list), but that they differ in their constraints (in the successive `rest` plan, the target is identified by counting from the front a specified number of positions whereas, in the `last` plan, the target is identified by its position from the end of the list). Figure 10 displays GIL's response to this type of bad-plan error.

The explainer contains approximately twenty frames describing different types of errors, such as strategic and legal errors concerning the input, output, or function, and a number of plan errors concerning various types of redundant effort or bad plans. The approach taken in this explainer is quite different, then, from the bug catalogs used in most rule- and plan-based tutors. Rather than requiring several hundred specific bug detectors, one for each type of misconception, GIL dynamically generates these explanations from knowledge contained in the closest matching rule or plan, or from general operator knowledge.

Knowledge in the Explainer

In order to summarize the explainer and its relation to the rest of the GIL system, it is instructive to consider the issue of the knowledge used by this module. The most important feature of the GIL explainer is that it draws directly upon the problem solving knowledge. The explainer constructs its explanations using the same knowledge that the problem solver uses to construct solutions to the problems: general knowledge of the operators characterizing the circumstances under which it is legal to apply each LISP function, the rule knowledge characterizing the situations under which it is strategic to apply each LISP function, and the plan knowledge specifying how individual steps can fit together to achieve a goal. In addition, the explainer reasons about entailment relations between clauses in order to avoid possible redundancies in its explanations (e.g., if something is not a list, then it is not necessary to mention that it does not have the proper first element).

Our focus on the explainer has been on the knowledge it manipulates rather than the manner in which it translates each proposition into English. The intelligence of the explainer is in selecting which clauses in the rules or operator knowledge and which relationships in the plans should be generated. The natural language generator that translates the clauses is very simple, and some awkwardness can occasionally result. For example, the generator does not currently make use of relative clauses, generating two individual sentences when a combined sentence might be smoother. To further improve the prose, it will be necessary to incorporate more knowledge about discourse to construct more smoothly flowing, coherent English text (e.g., Bienkowski, 1986; McKeown, 1985).

Research Issues

We have many difficult decisions in GIL's design, such as the timing of feedback, the content of the explanations, and the nature of the interface. Our decisions on these issues were in general based on theoretical motivations or pedagogical intuitions, but an important purpose of designing this intelligent tutoring system is to be able to test these predictions empirically. For example, one of the more controversial claims made by Anderson, Boyle, and Reiser (1985) is their argument that a tutor should respond with "immediate feedback." They argue that there are clear advantages for providing immediate feedback upon errors because the learning mechanism for adjusting a faulty rule or forming a new correct rule relies upon the problem situation being active in memory. Empirical evaluations of the effectiveness of feedback in procedural learning indicate that students learn procedures more quickly when provided with this feedback. Students can more easily utilize feedback and explanations when the reasoning that led to the error is still accessible. Furthermore, immediate feedback can prevent long episodes of counter-productive floundering. On the other hand, many educators share the intuition that learning is more effective when students are given the opportunity to experiment and thereby "discover" and correct their own errors (e.g., Bruner, 1961; Papert, 1980; Schank & Farrell, 1987). This view has motivated promising work on guided discovery systems and learning environments (e.g., Farrell, 1988; Foss, 1987; Glaser, Raghavan, & Schauble, 1988; Roschelle, 1987; Shute, Glaser, & Raghavan, 1989; White, in press) and underlies the design of many computer-based educational systems.

How then can the questions of immediate feedback versus the benefits of discovery be evaluated? A simple answer to this question is unlikely to arise. The answer will most certainly depend on the type of target knowledge desired, the student's current level of expertise, the possibilities afforded by the environment for the student to elicit explicit results from experiments, etc. One problem in evaluating the issue of immediate feedback is the definition of what constitutes "immediate" feedback. In the GIL tutor, students enter the input and output for a programming step and GIL responds immediately if a legal or strategic error is exhibited. This interaction is of a larger grain size than in LISPITS, in which feedback is presented after each word (function or argument). A model tracing system provides an opportunity to study an issue such as immediate feedback, keeping constant other aspects of the tutoring interaction. We plan to use the GIL tutor as a setting for a series of experiments examining these issues, by manipulations in which we vary the amount the student enters before feedback is provided and by making the feedback contingent upon student's request rather than obligatory.

A number of other interesting theoretical issues have arisen in the context of constructing the GIL tutor that we hope to explore empirically. Students working with GIL design their programs first using a concrete example rather than writing a general program using variables. This corresponds to the way in which we see good students working on difficult problems, but there are potential hazards to this technique. For example, students might not reason through an algorithm at the correct level of abstraction, or might construct programs that work for some examples but do not satisfy the general constraints for the problem. The advantages of reasoning about programs using specific examples versus general code is an important set of issues we hope to examine empirically, by comparing students working with the GIL interface and those working with a standard text-based editor. A related question is whether feedback and hints should be presented in the context of the example or in terms of general characteristics of the data. The feedback shown in Figures 6-10 combines the two types of information, explaining the general properties of the data (drawn from the rule) but illustrating them in the context of the specific example used in the program. An interesting issue suggested by the use of examples to construct a general program is whether examples rather than general principles might be used to provide hints about possible general strategies or next steps in a problem. Students can be effective in retrieving previous solutions from memory to help them construct new programs (Faries & Reiser, 1988). It may turn out to be a useful pedagogical strategy to remind a student who asks for a hint of particular problems he or she has solved that might be relevant to the current problem.

In general, in evaluating the intelligent tutoring systems approach, it is important to stress that particular tutoring systems such as LISPITS or GIL are designed not only as an end in themselves but also as a forum for research into the nature of learning and teaching.

CONCLUSIONS

We have argued that a truly robust intelligent tutoring system must be able to construct explanations directly from its problem solving knowledge. We have begun to build such a system in which students construct plans to achieve simple programming goals. In general, the simple explanation mechanisms we have implemented in the GIL tutor can construct explanations for a wide range of hints and error feedback. The content of the rules, combined with general knowledge about LISP functions, is used to generate explanations tailored to the particular problem situation. We are currently conducting experiments to evaluate the effectiveness of this system, including tests of the graphical forward and backward reasoning interface and an evaluation of the effectiveness of GIL's explanations. (See Reiser, Ranney, Lovett, & Kimberg, 1989 for some initial results.) We expect research on the construction of explanations to become an important focus in research on cognition and instruction.

ACKNOWLEDGEMENTS

We are grateful to Jody Gevins, Patricia Friedmann, Adnan Hamio, Eric Ho, Antonio Romero, and Alka Tyle for assistance in programming GIL. We also thank Jill Larkin and the participants in the Conference on Computer-Assisted Instruction and Intelligent Tutoring Systems for their suggestions on the GIL Interface. The research reported here was supported in part by contract MDA903-87-K-0652 from the Army Research Institute and by a research grant from the James S. McDonnell Foundation to Princeton University. The research was performed using equipment donated to Princeton University by the Xerox Corporation University Grant Program. The views and conclusions contained in this chapter are those of the authors and should not be interpreted as necessarily representing the official policies, either expressed or implied, of any of these supporting organizations.

REFERENCES

Anderson, J. R. (1983). *The architecture of cognition.* Cambridge, MA: Harvard University Press.

Anderson, J. R. (1987). Skill acquisition: Compilation of weak-method problem solutions. Psychological Review, 94, 192-210.

Anderson, J. R. (1988). The expert module. In M. C. Polson & J. J. Richardson (Eds.), *Foundations of intelligent tutoring systems.* Hillsdale, NJ: Erlbaum.

Anderson, J. R., Boyle, C. F., Farrell, R. G., & Reiser, B. J. (1987). Cognitive principles in the design of computer tutors. In P. Morris (Ed.), *Modelling cognition.* New York, NY: Wiley.

Anderson, J. R., Boyle, C. F., & Reiser, B. J. (1985). Intelligent tutoring systems. *Science, 228,* 456-462.

Anderson, J. R., Boyle, C. F., & Yost, G. (1985). The geometry tutor. *Proceedings of the Ninth International Joint Conference on Artificial Intelligence.* Los Angeles, CA.

Anderson, J. R., Farrell, R., & Sauers, R. (1984). Learning to program in LISP. *Cognitive Science, 8,* 87-129.

Anderson, J. R., Pirolli, P., & Farrell, R. (1988). Learning to program recursive functions. In M. Chi, R. Glaser, & M. Farr (Eds.), *The nature of expertise.* Hillsdale, NJ: Erlbaum.

Anderson, J. R., & Reiser, B. J. (1985, April). The LISP tutor. *Byte, 10* (4), 159-175.

Bienkowski, M. A. (1986). A computational model for extemporaneous elaborations (Tech. Rep. No. 1). Princeton, NJ: Princeton University, Cognitive Science Laboratory.

Bonar, J. G., & Cunningham, R. (1988). Bridge: Tutoring the programming process. In J. Psotka, L. D. Massey, & S. A. Mutter (Eds.), *Intelligent tutoring systems: Lessons learned.* Hillsdale, NJ: Erlbaum.

Bonar, J., & Soloway, E. (1985). Preprogramming knowledge: A major source of misconceptions in novice programmers. *Human-Computer Interaction, 1*, 133-161.

Brown, J. S. (1985). Process versus product: A perspective on tools for communal and informal electronic learning. *Journal of Educational Computing Research, 1*, 179-202.

Brown, J. S., & Burton, R. R. (1978). Diagnostic models for procedural bugs in basic mathematical skills. *Cognitive Science, 2*, 155-192.

Bruner, J. S. (1961). The act of discovery. *Harvard Educational Review, 31*, 21-32.

Burton, R. R. (1982). Diagnosing bugs in a simple procedural skill. In D. H. Sleeman & J. S. Brown (Eds.), *Intelligent tutoring systems.* London: Academic Press.

Chi, M., Feltovich, P., & Glaser, R. (1981). Categorization and representation of physics problems by experts and novices. *Cognitive Science, 5*, 121-152.

Clancey, W. J. (1982). Tutoring rules for guiding a case method dialogue. In D. H. Sleeman & J. S. Brown (Eds.), *Intelligent tutoring systems.* London: Academic Press.

Clancey, W. J. (1983). The epistemology of a rule-based expert system—A framework for explanation. *Artificial Intelligence, 20*, 215-251.

Clancey, W. J. (1987). *Knowledge-based tutoring: The Guidon program.* Cambridge, MA: MIT Press.

Clancey, W. J. (1988). The knowledge engineer as student: Metacognitive bases for asking good questions. In H. Mandl & A. Lesgold (Eds.), *Learning issues for intelligent tutoring systems.* New York, NY: Springer-Verlag.

Collins, A., & Brown, J. S. (1988). The computer as a tool for learning through reflection. In H. Mandl & A. Lesgold (Eds.), *Learning issues for intelligent tutoring systems.* New York, NY: Springer-Verlag.

Corbett, A. T., Anderson, J. R., & Patterson, E. J. (1988). Problem compilation and tutoring flexibility in the LISP Tutor. *Proceedings of ITS-88: The International Conference on Intelligent Tutoring Systems* (pp. 423-429). Montreal, PQ.

Cunniff, N., & Taylor, R. P. (1987). Graphical vs. textual representations: An empirical study of novices' program comprehension. In G. M. Olson, S. Sheppard, & E. Soloway (Eds.), *Empirical studies of programmers: Second workshop.* Norwood, NJ: Ablex.

du Boulay, B. (1986). Some difficulties of learning to program. *Journal of Educational Computing Research, 2*, 57-73.

du Boulay, B., O'Shea, T., & Monk, J. (1981). The black box inside the glass box: Presenting computing concepts to novices. *International Journal of Man-Machine Studies, 14*, 237-249.

Ehrlich, K., & Soloway, E. (1984). An empirical investigation of the tacit plan knowledge in programming. In J. C. Thomas & M. L. Schneider (Eds.), *Human factors in computer systems.* Norwood, NJ: Ablex.

Faries, J. M., & Reiser, B. J. (1988). Access and use of previous solutions in a problem solving situation. *Proceedings of the Tenth Annual Conference of the Cognitive Science Society.* Montreal, PQ.

Farrell, R. (1988). Facilitating self education by questioning assumptive reasoning. *Proceedings of AAAI-88, Seventh National Conference on Artificial Intelligence* (pp. 2-6). St. Paul, MN.

Foss, C. L. (1987). Learning from errors in Algebraland (Tech. Rep. IRL87-0003). Palo Alto, CA: Institute for Research on Learning.

Glaser, R., Raghavan, K., & Schauble, L. (1988). Voltaville, a discovery environment to explore the laws of DC circuits. *Proceedings of ITS-88: The International Conference on Intelligent Tutoring Systems* (pp. 61-66). Montreal, PQ.

Hollan, J. D., Hutchins, E. L., & Weitzman, L. (1984). STEAMER: An interactive inspectable simulation-based training system. *AI Magazine, 5*, 15-27.

Hutchins, E. L., Hollan, J. D., & Norman, D. A. (1986). Direct manipulation interfaces. In D. A. Norman & S. W. Draper (Eds.), *User centered system design: New perspectives on human-computer interaction*. Hillsdale, NJ: Erlbaum.

Johnson, W. L. (1986). *Intention-based diagnosis of errors in novice programs*. Palo, Alto, CA: Morgan Kaufmann.

Johnson, W. L., & Soloway, E. (1984). Intention-based diagnosis of programming errors. *Proceedings of the 1984 National Conference on Artificial Intelligence*. Austin, TX.

Johnson, W. L., & Soloway, E. (1987). PROUST: An automatic debugger for Pascal programs. In G. Kearsley (Ed.), *Artificial intelligence and instruction: Applications and methods*. Reading, MA: Addison-Wesley. (Originally published in 1985 in *Byte, 10*, (4), 179-190).

Kieras, D. E. (1988). What mental model should be taught: Choosing instructional content for complex engineering systems. In J. Psotka, L. D. Massey, & S. A. Mutter (Eds.), *Intelligent tutoring systems: Lessons learned*. Hillsdale, NJ: Erlbaum.

Kieras, D. E., & Bovair, S. (1984). The role of a mental model in learning to operate a device. *Cognitive Science, 8*, 255-273.

Klahr, D., & Carver, S. M. (1988). Cognitive objectives in a LOGO debugging curriculum: Instruction, learning, and transfer. *Cognitive Psychology, 20*, 362-404.

Laird, J. E., Rosenbloom, P. S., & Newell, A. (1986). Chunking in SOAR: The anatomy of a general learning mechanism. *Machine Learning, 1*, 11-46.

Larkin, J. H., McDermott, J., Simon, D., & Simon, H. A. (1980). Expert and novice performance in solving physics problems. *Science, 208*, 1335-1342.

Larkin, J. H., & Simon, H. A. (1987). Why a diagram is (sometimes) worth ten thousand words. *Cognitive Science, 11*, 65-99.

Lewis, M. W., Milson, R., & Anderson, J. R. (1987). The TEACHER'S APPRENTICE: Designing an intelligent authoring system for high school mathematics. In G. Kearsley (Ed.), *Artificial intelligence and instruction: Applications and methods*. Reading, MA: Addison-Wesley.

McKeown, K. R. (1985). *Text generation: Using discourse strategies and focus constraints to generate natural language text*. New York: Cambridge University Press.

Miller, J. R. (1988). The role of human-computer interaction in intelligent tutoring systems. In M. C. Polson & J. J. Richardson (Eds.), *Foundations of intelligent tutoring systems*. Hillsdale, NJ: Erlbaum.

Musen, M. A., Fagan, L. M., & Shortliffe, E. H. (1987). Graphical specification of procedural knowledge for an expert system. In J. A. Hendler (Ed.), *Expert systems: The user interface*. Norwood, NJ: Ablex.

Newell, A., & Simon, H. A. (1972). *Human problem solving*. Englewood Cliffs, NJ: Prentice-Hall.

Papert, S. (1980). *Mindstorms: Children, computers, and powerful ideas*. New York, NY: Basic Books.

Pea, R. D. (1986). Language-independent conceptual "bugs" in novice programming. *Journal of Educational Computing Research, 2*, 25-36.

Pirolli, P. (1986). A cognitive model and computer tutor for programming recursion. *Human-Computer Interaction, 2*, 319-355.

Putnam, R. T., Sleeman, D., Baxter, J. A., & Kuspa, L. K. (1986). A summary of misconceptions of high school BASIC programmers. *Journal of Educational Computing Research, 2*, 459-472.

Reiser, B. J. (1987). *Causal models in programming*. Paper presented at the Third International Conference on Artificial Intelligence and Education, Pittsburgh, PA.

Reiser, B. J., Anderson, J. R., & Farrell, R. G. (1985). Dynamic student modeling in an intelligent tutor for LISP programming. *Proceedings of the Ninth International Joint Conference on Artificial Intelligence*, Los Angeles, CA.

Reiser, B. J., Friedmann, P., Gevins, J., Kimberg, D., Ranney, M., & Romero, A. (1988). A graphical programming language interface for an intelligent LISP tutor. *Proceedings of CHI'88, The Conference on Human Factors in Computing Systems*. Washington, D.C.

Reiser, B. J., Friedmann, P., Kimberg, D., & Ranney, M. (1988). Constructing explanations from problem solving rules to guide the planning of programs. *Proceedings of ITS-88: The International Conference on Intelligent Tutoring Systems* (pp. 222-229). Montreal, PQ.

Reiser, B. J., Ranney, M., Lovett, M. C., & Kimberg, D. Y. (1989). Facilitating students reasoning with causal explanations and visual representations. In D. Bierman, J. Breuker, & J. Sandberg (Eds.) *Proceedings of the Fourth International Conference Artificial Intelligence and Education*. Springfield, VA: IOS.

Rich, C., & Shrobe, H. (1978). Initial report on a LISP Programmer's Apprentice. *IEEE Transactions on Software Engineering, 4*, 456-466.

Richer, M. H., & Clancey, W. J. (1985). GUIDON-WATCH: A graphic interface for viewing a knowledge-based system. *IEEE Computer Graphics and Applications, 5* (11), 51-64.

Roschelle, J. (1987). *The Envisioning Machine: Facilitating students' reconceptualization of motion*. Paper presented at the Third International Conference on Artificial Intelligence and Education, Pittsburgh, PA.

Schank, R. C., & Farrell, R. (1987). Creativity in education: A standard for computer-based teaching. *Machine-Mediated Learning*, 2, 175-194.

Shute, V., Glaser, R., & Raghavan, K. (1989). Inference and discovery in an exploratory laboratory. In P. L. Ackerman, R. J. Sternberg, & R. Glaser (Eds.), *Learning and individual differences*. San Francisco, CA: Freeman.

Shneiderman, B. (1983). Direct manipulation: A step beyond programming languages. IEEE Computer, 16, 57-69.

Simon, H. A. (1973). The structure of ill-structured problems. *Artificial Intelligence, 4*, 181-201.

Sleeman, D. H. (1982). Assessing aspects of competence in basic algebra. In D. H. Sleeman & J. S. Brown (Eds.), *Intelligent tutoring systems.* London: Academic Press.

Sleeman, D. H., Putnam, R. T., Baxter, J., & Kuspa, L. (1986). Pascal and high school students: A study of errors. *Journal of Educational Computing Research, 2*, 5-23.

Soloway, E. (1985). From problems to programs via plans: The content and structure of knowledge for introductory LISP programming. *Journal of Educational Computing Research, 1*, 157-172.

Soloway, E., & Ehrlich, K. (1984). Empirical studies of programming knowledge. *IEEE Transactions on Software Engineering, 5*, 595-609.

Soloway, E., Ehrlich, K., Bonar, J., & Greenspan, J. (1982). What do novices know about programming? In A. Badre & B. Shneiderman (Eds.), *Directions in human/computer interaction.* Norwood, NJ: Ablex.

Spohrer, J. C., & Soloway, E. (1986). Novice mistakes: Are the folk wisdoms correct? Communications of the ACM, 29 (7), 624-632.

Spohrer, J. C., Soloway, E., & Pope, E. (1986). A goal/plan analysis of buggy Pascal programs. *Human-Computer Interaction, 1*, 163-207.

Waters, R. C. (1985). The Programmer's Apprentice: A session with KBEmacs. *IEEE Transactions on Software Engineering, 11*, 1296-1320.

White, B. Y. (1990). ThinkerTools: Causal models, conceptual change, and science education. *Cognition and Instruction*, 42, 99-157.

White, B. Y., & Frederiksen, J. R. (1987). Qualitative models and intelligent learning environments. In R. Lawler & M. Yazdani (Eds.), *AI and Education.* Norwood, NJ: Ablex.

White, B. Y., & Frederiksen, J. R. (in press). Causal model progressions as a foundation for intelligent learning environments. To appear in *Artificial Intelligence.*

Wight, S., Feurzeig, W., & Richards, J. (1988) PLURIBUS: A visual programming environment for education and research. *Proceedings of the IEEE Workshop on Languages for Automation,* College Park, MD

5 A Practical Guide for the Creation of Educational Software

Ruth W. Chabay and Bruce A. Sherwood
Center for Design of Educational Computing
Carnegie Mellon University

PURPOSE

This chapter articulates and gives concrete examples of some of the important practical considerations in writing educational software. In the absence of a comprehensive theory, much of our advice must consist of assertions based on our experience with things that work, and don't work, in educational computer activities. We hope that these empirically derived guidelines may be useful not only to developers of computer-based instruction, but also as input for the formulation and testing of more rigorous models of human-computer interaction.

Some of what we say may seem utterly obvious and banal, yet we have often seen these "obvious" points missed by intelligent but inexperienced authors, including people who are very skilled both in teaching and in using computers, but who are new to the use of computers as an instructional medium. Diligent, committed authors will eventually come to many of the conclusions discussed here. By offering guidelines and suggestions, we hope to shorten the time required to discover what works and what doesn't. Nevertheless, there is no substitute for your own experience. We can help you reach the foothills, but you must reach the summit on your own.

What experiences have influenced our views on software? We have developed and published entire computer-based courses in chemistry and physics

(Chabay & Smith, 1977; Jones, Kane, Sherwood, & Avner, 1983; Kane & Sherwood, 1980; Smith & Chabay, 1977; Smith, Chabay, & Kean, 1983-86) which have been used by thousands of students. We have carried out formal and informal evaluations of these courses. Chabay has studied motivational factors in both computer-based and human tutoring. Sherwood has used computer-based materials for learning and teaching foreign languages. We are acquainted with a large amount of good and bad educational software. We have often been asked by novice and experienced authors for critiques of their work. It is this range of experience that encourages us to attempt a synthesis of what we think we have learned so far. We ourselves, however, feel that even after twenty years of experience we are still learning about this new medium, and we hope in the future to be able to create educational software much better than anything we have produced previously.

In this chapter, we will first discuss in general terms how the computer medium differs from other media and enumerate design challenges unique to this medium. Second, we will present specific guidelines for solutions to some of these problems in the areas of display, interactivity, input analysis, and control. We will close with a few hints on how to make the development of materials itself an interactive process.

A UNIQUE MEDIUM WITH UNIQUE DESIGN CHALLENGES

The Medium

Interactive software is a new medium and needs time to mature (Sherwood, 1976). It took several decades for cinema to mature, moving away from simply filming stage productions to a realization and exploitation of capabilities radically different from those of the stage. In the same way, interactive software differs dramatically from all previous media, because it is a two-way, dynamic, modifiable medium, requiring active input from the user, while previous media were primarily passive and one-way. The only model we have for this new interactive medium is human conversation. This model has limited utility, since on the one hand computers are not yet capable of complex, open-ended verbal interaction, while on the other, conversations do not exploit the dynamic, modifiable visual representations which computers can easily support. As a result, there is little past experience to draw upon for guidance.

The computer medium is unique in requiring inputs from the user. Exploiting this interactive character is a major reason for using a computer in instruction. But interaction creates a set of design problems that differ significantly from those of non-interactive media. For example, although graphic designers know a great deal about how to lay out an advertisement for a magazine, they need not worry about how to make such a display dynamic or interactive. In contrast, a computer display is often constructed a little at a time in response to inputs, instead of appearing all at once as does a magazine page. Perhaps the closest analogy is offered by informational video, which often builds up displays in a dynamic manner. However, its sequence is strictly linear, and there is no opportunity for user input or control of pace or content. In contrast, a computer display not only must look attractive but must also explain, or better, imply, how the reader might interact (e.g., touch a particular portion of the screen, or choose a menu option). In fact, since the actual content of a display may depend on user inputs, the program developer may not entirely know what will ultimately appear on a display. Such dynamic presentations, with pace and content influenced by the user, have an entirely different esthetic both from all-at-once pages in a book or magazine and from linear video or film.

In other media, physical characteristics provide context and control. For example, television programs have established lengths (30 or 60 minutes), and viewers can change channels at will. Readers can tell at a glance how far they've gotten in a book and can easily skip to a different part. The computer medium, however, does not automatically provide such information and options. These must be explicitly provided by the author.

In the specific case of instruction, how does the computer medium differ from traditional materials? In some ways the computer is more limited. Flipping between pages in a book is a rapid, intuitive process, and each page has significantly higher resolution and capacity than most current computer screens. Only very recently have there emerged computer-based materials which even approximate the easy access and high-quality text and graphics of a textbook. However, the computer has some advantages over the textbook. Static texts are rarely able to represent dynamic phenomena adequately, and they certainly cannot allow readers to experiment with the effect of parameter changes on figures in the text. Perhaps more importantly, the one-way nature of the textbook severely limits its effectiveness. Lacking inputs from the student, a textbook cannot notice that several pages have flowed by without the student understanding anything at all!

The computer medium offers more precision and more dynamic representations than a blackboard. Lectures plod or race inexorably forward in a straight line at a pace which may suit only a minority of the students. Compared with lectures, computer materials are inherently self-paced and repeatable, and they offer the potential for useful non-linearity (e.g., review, additional explanation, or experimentation). In favorable cases a computer program may be able to detect an individual student's difficulties and offer appropriate help, something rarely possible in a large lecture and too seldom available even in a small-group discussion class.

Design Challenges

Developing programs presents a series of challenging design problems. On each topic we offer suggestions on what to strive for and what to avoid. Situations do invariably arise where these guidelines conflict, and while we cannot provide general strategies for resolving such conflicts, we will at least note common dilemmas and trade-offs. Throughout the discussion, the following themes will recur with variations: displays, interactivity, input analysis, and control. They identify particularly challenging and critical aspects of interactive instructional programs.

Displays: A visual medium

The computer is inherently a visual medium. Because of its strong graphical capabilities, and because natural language interaction with a computer is so difficult, communication with the user will rely heavily on pictures and diagrams. Even text, in this medium, is best thought of as graphics. It is not effective to produce and lay out text for an interactive program as one would for a book. On the other hand, the dynamic nature of the medium offers new possibilities for presenting and making use of text.

Interactivity: Intuitive, transparent interactions with displays

The uniquely interactive, two-way nature of the medium has a striking impact even on seemingly non-interactive components such as static displays. Not only *can* the user interact with the program, he or she *must* interact for anything to happen at all. How does the user know what to do? One might think it sufficient to write instructions on the screen. But sad experience proves that even experienced users, including ourselves, often do not read or attend to such instructions. A major challenge is to produce graphics and text displays that make intuitively obvious what next moves are possible. This *interactivity* is part of the unique esthetic of good computer displays.

Input analysis: Communication problems

While modern computers offer exciting capabilities, they do sharply constrain the breadth of interaction compared with what a human provides. Through tone of voice, facial expression, and other body language, a human teacher provides important extra information, both cognitive and affective, that a computer cannot express. In the other direction, the computer's ability to guess a student's intentions is limited. Overcoming the constrained communications between computer and student constitutes a challenge to the author.

Control: Many paths

Unlike other media, the behavior of an interactive program is not entirely predictable, since it depends on user inputs. In extreme cases, every user of the same program might have a different experience—different paths through the material, different kinds of messages in response to inputs, different types of exercises, etc. The program must provide sensible context and responses for any path the user may follow; conversely, users must not be allowed to follow paths that the program is not prepared to deal with.

Using the framework described above, we now discuss major design issues related to display, interactivity, input, and control. We will close with advice on the development process itself.

DISPLAYS

There exist only the beginnings of a theory of what constitutes a good computer display, but some useful general points can be made. You want the user to pay attention to the most important things, and there is a limit on how many things the user can attend to simultaneously. This suggests keeping the display sparse and uncluttered, highlighting the most important aspects, and regularly removing from the screen those things which are of less importance and might distract the user. Since most computer screens are relatively small, with relatively low resolution compared to paper, displays can easily get crowded if one is not careful.

We offer the following suggestions for good, useful displays.

Basic Display Considerations

Let display determine structure

Make display central to program structure. Try to tie internal data structures to the external displays. Think of the display screen as the dominant element which drives your program and data structures. Don't think of the display aspects as a mere "user-interface" veneer grudgingly pasted over the "real" program. In an interactive program, the display is not the icing, but the cake; routines and data take second place to the screen (Larkin, 1988).

Simpler is better

This is perhaps the most important rule of display design. It is often a good rule in any medium, but it has special force in an interactive medium where the viewer must do more than passively observe the displays go by. But what is "simpler?" It is possible to characterize some aspects in detail.

Blank space

Leave lots of blank space. Leave borders, space between paragraphs, etc. Blank space in a computer display costs nothing, yet it is a powerful tool for making the important material stand out. Use two or three sparse displays rather than one dense display to present material that need not appear all at once. It is an unfortunate fact of life that most current computers have rather small screens which can easily get quite crowded if care is not taken in designing the displays.

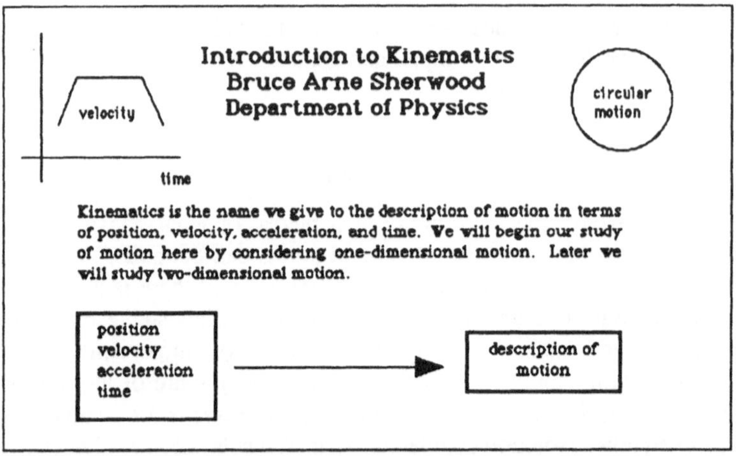

Compare the busy, crowded display above with the following display:

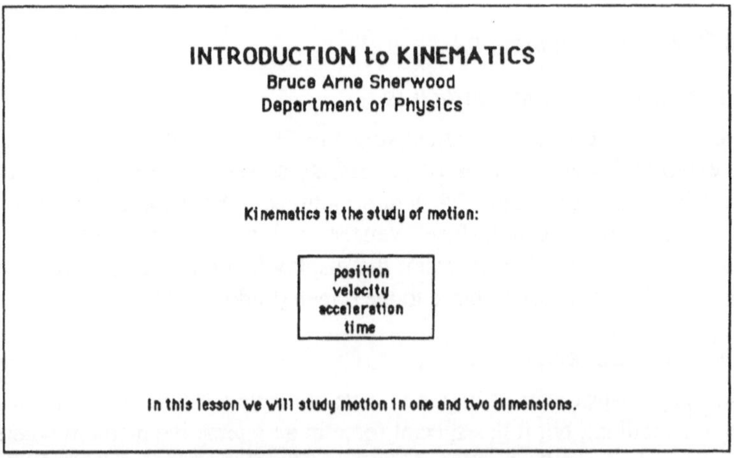

Information in the second display is clearer and easier to find.

About Text

Text IS graphics

Text serves two important functions in graphical displays. First, it presents basic information, and clarifies and explains pictures and diagrams. Second, it provides general instructions for using the program and specific instructions for performing particular tasks. Both uses are critical to the successful functioning of a program. But recall the discussion at the beginning of this paper: a computer is not a book. The sort of text that is appropriate to books does not work in dynamic interactive programs.

Don't use paragraphs

When you present text, don't use book-like paragraphs but rather set off words and phrases with plenty of white space. Even well-intentioned, diligent users have difficulty reading and retaining paragraphs of text displayed on the computer screen. Compare this paragraph with the following format:

When presenting text:

- don't use paragraphs
- do set off words and phrases
- compare with the format above

This terse, open, telegraphic presentation of the key points is particularly appropriate in an interactive medium and one in which blank space is cheap (in contrast to a book or article).

Mix text and pictures

In scientific or technical programs, authors often make the mistake of omitting explanatory text for diagrams. A picture may well be worth a thousand words, but a few well-placed words can enormously increase the impact of a picture. For example:

- Label the axes of your graphs.
  (Is the horizontal axis time or distance?)
- Label each curve plotted on a graph.
  (Which parameter value generated which curve?)
- Identify important components of diagrams.
  (Which angle is theta?)

Likewise, in verbal, text-oriented applications, a few pictures can vivify concepts and add interest.

This display makes vivid the importance of the final "n" in identifying the direct object of an Esperanto verb.

Strive for clarity

Time spent searching for clear, concise wording is time well invested. Very clear wording is essential both for subject matter and for instructions. Most teachers have had the sad experience of discovering while grading an exam that students misread a problem statement that had seemed perfectly clear to the teacher. The misunderstanding might never have been discovered, had the student not been asked to perform an action based on that text. In a textbook, by contrast, unclear or misleading wording may go undiscovered through several editions, because there is little direct evidence of the fact that students are not understanding some paragraph. The interactive computer medium, which demands inputs and responses from users, requires clear, unambiguous wording.

Highlighting

Ideally, it should be vividly clear at all times which parts of the display are most important. Various forms of highlighting can be used to emphasize what is salient.

Highlighting provides a focus

Use highlighting to provide a focus on the most important points. It can be achieved by the use of italics, by making something blink, by putting a box around a major item of text, by pointing at something, by using "inverse video" (e.g., white letters on a black background instead of black on white), by using distinctive colors, etc. Highlighting can be dynamic and temporary. That is, once the user has done something which indicates that attention is being paid to the highlighted area, you might remove or reduce that highlighting.

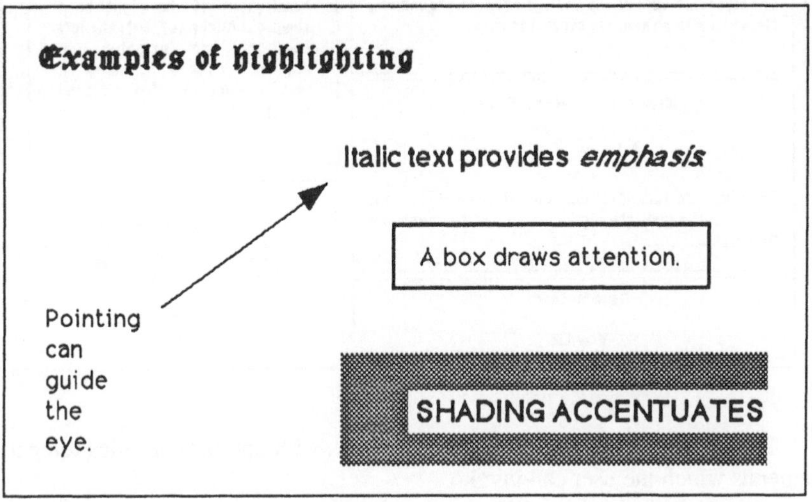

Highlight sparingly

If everything is highlighted, nothing is important, as in a student's textbook where every sentence has been marked yellow with a highlighting pen. **Moreover,** *using too* **many** *colors* or too many text styles **can be** *VERY* **DISTRACTING!**

Make important display components BIG

If the critical element of the display is a circuit diagram, it should normally be at the center of the display and large, while peripheral matters such as lists of options or explanatory text should be relegated to the periphery or to menus which are displayed only when invoked by the user.

Compare the following examples. In the first version, the central element (the circuit) is overwhelmed by non-critical information. The user must sort through the text to find out what, in fact, is the task posed by the display. Extra text is required to refer to and identify the headlights, which are not visually distinguished as the elements of interest in the circuit.

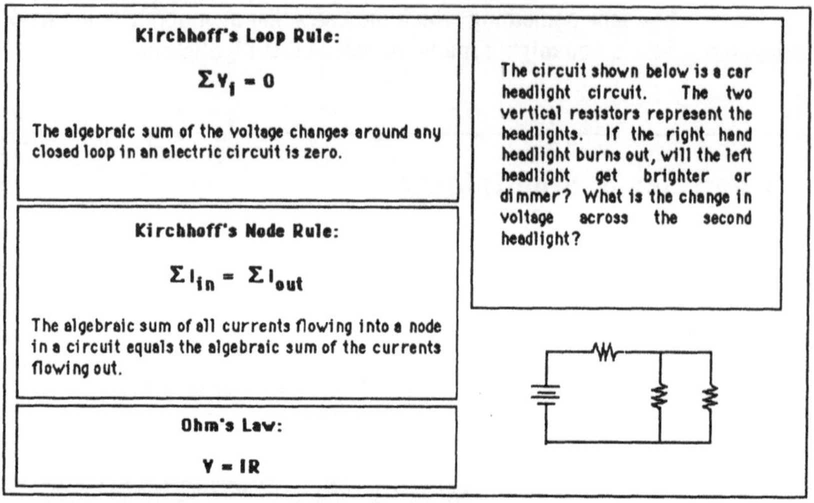

The circuit is central to the second display, with options and rules relegated to menus which the user can invoke.

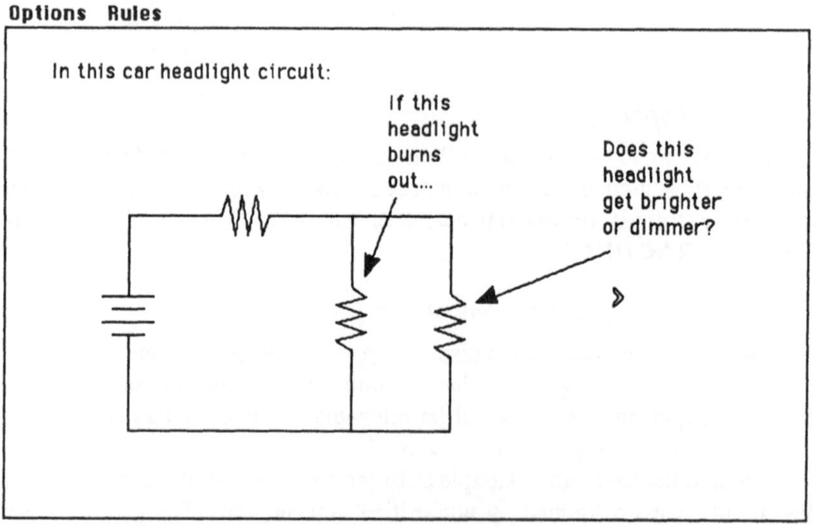

Remove unnecessary elements

Many of your displays will be dynamic rather than static: elements come and go in the course of the interaction with the user. It is important to remove text or graphics no longer needed, to make it easier for the user to pay attention to that which is still important or newly important.

Incremental Display-Building

Another way to provide emphasis and focus is by building up a display a little at a time. Here are some considerations in this regard.

Build up displays piece by piece

Do not flood the display with a great deal of information all at once. Constructing the display one element at a time, and waiting for a signal (a keypress or mouse click) before adding the next element, gives the user time to identify and comprehend the components of a complex display.

Maintain visual context, but avoid clutter

Leave enough older information on the screen to provide a context for the current activity. Such context is typically more needed here than in a book because it is usually easier for a book reader to flip back and forth to review the context.

However, here is one of the conflicts to which we alluded earlier. It is necessary to retain enough of a display to maintain context for the activity. It is also necessary to remove all but essential elements in order to help the user focus attention on salient features. What should you do, remove older output to provide focus, or leave it on to provide context? Of course there is no answer valid for all circumstances. One must seek a balance between these competing needs. But it is important to be consciously aware of both the needs and the conflict.

Use multiple "pages"

Many programs have only one "page" in the sense that only small modifications in the display ever take place, and the screen is never erased as a whole. This display strategy has the advantage of keeping a strong contextual framework visible at all times. However, one should not always slavishly follow this model. For example, your program might detect a major misunderstanding on the part of the student which requires extended discussion. Trying to squeeze this somewhere onto the current "page" may cramp things too much. It may be much better to clear the screen entirely, display only the bare minimum of context extracted from the situation, and proceed to exploit the much larger display space now available. When you have completed this digression, go reconstruct the original display to re-establish the full context. Other uses of multi-"page" strategies include having title pages and tables of contents, or separate sections of the program with quite different contents and formats.

Break up long texts

It is often helpful to the user to break up text into separate pieces, waiting for a keypress before adding the next item to the growing list. Building up the list a little at a time maintains emphasis (of the most recent item) while maintaining context (because the previous items are still visible).

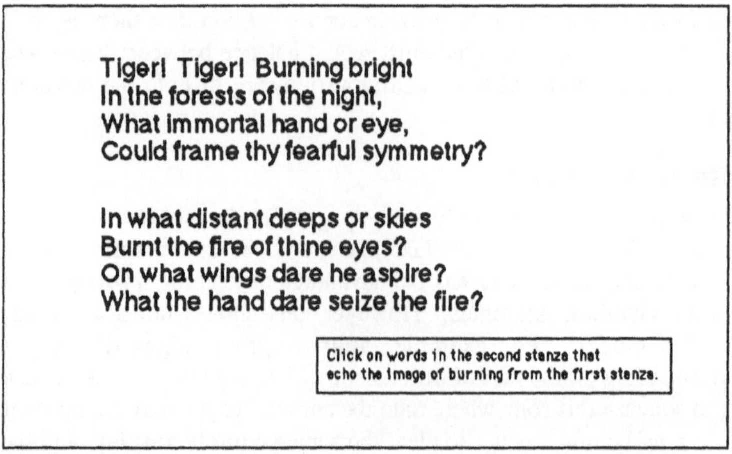

Building up the display a little at a time is a very simple but effective technique, and one which a book cannot offer.

Connections Among Display Elements

In this section we discuss the importance of connections among the various parts of a display.

Connect text with graphics

A general principle is to avoid describing in words that which is better shown with graphics, and this includes tying together pieces of text. It is much better to point graphically to the relevant words in a cited passage than to attempt to describe its location verbally:

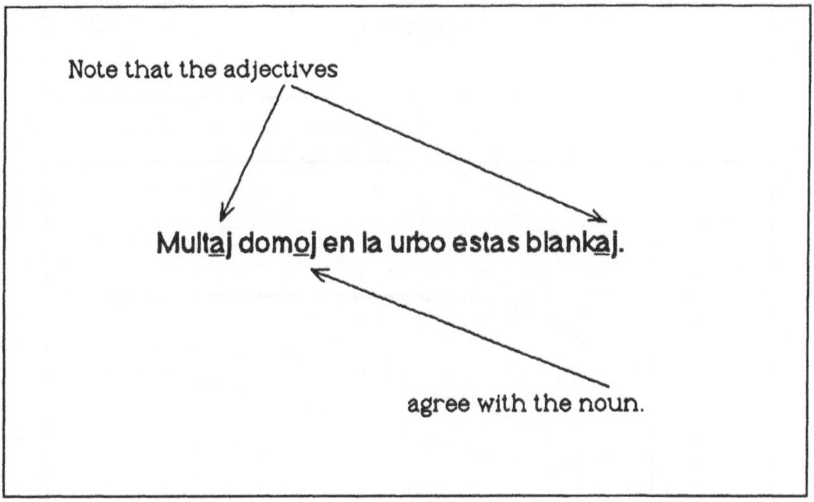

Connect graphics with text

Text and sequencing are needed to make connections among the elements of a graphical display. For example, remember to title the axes of a graph. You may know very well what the graph depicts, but you're not writing the program just for yourself. If there are several functions displayed on the graph, consider distinguishing them with their own neighboring titles, and/or plotting them one at a time in diverse colors or textures, waiting for user acknowledgement with a keypress before displaying another in the series. As with text, this incremental approach to building the final display is an excellent mechanism for providing both emphasis and context.

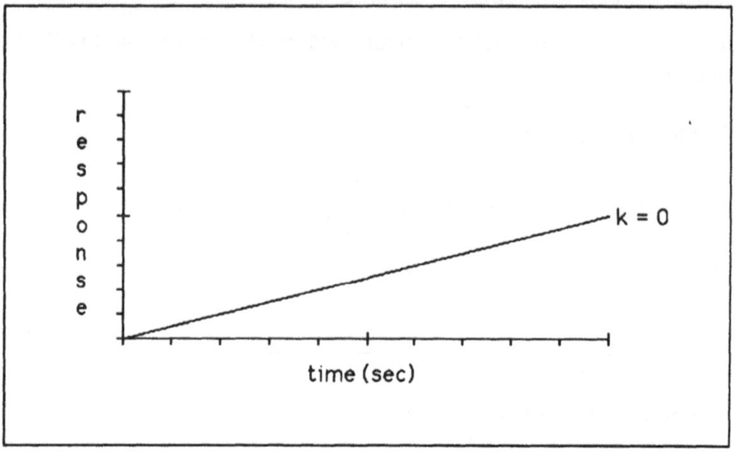

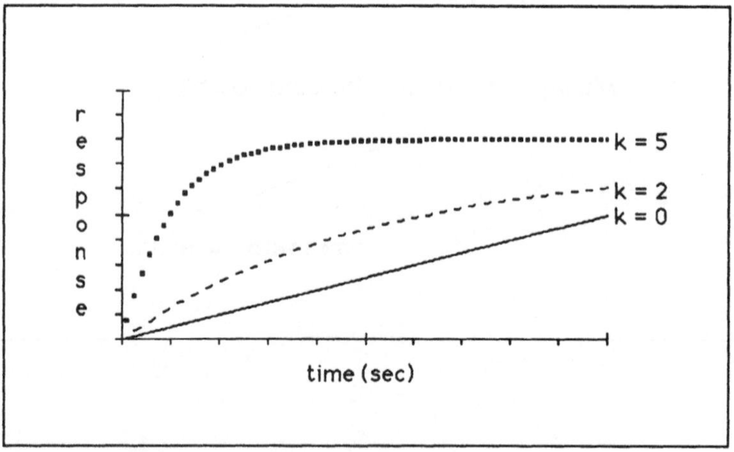

Adjacency

Generally speaking, work down and to the right as you add to a display, to provide some consistency in where to look for new information. A more general way to state this principle is that new information should be near the most recently displayed information. Adjacency on the screen is an important tool for making a complex display understandable. But when it isn't possible to use adjacency, or you need to make a link back to earlier information, use sequencing or graphic cues to make that connection.

Here is an example of the confusion which results when these principles are violated:

```
Here is a bad example that does not use adjacency.
The discussion is begun up here.
```

```
Here is a bad example that does not use adjacency.
The discussion is begun up here.









The user inputs a function down here:
» y = sin(x)exp(-x)
```

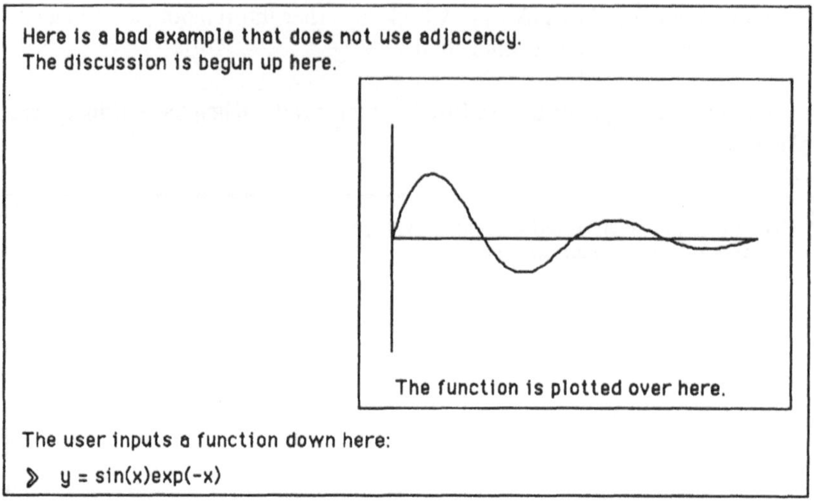

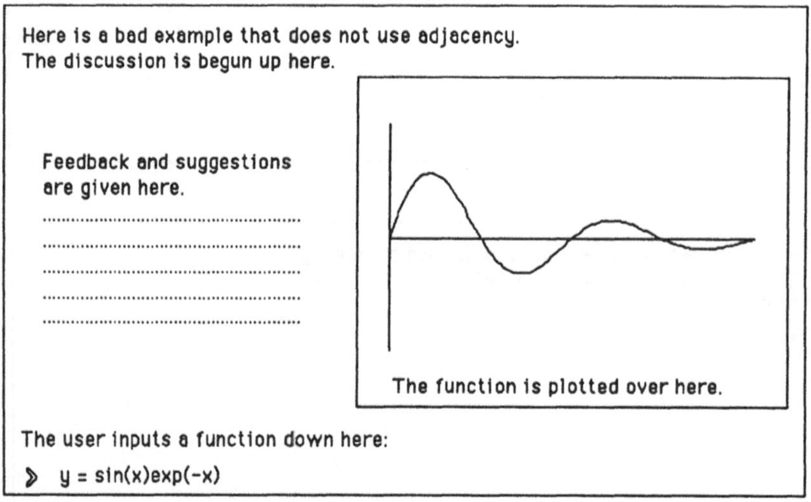

Input: adjacency versus consistency

It is desirable to establish a clear convention for input. One strategy, which is frequently appropriate, is to decide on a single, consistent screen location for input throughout the program. Given such consistency, the user will always know where to look when input is requested. However, the requirement for consistency may conflict with other principles. For example, for the sake of consistency, you might decide that input typed by the user should always be entered at the bottom of the screen, so the user will always know what to expect when input is requested. Suppose, as in the figure below, you have displayed a list of numerical parameters at the top of the screen and have invited the user to vary them. In making the change, the user's focus of attention must drop way down to the bottom of the screen, where the value is entered. This is consistent. It is not good, since the context (the current parameter value) is lost, as shown below.

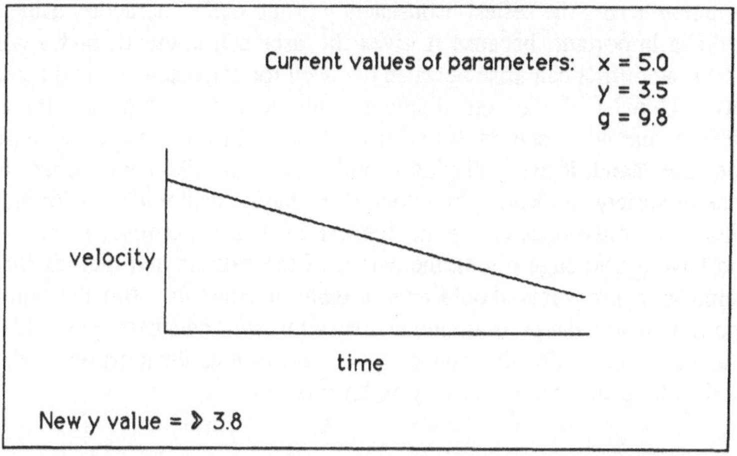

It is far better to have the user's typing appear right beside the chosen item, as in the next figure.

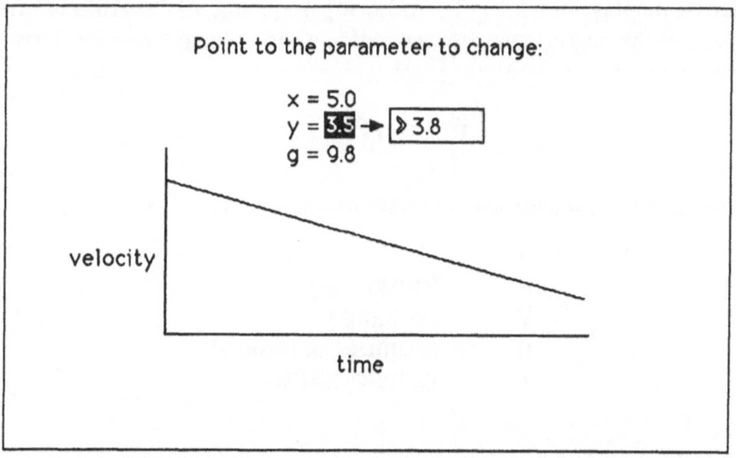

This automatically maintains the context: the current value is shown for comparison, and the location of the typing in and of itself indicates which parameter is being changed. Here absolute consistency is far less important than *adjacency*—placing new items adjacent to logically related items (though this, too, may be thought of as a form of consistency). Adjacency cuts down on the time the student needs in order to identify the next task, thus reducing the processing load and the possibility for confusion.

Consistency versus variety

If you write a series of programs, try to maintain consistency of presentation across the series. Consistency of the main interaction aspects and notation is important, because it gives the user a framework and a context. However, a conflict can arise between the need for consistency and the need for variety. Consistency in the displays (and interactions) builds the user's confidence that he or she knows what to expect and how to use the materials. On the other hand, if every display is laid out exactly like every other display, the lack of variety can lead to boredom. One way to deal with this conflict is to provide strict consistency only at the highest level. For example, every program should have a title page giving the names of the authors and their affiliations, and multi-part programs should have a table of contents. But the individual components inside the program might vary a lot, with consistency provided in a general way (e.g., by drawing new display elements near the most recent display) rather than by using specific unvarying layouts.

Example

As an illustration of balancing the multiple issues in building a good interactive display, consider the following sequence of "snapshots" from a discussion of the relationship between pressure and volume for an ideal gas.

$$PV = nRT$$

The ideal gas law expresses the relationship between these variables:

P	(pressure)
V	(volume)
n	(number of moles)
T	(temperature)

for an ideal gas.

Note that context is maintained by the retention of the original equation at the top of the screen.

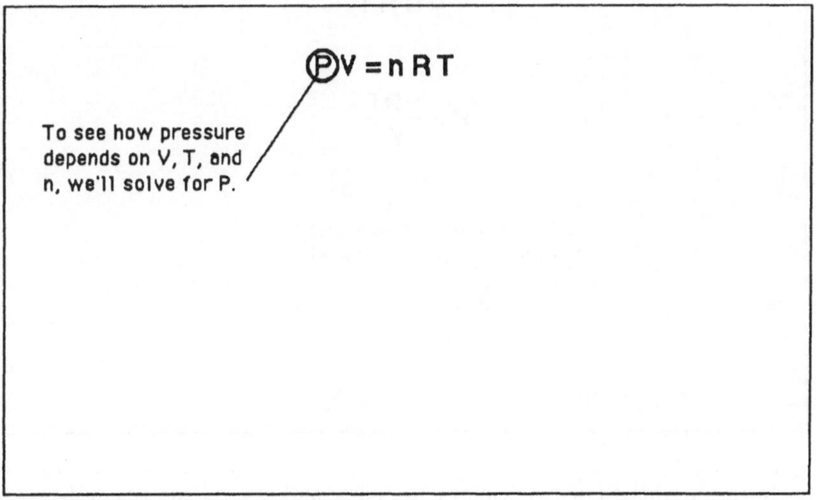

Important elements, and their connections, are highlighted temporarily; comments and explanations are presented, then removed.

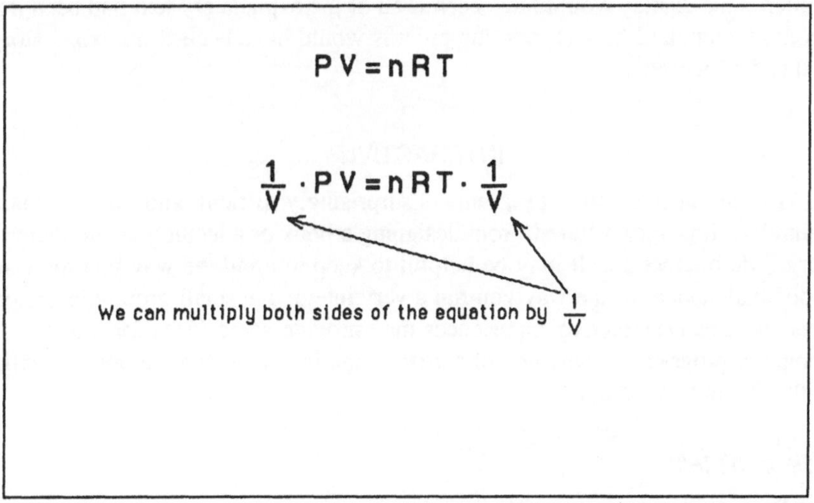

The step-by-step process makes it possible to check students' understanding along the way:

$$PV = nRT$$

$$P = \frac{nRT}{V}$$

If the volume decreases, will
the pressure go up or down?

»

Note, too, that all of the displays are sparse and have plenty of empty space. Explanatory text is provided, then erased when it is no longer relevant to the current step. The sparseness of the displays makes it easy for the student to focus on the most important points in the discussion. Consider how the how cluttered the display would have been if all of the explanatory text had been left on the screen, and how cryptic the process would have been if no explanatory text had been used.

INTERACTIVITY

Designing interactive programs is surprisingly difficult and doesn't come naturally. It is very different from designing a book or a lecture, where there is very little interaction. It may be helpful to keep in mind the way you tutor an individual student or the way you run a very interactive small-group discussion session. Such interactive experiences may provide some ideas for interactive computer programs. There are, of course, some factors which are quite specific to the computer medium.

Ask, don't tell!

Perhaps the most generally useful guideline is, "Never tell when you can ask." For example, an author drew a distribution of points on a graph and wrote on the screen, "The average weight of this group of puppies is 3 pounds."

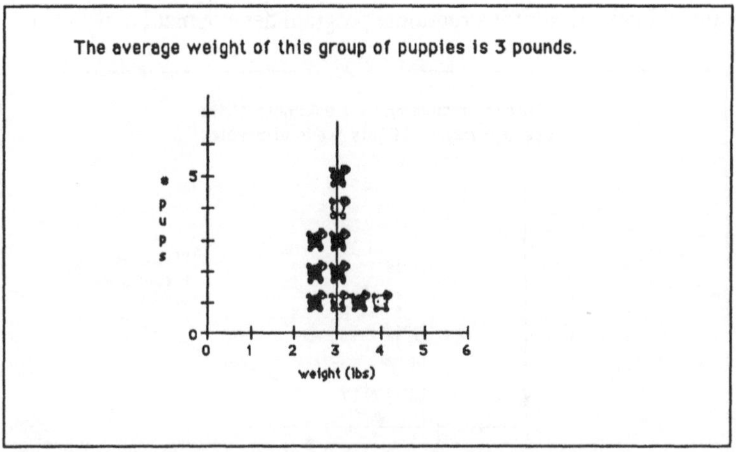

A major improvement was to instruct the student, "Click the mouse on your estimate of the average weight of this group of puppies." Of course, this made it necessary to provide clear feedback if the student's response was far from the appropriate answer. (In this case, a click anywhere near the line x=3 is accepted as a correct answer).

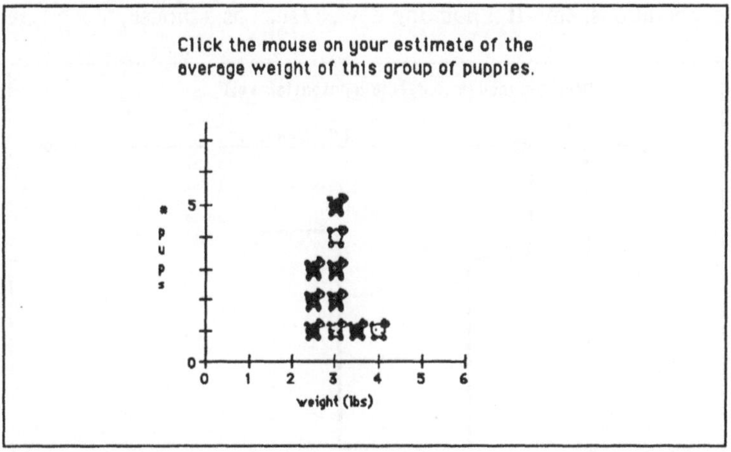

This is active; the earlier version, passive. The active version usefully exploits the unique qualities of the medium. The passive version makes the student wonder why the teacher didn't just hand out some written notes. We say again, "Designing interactive programs doesn't come naturally." This particular example involved an intelligent author with a lot of knowledge about the field, but without a great deal of instructional program development experience.

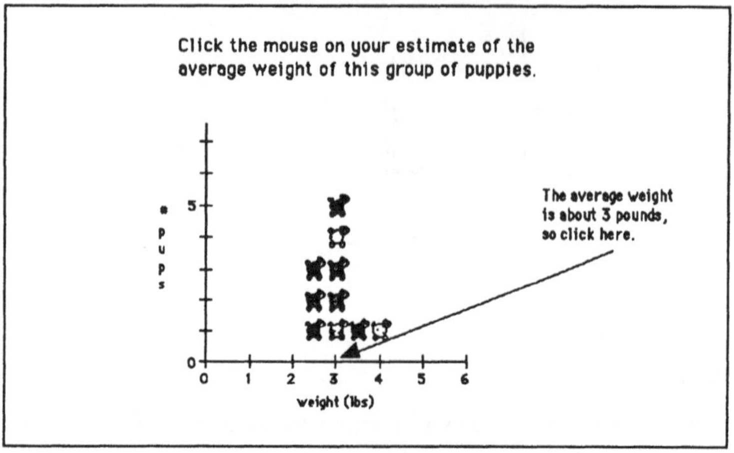

Direct manipulation

Where possible, let the user manipulate things directly—parameters, objects, conditions, etc. If a pointing device (such as a mouse, touch screen, or

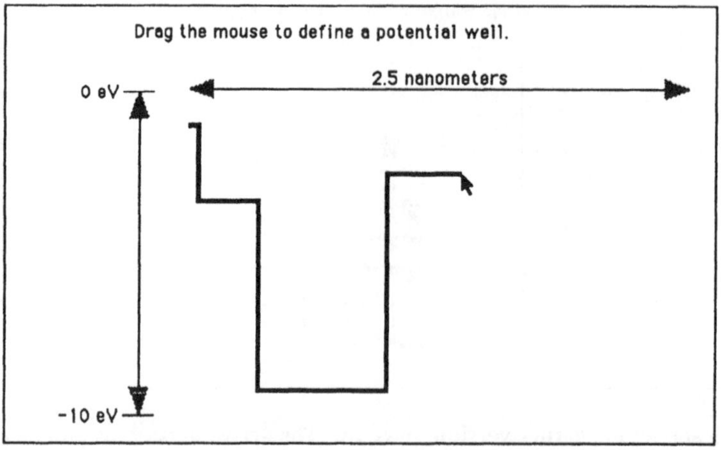

joystick) is available, don't ask the user to type "right" or "left" to choose between two pictures; have the user touch the desired picture. If you want the user to position a ball somewhere on a sloping track, let the user do it directly by pointing, rather than asking for a numerical distance. Without such direct manipulation, there is a real danger that the user will be deflected from thinking directly about the task into thinking about the interface. The interface should be as "transparent" as possible. In the potential well example above the student uses a mouse to enter information graphically, rather than typing in a series of numbers. This is appropriate because the emphasis of the program is qualitative; it is the shape of the well that matters, not the precise numerical values. Requiring numerical input would create an extra, and distracting, mental load for the user.

Avoid typing

Bear in mind that typing is usually harder than pointing. Certainly there are many situations where it is appropriate or even necessary to require keyboard input. But every time you require the keyboard you should ask yourself whether there is an easier, more direct way to handle the interaction. Remember that most students are not skilled touch typists.

No mouse?

A pointing device such as a mouse facilitates input to such an extent that it is practically a requirement for interactive programs. You may, however, need to work with older computers which do not have such a device. Many older programs incorporate quite successful schemes for using the keyboard to move a screen pointer. Typical approaches include using arrow keys or a key cluster such as "i j k m" to move a cursor, or using the space bar to cycle through possible selections on a menu or diagram. In situations where "pointing" input is important, using the keyboard in this fashion is much better than requiring extensive or complex typing.

Don't mix input modes

Avoid mixing keyboard and mouse actions for the same input. It can be quite annoying to have to move rapidly between two different input devices. This is a matter of consistency as well: stay with one or the other for a while.

Wait for the user

Don't use timed pauses (a pause for a specific amount of time) except for very special purposes such as animations. A common mistake is to display some text, pause three seconds, draw a graph, pause three seconds, then erase the entire screen in preparation for something else. This is disastrous. If the user glances out of the window, or sneezes, or is interrupted by a friend, the whole sequence may be missed. Even without that fatal full-screen erase, this kind of presentation is frustrating. Some users will wish that the pauses had been shorter. Other users will wish that the pauses had been longer. There may not exist one single individual (other than the author!) for whom the pauses are the right length.

It is far better to wait for a signal from the user (typically a mouse click or a keypress) before moving on to the next item, thus making the display go at the user's own pace. Note the comparison with a lecture for a large group of students, where the lecture necessarily bores some students because it goes too slowly, and swamps other students for whom it goes too rapidly. There is no need to carry over this common source of frustration to an interactive medium.

Provide instructions

In a research program written and used only by yourself, little or no explanatory text is required because you know what the program is supposed to do. But someone else might not be able to use the program at all without an instruction manual. Since instruction manuals quickly get out of date as a program is revised and are seldom around when one needs them, it is important that the program be usable on its own, without a manual, which mandates that adequate instructions should be found in the program itself.

On the other hand, you should and can avoid excessive amounts of text. Long paragraphs *telling* the user what to do are much less effective than *showing* the user interactively what to do. Telling is ineffective because the user won't read long instructions and because it is difficult for the user to translate written instructions in one context into actions in a different context. Showing is direct and context specific, and it is possible because of the interactive and dynamic nature of the medium. Here are some specific suggestions for handling instructions:

- Provide instructions for a task as part of its display.
- Keep instructions terse and telegraphic.
- Show, don't tell, the user what to do.
- Step the user through a complex input sequence once.

On-screen instructions

Ideally, instructions for user input should be on the display where the task is performed, not on an introductory page at the beginning of the program. Before encountering the actual task, a user cannot digest or remember a long paragraph describing a sequence of operations or mechanisms for providing input. Do not expect a user to remember complex input conventions. Very frequently used control options are an exception; it is not only unnecessary to put "Press

RETURN to go on" on every display, it is distracting and eventually even annoying.

Teach the interface

If the interface has some unusual features, teach these features explicitly, in a step-by-step manner. Treat this as another teaching task: showing how to use an unusual interface should be just as interactive as teaching the content. *Ask, don't tell.* Have the user exercise the various options while your program watches in detail. It is not adequate to discuss the interface conventions in several pages of passive text at the start of the program. Such instructions will certainly not be remembered. If you are pressed for time and must nevertheless resort to mere textual description, at the very least don't forget to provide an easy mechanism for reviewing those instructions at a later time!

INPUT ANALYSIS

Inputs must *always* be analyzed to see whether they are valid, and invalid inputs should be handled in a sensible way. This may sound obvious, but it is quite common for new authors to violate this rule. For example, suppose you let the user choose the initial speed and angle for a kicked football, and you then display the trajectory of the ball. You should normally tell the student what range of values your program will handle; you definitely must check to make sure that the inputs are indeed within range. If you just blindly use whatever values are input, without checking their validity, the trajectory might go off the screen in a confusing way. In some situations, failing to check the input could even cause the program to crash (e.g., trying to take the square root of a negative input value, when you were expecting a positive input).

Basic checks

Validity

First, check that the input is the kind you expect. If you ask for a number, you should first check to see that the input *is* a number, not some non-numerical word or sentence, or a numerical expression which is ill-formed (such as "3+*5-"). If you detect a mouse click, you should check to see whether the mouse cursor is indeed on a meaningful display object. What do you do if you find the input is invalid? To prevent frustration and confusion, you must provide immediate feedback to the user, stating why the input is not a valid one. For example, if the input is a number but not in the desired range, you can remind the user of the specified range restrictions and ask for different input. If the mouse click is in an inappropriate region, you can tell this to the user and reiterate or rephrase your instructions "That's not on the graph. Click on one of the curves on the graph."

Ignore blank inputs

Users frequently press the RETURN key accidentally before typing anything at a prompt. The consequences can be disastrous if the program simply accepts this and proceeds to judge the response incorrect, assume a default value, or take some other action. Usually blank inputs should be ignored when typing is requested.

Verbal input

As Culley (this volume) eloquently describes, the machinery for analyzing free-form sentence inputs is massive, complex, and requires that the computer "know" a great deal about the specific context. Constructing such natural-language understanding programs is still very much a research endeavor. Unless language itself is the focus of your program, it is unlikely to be practical to provide this kind of resource. Lacking such intelligence, it is very difficult for a computer program to analyze sentence inputs correctly, and one should avoid asking the student for words or sentences unless absolutely necessary. Nor is it appropriate to pretend or imply to the student that sentence input will be understood if it won't be, because this creates expectations which cannot be met. If asked for free-form input, the student will become very frustrated if it becomes apparent that the program can't actually process free-form input. Even if the student is asked a yes/no question to be answered with a typed response, the program had better be prepared for a wide range of inputs such as sure, yep, yeah, yup, I believe so, I think so, nope, etc. And what do you do with "I don't think so" or "maybe"? It is far better in this case to ask for a mouse click on a YES box or a NO box, or else to ask explicitly for "y" or "n" as the only acceptable typed response.

This is not to imply that sentence input is never appropriate. There are successful foreign-language sentence translation drills (Culley, this volume) which do function quite well. But these drills have typically placed very tight constraints on the range of analyzable sentence forms, given the context of a particular lesson in a particular elementary course, where the student knows only a small vocabulary and only a few forms of syntax.

Allow synonyms

Even for simple numeric or one-word answers, do try hard to accept a broad range of equivalent responses. If the input is a number, you should accept equivalent expressions (e.g., "30/6" should normally be taken as completely equivalent to 5, except in a drill on division). If the input is a word, try to accept its most common synonyms (e.g., "car, auto, automobile"). If a response is close to being acceptable, it is advisable to indicate this explicitly even if you are unwilling to accept this near miss. For example, if you want the student to identify "acetylene" and the student types "acetalene," it would be disastrous merely to say "You're wrong," because the student will then think that it *isn't* acetylene and will go off on a wrong track. You really should say something like "You have the right idea, but your spelling isn't quite right—please try to spell it in the standard form." Of course the ability to handle such near misses depends critically on the authoring tools available to you.

Feedback

Give clear, explicit feedback

Students who believe they have understood what to do can become frustrated very quickly if their actions do not produce the results they expect. It is essential to provide feedback that makes it clear that the computer has detected input, and how the input has been interpreted.

Avoid cuteness

In part because of a need for accuracy, in part because of the lack of clear emotional and personal context, it is important to avoid being cute. In our experience, it just doesn't work. It may have effects opposite to those you intend. Your personality will come through in your materials, just as it will if you write a book. Yet there are constraints imposed by the medium on how you can express that personality. Be polite and friendly, but avoid cuteness.

A related point is that one should avoid cute "rewards" in the form of lengthy unrelated graphics or music, especially if they recur often. After the third or fourth delay caused by having to sit through yet another irrelevant sequence of this kind, the user may be ready to scream. If short sounds are used only to augment other kinds of highlighting, offer the user an option to turn this off, so as not to disturb others when the materials are used in a public place.

Analyze for misconceptions

Unfortunately, most input analysis problems are far more complex and subtle than the examples in the preceding section suggest. A particular "invalid" input may be indicative of an important misconception which should be dealt with extensively. As such, "invalid" inputs are not mere nuisances which need to be checked for, but critical indicators of student understanding to be used for guiding the following interaction. In some heavily algorithmic areas such as mathematics or science, the program can often diagnose problems in a general way. For example, all numerical inputs can be checked for an overall sign error. Numbers resulting from division can be checked for inversion (4/3 instead of 3/4).

However, even with a precise diagnosis of a student's problem, there remains the pedagogical and motivational enigma of what to do about it (Lepper & Chabay, 1985, 1988). Should you immediately tell the student what the "right" answer is? Should the program say "You're kinda on the right track, but have you considered such-and-such?" These problems arise when tutoring a student in person, and they arise when a computer is helping the student. The challenge must be faced somehow, even though there is little theory or practice to guide the attempt.

Avoid dead ends

One important guideline can be offered: Do not let the student get trapped in a blind alley, where he or she must answer a question in order to proceed but cannot find an input that is satisfactory to the program. This is without a doubt the most frustrating aspect of poorly written materials. Often the underlying fault is a failure of the program to accept alternative valid forms of the answer. But even if the student can't come up with a valid answer, the program must provide some way to request help or to bypass the question, or at least to back up and review before trying again. If no other scheme seems feasible, at least provide some way for the student to request what the correct answer is. You might give increasingly detailed hints after each wrong response, until finally saying explicitly what you were looking for. Even with such an incremental scheme in place, you still might provide a way to see the correct answer without going through all those levels of hints.

No browsing

It is tempting to provide an easy way to browse through a tutorial program with essentially no effort, by letting the user just press RETURN in order to proceed without answering a question. This may be useful to an instructor who wants to get a quick overview of the material. It is rarely appropriate for students because it is undermines the interactivity which is the hallmark of good educational programs. We have even seen students complain about a browsing mode or easy help, claiming that it was the author's fault for allowing them to breeze through the material without paying attention or learning anything! There are other, more appropriate mechanisms for giving students control and allowing them to move about in a program.

Test and observe

Above all, because of the great difficulties of handling user input well, it is vitally important that you watch students using your program, to see what kinds of difficulties they run into. Do not wait until your program is "finished" to do this. Invite two or three students to go through your program while you sit beside them taking notes. You will be utterly amazed the first time you do this. Student creativity in thinking up responses you hadn't imagined is limitless! After small-scale testing with two or three students and revision based on that testing, try automated collection of input from twenty or thirty students, if you have the appropriate computer tools to do this. Revise again based on this more extensive testing.

USER CONTROL

There are few things more frustrating to users of educational software than a feeling of lack of control over the program. Angry students, trapped in sequences that they feel are inappropriate (too easy, too hard, confusing, irrelevant), are not receptive learners. As a teacher and author, you may in fact know better than your students what material they need to cover and in what order. However, it simply does not work to force students through a sequence of activities. You should make your overall plan clear with maps, suggestions, and reminders, but you must allow students to make choices of activities and to change their minds in the middle.

Books provide an analogy helpful for designing good user control. The author's overall plan and organization is clearly embodied in the sequence of chapters and the order of topics within a chapter of a book. The most natural course for the reader is simply to read the material in the order in which it occurs in the book. It is, however, possible to skip sections or whole chapters, to read them in a different order, to stop in the middle of a section and go back and review a previous section, and so on. Books provide tools to help readers make such choices: a table of contents, an index, and chapter headings on each page. Analogous maps and control options must be provided in educational computer activities as well.

Moving around in the program

Give the user lots of control over the program. One of the most important aspects of control is the ability to move around inside the program—to be able to skip to a later section or to review an earlier section. In order to allow the user to exercise control, though, it is necessary to make clear both the current and overall context and location in the program.

A multi-section program might include displays like these:

Title page (names and affiliations of the authors)
Brief statement of purpose
Table of contents
Section 1 (displays marking transitions between sections)
Section 2, etc.

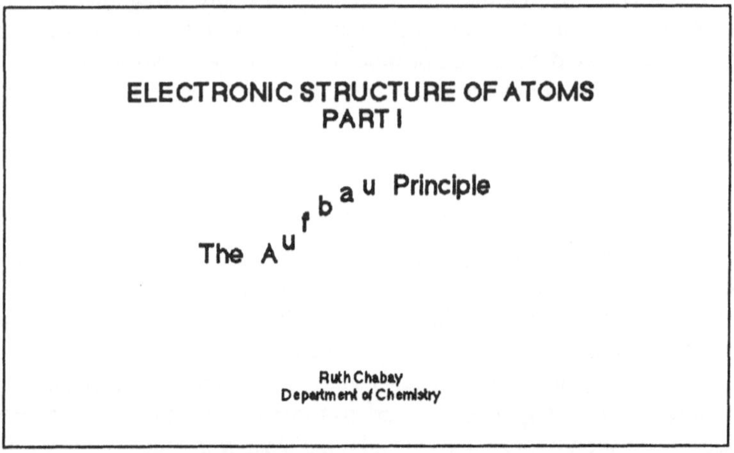

The title page establishes the basic context and identifies who is responsible for the material.

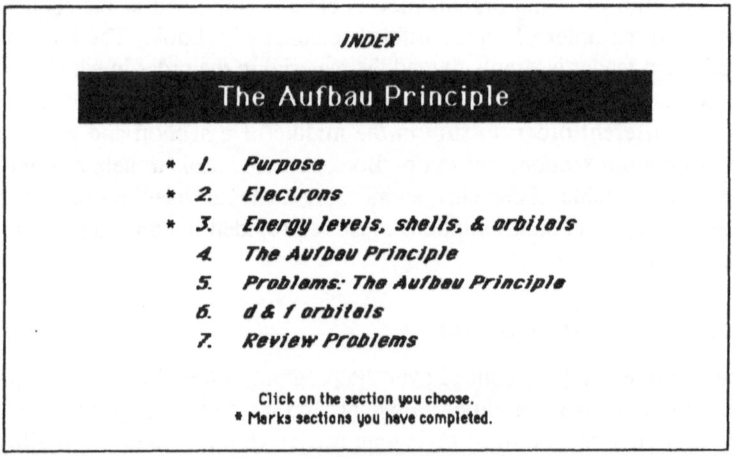

A table of contents provides transportation among sections of the program and may also indicate student progress, reminding the student of what sections have already been completed. The student need only point to a section or type its number to go to the chosen section. Provide a menu or other well-advertised option to permit the user at any time to get to the table of contents.

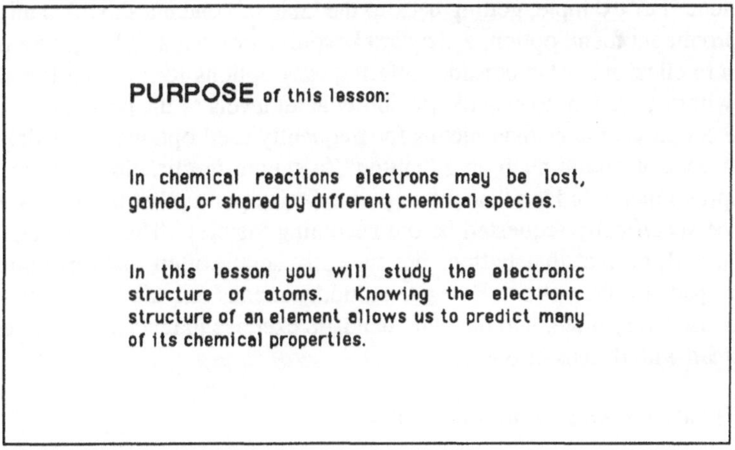

A statement of purpose provides additional context and goals, and may also list prerequisites.

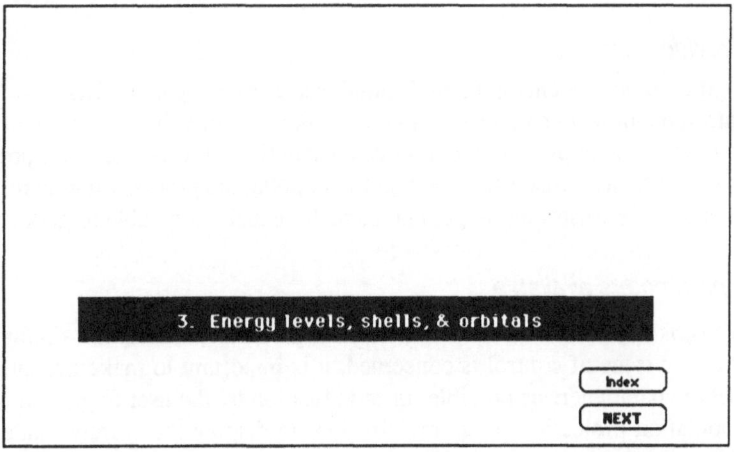

In passing from one section into the next, indicate this with a characteristic section title, just as is done with chapters in a book. If you don't point out this transition between sections, the user has no sense of progress and flow.

Advertise control options

It is very important that control options be not only easy to use but obvious. Don't hide them, and don't expect that a single mention at the start is sufficient. For example, getting back to the table of contents should at all times be a prominent menu option, a standard keypress, or even a little symbol on the screen to click on. Also consider offering easy options for moving forward or back within a section, to provide flexibility at all levels of the program.

Use buttons rather than menus for frequently used options. A visible, on-screen control option such as a "button" (a square to click in) is often more appropriate than a hidden "menu" (a pull-down or pop-up list of options which must be specifically requested before becoming visible). The immediacy of a button, and the fact that buttons are typically small, often justifies taking up screen space for the option. Relegate to hidden menus only those options which are not used very often. On the other hand, do exercise judgement: don't clutter the screen with dozens of buttons.

Remove inactive control options

Remove or visually deactivate (e.g., "gray out") any control options that have become inactive or are not relevant at this time, such as buttons, menu items, or reminders of control keys. Users invariably will try to make use of these options and will become frustrated or confused when they don't work.

Provide a way out

Bear in mind that changing one's mind is a user prerogative. Don't lock the user into something, even under user choice. For example, if a process will take a long time, such as plotting a complicated satellite orbit, be sure you provide and prominently advertise some method for stopping the process prematurely. It can be extremely frustrating to get into something and not be able to get out.

Make parameters available

We spoke earlier about checking for valid parameter values in a simulation. As far as the issue of control is concerned, it is important to make available as many of the parameters as possible for modification by the user (e.g., birth rates in a population projection program). Be sure to display the current values, to give the user adequate context for changing them.

Where am I?

It is often difficult in the computer medium to have a good sense of where you are in the material, which leads to uneasiness and a feeling of lack of control. With a book, it is physically obvious when you are coming to the end, and it is quick and easy to flip a few pages and estimate where the end of the chapter is. The computer screen doesn't automatically give these visual cues, so they must be provided some other way. Even better than a usage-marked table of contents may be an easily accessible graphical "map" of the program, indicating with boxes and arrows where the user is, where he or she may go, and what the connections are between sections.

Within a section, a local indicator is important. In a twenty-item drill on balancing chemical equations, be sure to display prominently "7 right, 13 to go," updating this message after every item.

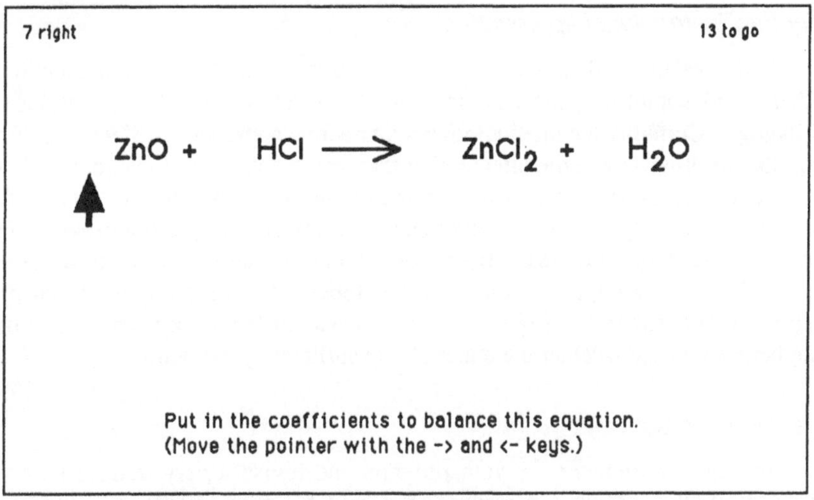

Note also in this example the blank space left for comments and feedback in the middle of the screen, and the avoidance of mixed input modes; all input, including cursor movement, is done with the keyboard.

HINTS FOR DEVELOPMENT

Explore the medium

A good way to get a feel for a new medium is to immerse oneself in existing examples. It is not enough to dip into instructional programs or to watch demonstrations. Work *completely* through some good instructional programs. Probably the vast majority of instructional programs are of poor quality, because the field is still so new. There do, however, exist good programs, and one can learn a great deal about the strengths and weaknesses of the medium by experiencing these programs directly. When trying out such a program, don't just skim it, but put yourself as much as possible in the shoes of the students for whom it was designed, and go through the whole thing. Make mistakes and note how they are handled. Even with very good materials you are likely to find troublesome or even aggravating aspects, partly due to current limitations of the medium and partly due to limited understanding on the part of even the best and most experienced authors. When you write your own materials, remember the frustrations you experienced when playing student, and try to anticipate and overcome such feelings on the part of your users.

Try new instructional approaches

Some pedagogical approaches are better suited to the computer medium than others, and sometimes the new medium suggests completely new styles of pedagogy. Certainly the medium favors interactive approaches. Since it is often possible to show a dynamic effect rather than being constrained just to talk about it, you might preface a formal exposition with an interactive, qualitative overview of the topic. As with any medium, think critically about exactly what you hope students will learn from your materials, and go after these goals explicitly. For example, if you want the student to learn planning, teach this explicitly rather than leaving it to chance. Detailed feedback from student use can help determine whether the materials are sufficiently explicit.

Develop interactively

During development, try your program and revise it very frequently, on a scale of minutes, not days or weeks (Sherwood & Larkin, 1989). It is useful to make a few rough sketches of screen displays and flow of control before starting work, but try to do as much of the work as possible in an interactive manner. Treat the medium as plastic, and think of yourself as a sculptor. Try this, try that, discard this, follow up that. Since the medium is itself an interactive one, let its interactivity suggest things to you. An idea you wrote down on paper may turn out to be all wrong when you try it on the computer, yet in playing with the medium you may find a different twist which suits the medium very well. Be open to throwing away initial ideas and even sizable chunks of programming whenever experimenting with the medium suggests a better way.

Move from the specific to the general

Try very simple things first to see how they "feel" before investing a lot of effort in complex versions. The bigger an investment you have made, the less likely you are to admit to yourself that it isn't working out. A closely related point is that while very general procedures have great power, it is frequently prudent to start with specific, special-case schemes which can be implemented quickly and easily. Only after you are convinced that you are on the right track might you extract what is common to your several procedures and combine them into one general case. In some cases you may even find that there is no need later to replace your specific routines with a general one, and that using specific rather than general procedures offers useful variety and specificity.

Initial testing

As discussed earlier, do try out your experimental program with a few students and revise it accordingly. Do this rather early, long before you have talked yourself into believing that your program is wonderful and finished, because after that point it will be much more difficult to accept contrary evidence!

If students have difficulty with parts of the program, try to change the program, not the students. Experiment with ways to simplify control and interactions, add more background, or break tasks into smaller parts, rather than providing more and more detailed instructions on how to work around the program's shortcomings.

Later testing

After your program has been through testing and actual use by real students, revise again to turn it into a finished product you would be proud to distribute to colleagues. Robustness is crucial at this stage: the program should certainly not crash, and it should react well to varied kinds of usage and a wide range of observed inputs. A program sufficiently robust for you is not necessarily robust enough for your students, and even that program may not be sufficiently robust for someone else's students, who may have different backgrounds. Do take the time to be finicky about display details. Even a single unwanted dot on the screen due to faulty erasing can seem quite annoying or confusing to many people. Be sure to remove spelling errors and other typos. Failure to pay sufficient attention to such details can seriously mar an otherwise excellent product.

Be flexible

We hope that our suggestions will be helpful to you. We should admit that in our own work we have not always lived up to these guidelines. Moreover, we occasionally violate them deliberately. This is a new field, and experimentation should be encouraged, because no one knows precisely what works well in all cases.

CONCLUSION

We have emphasized the novelty of the highly interactive computer medium, with its own distinctive esthetic. The key issues a developer must address are in the areas of display, interactivity, input, and control. Creative use of the new capabilities may lead not just to improvements in education but possibly even to new kinds of education.

REFERENCES

Chabay, R. & Smith, S. (1977). The use of computer-based chemistry lessons: An individualized component of a large lecture course. *Journal of Chemical Education, 54:* 745-747.

Jones, L. M., Kane, D., Sherwood, B. A., & Avner, R. A. (1983). A final-exam comparison involving computer-based instruction. *American Journal of Physics, 51:* 533-538.

Kane, D. & Sherwood, B. (1980). A computer-based course in classical mechanics. *Computers & Education, 4:* 15-36.

Larkin, J. H. (1988). Display-based problem solving. In D. Klahr & K. Kotovsky (Eds.), *21st Carnegie Mellon Cognitive Symposium.* Hillsdale, NJ: Erlbaum.

Lepper, M. R. & Chabay, R. W. (1985). Intrinsic motivation and instruction: Conflicting views on the role of motivational processes in computer-based education. *The Educational Psychologist, 20:* 217-230.

Lepper, M. R. & Chabay, R. W. (1988). Socializing the intelligent tutor: Bringing empathy to computer tutors. In H. Mandl & A. Lesgold, (Eds.). *Learning Issues for Intelligent Tutoring Systems.* New York: Springer. Pp. 242-257.

Sherwood, B. A. (1976). The esthetics and economics of computer-based education. In D. T. Tuma, (Ed.), *Innovation and Productivity in Higher Education.* San Francisco: San Francisco Press. Pp. 51-55.

Sherwood, B. A. & Larkin, J. H. (1989). New tools for courseware production. *Journal of Computing in Higher Education, 1:* 3-20.

Smith, S. & Chabay, R. (1977). Computer games in chemistry. *Journal of Chemical Education, 54:* 688-689.

Smith, S., Chabay, R., & Kean, E. (1983-1986). *Introduction to General Chemistry.* Wentworth, NH: Falcon Software Inc.

6 Realizing the Revolution: A Brief Case Study

George Brackett
George Brackett Associates, Cambridge, Massachusetts

It is a commonplace that computers and computer-controlled devices offer great promise for revolutionizing education. It is also a commonplace that education is in need of revolutionizing. In the United States, the land of the technological fix, optimists might hope that this situation neatly matches tool and task, with a guaranteed positive outcome. I share the vision, but not the optimism.

Realizing the revolution will require solutions to many knotty problems. There are, of course, a host of technical problems to be overcome in hardware and software design. More challenging, at least to me, are the pedagogical issues raised by the power of computer-based educational technologies: what should be taught, in what order, with what overarching conceptual structures and representations, by what mix of media, in what modes of interaction, and with what roles for student, software, ancillary materials, and teacher? At the root of these pedagogical issues lie even more fundamental questions, questions about how people think, communicate, and learn, questions about the mental processes and data structures we so often take for granted but about which we know so little.

As ably illustrated by the other chapters in this volume, such technical, pedagogical, and fundamental problems are challenging but probably tractable; with hard work, cleverness, and the usual portion of luck, they can and will be solved. In this chapter, I would like to examine an entirely different set of problems. These problems are practical, mundane, and easily overlooked, but they may ultimately prove to be the most difficult ones we face.

As a small-scale commercial developer of educational software, I am forced to look at realizing a computer based educational revolution from a business point of view. I find this perspective often sobering, but always instructive. In this view, software development forms only a small part of a much larger system of activities which jointly determine the success—or failure—of educational computing.

The people involved in this system range from basic researchers in university and government laboratories at one extreme, to administrators, teachers, parents, and students in a wide variety of educational settings at the other. In between lie a motley collection of hardware manufacturers, software developers, publishers, distributors, and retailers; hovering in the background are various government agencies with missions in education. (See Figure 1.)

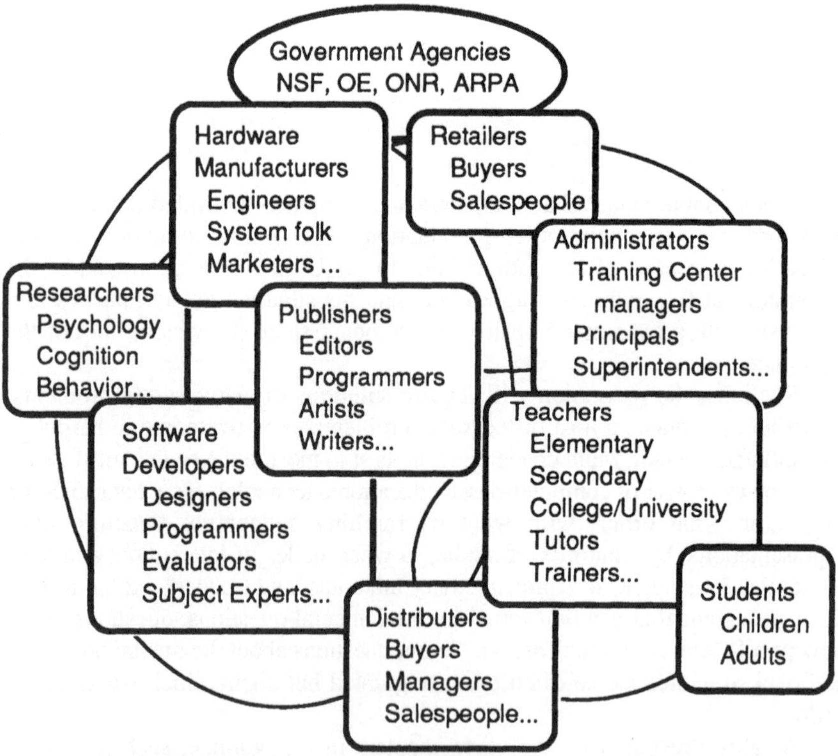

Figure 1: The educational research, development, distribution and delivery system.

Like some giant Rube Goldberg device, all the parts of this complex system must somehow work together to transform advances in computer-based pedagogy into improved learning for students. Outputs must mesh with inputs, and there must be enough energy (recognition, profit, satisfaction) to make all the wheels go 'round.

Unfortunately, this system tends to wheeze, gasp, and stop rather than hum. As with the original Rube Goldberg inventions, some of the parts were intended for other purposes, many are fragile or balky, and all work only when local conditions are right. Indeed, local conditions have been bad enough in recent years that many manufacturers, developers, publishers, distributors, and retailers have either vanished or greatly curtailed their activities.

If we are to realize the promise of a computer based educational revolution, we must find ways to make this complex system work better, and that means trying first to understand the system itself a little better. Accordingly, I propose in the remainder of this paper to present a case study outlining a software development project in which I am now engaged. In describing this project, I hope to depict more clearly the workings of my own small part of the system. I also hope to highlight some key issues we all face in making the larger system work as we wish it would.

It is worth saying at the outset that the following case applies particularly to the development of commercially distributed educational software for elementary school, secondary school, and home use. Some of the decisions described and the issues raised may not arise in other contexts: for example, in corporate or military training, or in software development within higher education. Still, in the absence of massive governmental support, educational software must survive in the environment described here if it is to reach the many people who could and should benefit from it.

SLIDE SHOP

Currently in the last stages of development, *Slide Shop* (Brackett, 1988) is a program for creating slide shows generated and displayed via computer—"presentation graphics" in the present marketing jargon. People can use the program to create a set of slides incorporating multi-font text, freehand drawings, selections from libraries of clip art, full screen templates and backgrounds, borders, music, digitized speech, and sound effects. They then create scripts which specify a sequence of slides and slide-change special effects, including cuts, wipes, fades, dissolves, and such exotic transitions as checkerboard wipes and screen smears. The resulting slide shows are stored on auto-run disks created by the program, from which they can be displayed automatically or manually on the computer, printed on paper, or transferred with narration to videotape.

Issue: Hardware Requirements

No description of educational software is complete without a statement like this:

> *Slide Shop* runs on Apple II™ computers with a minimum of 128K memory, on IBM™ PC, XT, and AT computers and true compatibles equipped with a graphics card and a minimum of 256K memory, and on Tandy™ 1000 series computers with a minimum of 256K memory.

That it should be necessary to make such a statement underlines an important fact: unlike any other successful educational medium, educational software is useless without access to a machine, and a highly specific machine at that.

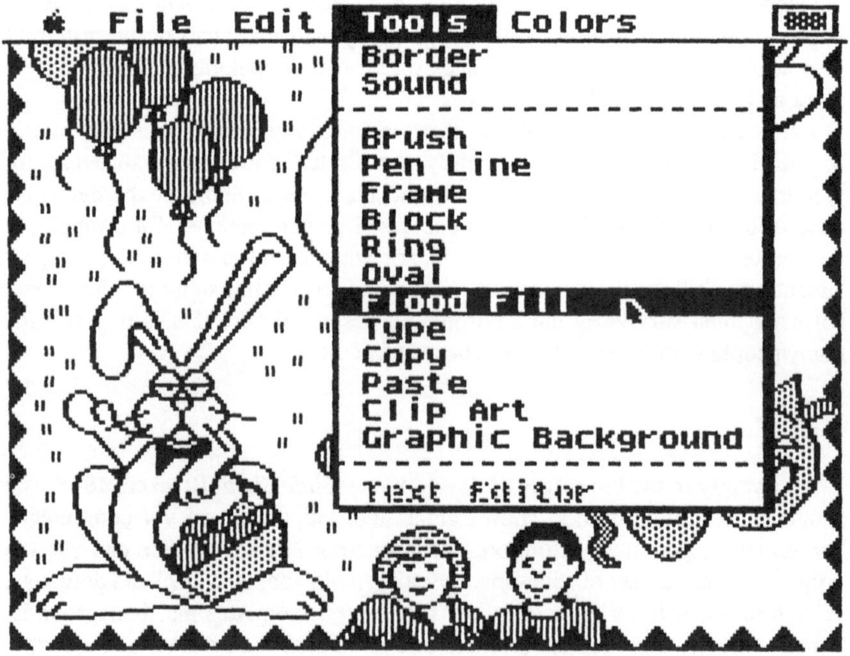

Figure 2: The pull-down Tools menu in *Slide Shop*.

This stricture has several serious consequences which are often overlooked in the enthusiasm for the latest clever or powerful program. First, hardware requirements severely limit the size of the available market for educational software. (Or, viewed another way, they severely limit the number of people who can benefit from educational software. Take your pick.) A 1987 survey (Educational Technology, 1987) found just under a million microcomputers in public elementary and secondary schools, including a wide variety of incompatible types as well as outmoded or moribund machines. The same survey in 1986 reported an average of 38 students per microcomputer nationwide (Reinhold, 1986), ranging from 14 per machine in Alaska to 135 per machine in Georgia. Whether the aim is aiding a great many students or selling a great many programs, the small number of machines poses a serious barrier. And while this number increased by about 18% between 1986 and 1987, the emphasis in new expenditures is shifting toward software and training rather than hardware (Educational Technology, 1987).

Second, when administrators, parents, teachers, or students look for solutions to educational problems, hardware requirements place software at a substantial disadvantage compared to other educational media. The most successful media, books and other printed materials, require no hardware at all. And while audiovisual media do require hardware, format standards effectively eliminate restrictions to a single brand or configuration. Therefore, even when a program has penetrated the market and found its way into a school or home library, it may still be the solution of last resort because hardware logistics—finding the right machine and peripherals in sufficient quantity at the right time and in working order—are simply too much for busy people to contemplate.

A third consequence of hardware requirements is the fragmentation of the entire system which creates, distributes, and uses educational software. For each major machine type, there is almost a complete, separate subsystem operating in parallel with all the others. Every action is duplicated several times, with enormous wastage of resources.

Slide Shop, for example, consists of three separate, complete programs, one for the Apple II series, one for MS-DOS computers with CGA graphics, and one for the 16-color graphics of the Tandy 1000 computers. Apple, IBM, and Tandy machines together account for about 80% of the installed base of computers in schools: 56%, 14%, and 9% respectively (Reinhold, 1986). Each program requires different programming, documentation, fonts and clip art, and sample slide shows. Each will be advertised in different magazines and catalogs, distributed through different channels, and sold to people who must be identified in advance as Apple, IBM, or Tandy users.

In short, to have measurable impact (and to survive in a competitive marketplace of products and ideas), educational programs must not only be clever and powerful solutions to educational problems. They must also run on at least two of the most popular microcomputers. They must avoid where possible special hardware requirements (e.g., pointing devices, speech synthesis cards, extended memory or disk space). And they must present the fewest possible barriers to adoption as the solution of choice; in other words, they must be easy to learn and easy to use. Not surprisingly, all this takes work.

Issue: Time, Effort ... and Money

Slide Shop has required substantial time, effort, and money to produce. Between the first negotiations with the publisher (at which time some of the core programming was already complete) to delivery of the final master disk, more than eighteen months will have elapsed; at least three more will be required before *Slide Shop* appears in catalogs and on shelves. The Apple II program, exclusive of data areas, occupies about 60 kilobytes, corresponding to about 25,000 lines of 6502 assembly language which required over one person-year to design and write. The IBM and Tandy programs, written in 8086 assembly language under contract, are each about the same size as the Apple program, and together will require about fifty percent more time to develop. Taken together, the three versions of *Slide Shop* will have required about two and a half person-years and a budget of over $100,000 to complete.

Most of the design effort, and at least half of the programming effort, has been directed at making *Slide Shop* easy to learn and easy to use. The program uses a modified Xerox Star™ or Macintosh™ interface because of that interface's increasing familiarity to users and because its claim to ease of use appears well justified. Using this approach required substantial additional programming and design effort, ranging from programming and organizing pull-down menus (see Figure 2) to developing disk menus which simplify a novice's access to complex hierarchical file systems (see Figure 3).

Further, all of the interface was written from scratch because the corresponding software tools available on more sophisticated machines (such as QuickDraw™ graphics primitives, and cursor, menu, and dialog routines) are not available on the majority of the Apple (nor, of course, MS-DOS) machines now in schools. In addition, very few of the computers in schools are equipped with pointing devices. Those that are so equipped may have joysticks or a graphic pad instead of a mouse. Therefore, to minimize special hardware requirements, the *Slide Shop* interface is written to work with any pointing device and, optionally, with the keyboard alone.

I believe that *Slide Shop* is representative of the time, effort, and money required to produce commercial-grade educational software; in fact, it may even fall on the low-cost side of the distribution. Using a less sophisticated interface, which has been done in some good educational software, is one way to reduce development costs. Another is to work in high level languages, which speed programming by factors of between two and four (A. Crane, personal communication, October 1988), although the same results cannot always be obtained from high level languages as from assembly language. *Slide Shop*, for example, simply could not be written in BASIC, Pascal or C on an Apple IIe or IIc computer.

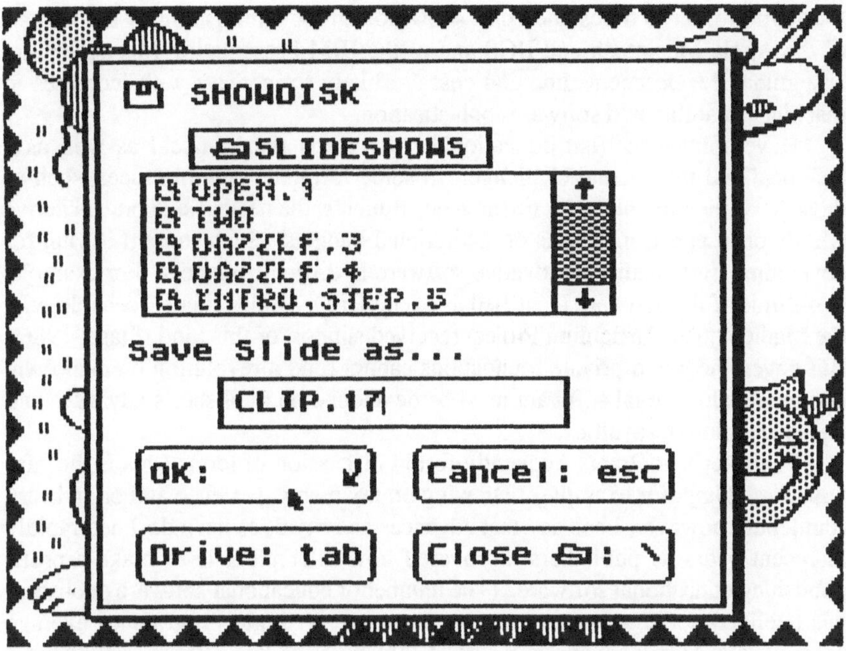

Figure 3: *Slide Shop's* disk menu, which provides easy access to multiple disks and hierarchically organized files.

On the other hand, *Slide Shop* is lacking one important and very costly ingredient of much educational software: *content.* Most subjects reveal new depth and subtlety when freshly viewed by people who are carefully rethinking how they should be taught. And when those people are also seeking ways to incorporate new models of learning and teaching, the effort required—including pedagogical design and the necessary formative research as well as interface design and programming—can be very large. (For some excellent software exemplifying these points, see the chapter in this volume by Sharon Dugdale.)

Based on my own experience and on conversations with a number of educational software producers,[1] I estimate that a single, high quality,

---

[1] Colleagues at Bank Street College, Education Development Corporation, Tom Snyder Publishing, Teaching Tools, Inc., Joyce Haakanson Associates, and Learningways, Inc. (personal communications, October 1987 to February 1988).

commercially published educational program now requires between three-fourths and three person-years to develop, and costs between $50,000 and $200,000; the mode is about one person-year and $60,000. Developing multiple versions of the software increases these figures by at least 50-75% per version. Furthermore, these times and costs show no sign of diminishing; if the lessons of the Apple Macintosh and IIGS and of the IBM Presentation Manager™ are any guide, development time and cost are likely to increase with increases in machine capability and software sophistication.

Developing excellent educational software is thus a fiscal as well as a technical and intellectual challenge. In some fortunate circumstances, such as those prevailing in university research departments, the needed support can derive wholly or in part from grants or institutional budgets. Such support is vital for developing high quality, innovative software in difficult subjects. For example, two-thirds of the software identified as exemplary by California's Technology in the Mathematics Curriculum Project received support of this kind (Stage, 1986). But government and private foundations cannot fund a revolution on their own, and much educational software must be developed on publisher's advances and the expectation of royalties.

Publisher's contracts frequently forbid discussion of terms (this is the case with *Slide Shop*, for example). Drawing on my own experience and on industry scuttlebutt, however, I can say that advances and royalties have declined rapidly in recent years as publishers discovered how difficult it is to make a profit publishing educational software. (The number of educational software publishers has declined for the same reason.) Currently, a single program of average promise might draw advances of $10-25,000, with the latter figure applying to a program from an established developer and royalties ranging between 8 and 12.5% of the publisher's net proceeds. In partial corroboration, publishers currently report investments in educational programs (including advances and internal development costs) averaging $14,000 for school (textbook) publishers, and $39,000 for consumer publishers (TALMIS, 1987).

This means, simply, that the average publisher's advance does not cover the average program development cost. Unless the developer is able to obtain unusually favorable terms (terms in which the advance equals the development cost), the difference must be made up from royalties. In a mix of direct school and retail distribution, the publisher's net proceeds average about 50% of retail price; proceeds from retail-only distribution are typically about 40%. Assuming the more favorable 50% return, a sale of one copy of a $40.00 program nets $2.50 for the developer at a royalty rate of 12.5%. To recover a typical development deficit of $25,000 therefore requires sales of 10,000 copies beyond the first 10,000 needed to recover a $25,000 advance.

To sell 20,000 copies, a program must be both a critical and a popular success. Very few programs, unfortunately, achieve this degree of success. For example, of the four published programs I have worked on, three have been critical successes in terms of reviews and awards, but only one has recovered its advances. Sales to date on these programs range from a low of about 3,000 copies over two years to a high of 34,000 copies over five years. Only the last-mentioned program (Brackett, 1983), however, has sold more than 15,000 copies.

These gloomy data underscore a simple observation: developing and publishing educational software is not a golden opportunity to advance education and make money simultaneously, as many once thought. It is instead a risky business where pedagogical sophistication and programming ingenuity are no guarantee of success. Sophistication in marketing, alas, becomes a very important ingredient of success.

Issue: The Effects of Market Orientation

Slide Shop is educational software in the same sense that a word processor designed for school use is educational software: it provides a tool-rich environment for educational activities such as writing, editing, organizing thoughts and symbols, and so on. *Slide Shop* does not teach history, for example, but teachers and students can each use it to make class presentations in a history course, or to create a videotape show on the American Revolution for younger students.

I chose to write *Slide Shop* in part because I enjoy making tools that enhance people's ability to be creative and to organize their thoughts and mental images into stories, pictures, and presentations. But I also chose *Slide Shop* as a project precisely because its status as a generalized tool gives it the widest possible educational market.

A focus on generalized tools, especially those which cannot be duplicated without a computer, is one important strategy for survival in the uncertain world of educational software. It is not lost on developers and publishers that the best selling school software, notably *Bank Street Writer* (Bank Street College of Education & F. Smith, 1987) and *Print Shop* (Balsam & Kahn, 1984), are such generalized tools. A related approach is evident in the rash of "problem solving" software available. "Problem solving" software normally confronts the student with a simulated environment where logical problems must be solved to succeed. One good example is *The Factory* (Kosel & Fish, 1982), where students are challenged to duplicate a target product by arranging processing machines and product orientation steps in a correct sequence. In problem solving software, the emphasis is on generalized skills rather than generalized tools, but the core strategy is the same: maximize the number of people who potentially need and have use for your program.

There are other strategies as well, of course, all aimed at maximizing the size of the potential market, minimizing development effort and cost or, preferably, both. Capitalizing on the market identified (and sometimes created) by an enormously popular program is one such strategy. The many printing utilities and shoot-em-up-style drill programs testify to the success of such programs as *Print Shop* (Balsam & Kahn, 1984) and *Math Blaster!* (Davidson & Eckert, 1983). *Slide Shop*'s name unblushingly alludes to *Print Shop*, because "... *Shop*" now implies a useful program for creating one's own materials; furthermore, *Slide Shop* allows people to draw on the very large existing libraries of *Print Shop* clip art in creating slides.

Another strategy is to develop software engines, program frameworks incorporating a standard interface and pedagogical approach which allow the rapid development of an entire series of programs. Although the effort and expense of developing the content of each program remains, the development of interface and approach can be amortized over the series. This strategy is particularly apparent in software produced by textbook publishers, who are forced by adoption requirements to include software with their texts, but without a significant corresponding increase in total package cost. It is also at the core of such software series as Tom Snyder Production's *Decisions, Decisions* (Snyder, Dockterman, & Lewbel, 1986). Not only can a series lower development effort, it can also lower marketing and adoption costs by grouping multiple purchase decisions and teacher training sessions into one. The obverse of this strategy underlies the relative rarity of single subject programs. They are difficult to market and, especially in the case of high quality tutorials, often very expensive to develop.

The most important current strategy is to emphasize software which fits as seamlessly as possible into the everyday life of schools. The reasons are legion, but they all boil down to an attempt to minimize resistance on the part of administrators and teachers who are not already computer enthusiasts. (Unfortunately, students generally do not make purchase decisions.) For example, this means developing software that does not require quantities or types of hardware not readily available in schools. It means developing software with interfaces that are recognizable and comfortable to teachers and students. And it also means developing software that teaches what is currently taught, in ways clearly similar to current methods. In short, it means developing software which solves recognized educational problems in understood ways without creating new problems in the process.

Individually, strategies like these may seem reasonable and necessary to ensure the survival of educational software. Together, however, they have a profoundly chilling effect on the potential of educational software to revolutionize education. Not all educational problems are solvable by generalized tools. "Me-too-ism" exacerbates the "hit" mentality of distributors and retailers, limits our vision of what computers can do, and wastes resources on the development of redundant materials. Cost cutting approaches such as series engines tend to shoehorn topics into the simplest frameworks available; they can also promote a centralized approach to educational computing, limiting its potential for more flexible uses. And taking the path of least resistance effectively prevents the kinds of quantum leap we might hope for from a powerful educational technology.

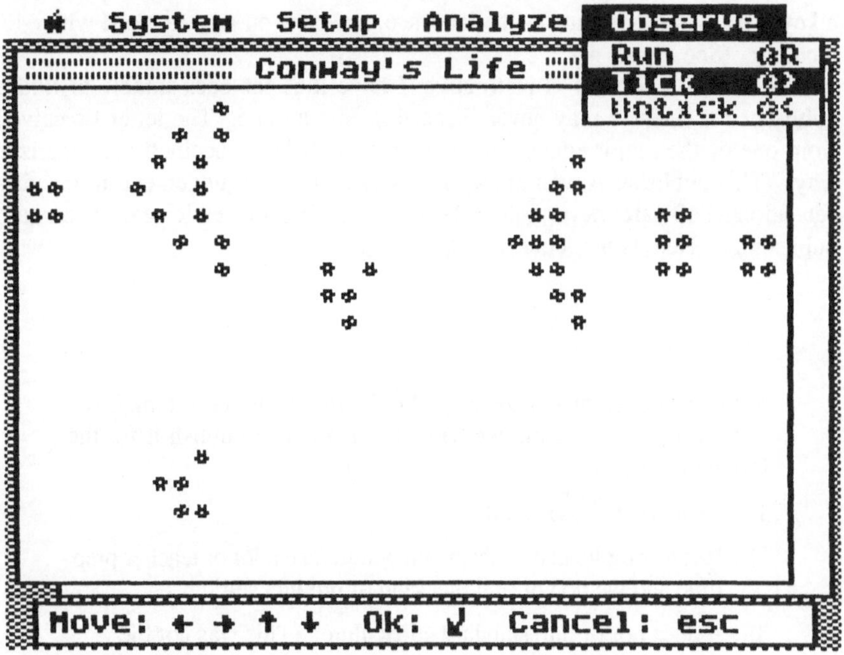

Figure 4: A complex system (called the "glider gun") ready for an experimental observation in *LifeLab*.

CONCLUSION

As a physicist by training, I am interested in finding ways computers can improve the learning and teaching of science. One result of this interest is a program called *LifeLab*, which I worked on for six months before starting *Slide Shop*. *LifeLab* is a simulated laboratory in which students can observe the behavior of cellular automata, creatures which live in a mathematical grid according to simple life and death rules. Students can create automata with many different rules, and can observe those created by others without having access to the rules. They can conduct experiments designed to discover the unknown rules, create model automata that behave according to their theories, compare the "real" and "theoretical" creatures' behavior, and continue until the theoretical model matches the observed behavior in every detail. The central idea was to create a microworld in which complex behavior was the consequence of simple laws, so that the process of science, the process of discovering laws from carefully contrived experimentation, could be the focus of activity. *LifeLab* uses a keyboard-based Macintosh-like interface, and runs on any Apple II with 64K memory. (See Figure 4.)

The fate of *LifeLab* is instructive: I have thus far been unable to find a publisher for it, and I may never succeed in finding one. The letter I received from one of the major educational software publishers succinctly summarizes why. (This publisher is well known for its excellence of judgement in selecting educational software; nevertheless, 1986 was its first profitable year of software publishing). Here is the letter, *in toto*:

> Dear George:
>
> We have looked at and considered *LifeLab*. Although I think it is a beautiful piece of work, we have decided not to publish it for the following reasons:
>
> 1) Its market is too small.
>
> 2) It is a complicated concept and would take a lot of teacher prep time and we do not find that kind of product selling.
>
> 3) It does not fit into standard curriculum. (This was not the deciding factor however.)
>
> Please consider us for future products.

The cases of *LifeLab* and *Slide Shop* represent to me the dilemma that faces us. Computer power does have the potential to revolutionize education, but the system through which that revolution must evolve is hardly optimized for revolutionary activity. In some ways, it is even inimical to it. To get more than gradual change out of this system, we must all—researchers, developers, publishers, teachers—seek ways to straighten the bent parts, grease the sticky ones, and enlarge the bottlenecks so that major improvements can make it through. The strategies for doing this are the subject for some future chapter. A key ingredient, however, must be developing better understanding and communication among the various parts of our system. This paper is one small attempt in that direction, but we will need to uncover and share many more goals, strategies, tools, and lore if we are to realize the educational revolution inherent in computer power.

REFERENCES

Balsam, D., & Kahn, M. (1984). Print Shop. San Rafael, CA: Brøderbund Software, Inc.

Bank Street College of Education, & Smith, F. E. (1987). *Bank Street Writer III*. New York: Scholastic, Inc.

Brackett, G. (1988). *Slide Shop*. New York: Scholastic, Inc.

Brackett, G. (1983). *Story Tree*. New York: Scholastic, Inc.

Davidson, J. G., & Eckert, R. K. (1983). *Math Blaster!* Rancho Palos Verdes, CA: Davidson & Associates, Inc.

Educational Technology 1987: A Report on EL's Seventh Annual Survey of the States. (1987, October). *Electronic Learning*, *7* (2), 39-44.

Kosel, M., & Fish, M. (1982). *The Factory*. Pleasantville, NY: Sunburst.

Reinhold, F. (1986, October). "Computing in America: Electronic Learning's 1986 Annual Survey of the States." *Electronic Learning*, *6* (2), 26-33.

Snyder, T., Dockterman, D. A., & Lewbel, A. (1986). *The Decisions, Decisions Series*. Cambridge, MA: Tom Snyder Productions.

Stage, E. (1986). Unpublished paper prepared for the Educational Technology Committee, California State Department of Education.

TALMIS report. (1987, October). Educational Suppliers of Electronic Media: The 1986 Market. Quoted in *Electronic Learning*, *7* (2), 8.

7 SHERLOCK: A Coached Practice Environment for an Electronics Troubleshooting Job

Alan Lesgold, Susanne Lajoie, Marilyn Bunzo, Gary Eggan
Learning Research and Development Center, University of Pittsburgh

SHERLOCK is a computer-based supported practice environment for a complex troubleshooting job in the Air Force. This chapter describes the training problem for which SHERLOCK was developed, the principles behind its development, and its implementation. The training problem is severe and representative of a problem common in our high-technology society. People who will fill a position for a brief period (four years or less for many in this Air Force job) carry out a set of routine tasks which are well supported by technology. However, periodically, a breakdown occurs—a novel situation requiring sophisticated problem solving for which little support is available. Expertise in solving such problems is difficult to acquire. Semi-automated, routinized jobs do not afford sufficient opportunities for complex problem-solving skills to develop, so their incumbents lack the skill required to handle novel problems. SHERLOCK is an environment in which this missing skill can be acquired for a specific troubleshooting job.

SHERLOCK was developed to raise the level of F-15 Manual Avionics Test Station Technicians' troubleshooting knowledge. These technicians repair electronic modules that have been removed from F-15 aircraft because of suspected malfunction. In their daily work, they follow detailed written troubleshooting procedures (part of their "Technical Orders") and use a test station to diagnose the failures in the modules that are sent from the flight line. The test station is a large (40 cubic feet) system of electronic equipment to which the module being diagnosed can be attached. By setting various switches on the front panels of the test station, the airman can quickly perform tests on the module. When a test in the prescribed test routine isolates the cause of the malfunction, the airman consults the Technical Orders for an appropriate repair.

A serious problem arises when the test station itself has a malfunction. Now, instead of following fixed procedures from a check sheet and making use of the substantial technological support of the test station, the airman is much more on his[1] own and must engage in complex heuristic problem solving. Because they may be working in the field far from help, these technicians have to be self-sufficient: they have to be able to repair their equipment. However, because the test station breaks down only about once a month (and even then may be diagnosed and repaired by an expert to minimize downtime), a first-term airman (someone in his first four years of duty) gets few opportunities on the job to learn this most difficult skill. The technical training airmen receive before reporting for work is oriented toward the conceptual knowledge and skill needed for the routine part of the work—which is all there is for perhaps 95% of the time. Yet this leaves the Air Force with a dilemma; its training supposes that test station repair will be learned on the job, but the job doesn't provide the relevant practice opportunities.

The subject matter addressed by SHERLOCK is not only highly technical, it is considerably more complex than that addressed by other ITS or CAI systems, making SHERLOCK's instructional problem a particularly interesting and difficult one. Central to SHERLOCK's architecture are the following design features needed to cope with this complexity. In contrast to other intelligent tutoring systems, such as LISPITS (Corbett & Anderson, this volume) and GIL (Reiser, Kimberg, Lovett, & Ranney, this volume), SHERLOCK does not incorporate a general problem space with every level of detail of every problem for which it provides instruction. Instead it limits the problem-space size by using "effective" problem spaces that are specific to individual problems, that include only operations concerning replaceable test-station components (e.g., whole circuit boards instead of individual electronic components), and that include only actions that expert instructors believe students or experts may plausibly take. Associated with the "effective" problem space is an abstracted goal structure representing expert and novice techniques for solving the problem. For each goal or subgoal, there is a special, small program, called an "object," that embodies detailed knowledge about measurements within a circuit board.[2]

---

[1]To simplify exposition, we use masculine pronouns. Most, but not all, of our trainee subjects were male.

[2]An object is an independent program unit that can take certain actions and keep certain data in response to messages from other objects.

Experimental testing has demonstrated the instructional effectiveness of SHERLOCK's approach. In an independent evaluation (Nichols et. al., in press), less experienced technicians who have practiced about 20 to 25 hours on SHERLOCK perform as well in troubleshooting test station failures as colleagues who have four more years of on-the-job experience.

SHERLOCK demonstrates a relatively speedy and efficient approach to teaching performance of cognitive tasks where:

1. There is a huge problem space, i.e., there are many possible actions that can be taken, many choices to be made in solving a problem.
2. The job is difficult largely because of its complexity rather than because of a few specific conceptual barriers.
3. On-the-job apprenticeship dealing with the difficult aspects of the job is not available.

This chapter first describes SHERLOCK's task domain—the electronic trouble-shooting task. We then discuss the principles guiding SHERLOCK's development, followed by examples of how experts and trainees think about the trouble-shooting task and of how SHERLOCK interacts with a trainee. The final sections describe SHERLOCK's implementation and its relation to some general pedagogical issues.

SHERLOCK'S TASK DOMAIN

To understand SHERLOCK, it is helpful to understand a bit more about the job for which it was developed. Routine troubleshooting generally is organized around a decision tree (or a set of nested multiple-choice questions). At each question, or branching point in a decision tree, one gets a piece of information and then makes a choice. Eventually, these choices lead to a repair action. If that action is successful, the task is completed. A decision tree can be generated any time that one can state a rule for detecting each possible fault in a system, where the rule specifies the conditions under which that fault is present and each condition can be verified by a measurement. The decision tree simply represents an organization of those rules that attempts to minimize the number of conditions that need to be verified before the fault is found. It is a labor-saving artifact. For the F-15 trouble-shooter, such decision trees are part of the written "Technical Orders" and are used routinely.

Like decision trees, the test station is a labor-saving artifact. When many electrical tests are to be made, time is taken up preparing test equipment, reconfiguring the system so that the needed test points are exposed, attaching any required electrical sources, and attaching instrument probes. The test station minimizes these time costs by acting as a large switchboard. By pushing a few buttons and turning a few knobs, a technician can configure a test circuit, specify a measurement to be made, and produce the value of the measurement on a display. Every test has the same basic form: an electrical circuit is created in which there is a stimulus (a source of patterned electrical energy or perhaps a power supply or a signal generator that propagates a "signal" through the system circuitry), a device being tested, and a measurement device. In essence, the technician is measuring the effect (or "signal"), at some point(s) in the device being tested, of applying the stimulus to some other point(s).

When a test "fails"—that is, when a test result is out of the expected range—this suggests a malfunction in the part of the device being tested. The Technical Orders tell what to replace for any given test failure. However, sometimes the mandated repair does not resolve the failure. This generally means that the intended test circuit was not properly created. Either something is wrong in the test station, or something is wrong in the cabling between the test station and the device being tested. A false and possibly misleading test value results. If a technician understands what test configuration is not being achieved correctly, then he has greatly constrained the troubleshooting problem. Because the test station is essentially a switchboard, he need only consider the circuit path through the test station that was (or should have been) created for the test that failed, plus the switching circuitry that is involved in producing that configuration.

So, an airman technician must learn several things to successfully diagnose test station failures. First, he must be able to figure out what test the station was attempting when it failed; he must have a model of the test. From this internal understanding of how the test should work, he can determine which circuitry, distributed throughout the test station, might be the locus of failure. Second, he must devise a strategy for searching this circuitry for the fault. This will involve narrowing the search space by performing various tests. For example, if no signal even gets to the device being tested, then none can get to the measurement module. In that case, the problem must be between the signal source and the connections of the test station to the device being tested, not in the path from the device to the measurement module of the test station. Third, he must be able to carry out the strategy. This requires repeated exercise of certain skills of measurement and of circuit diagram interpretation. So the technician must be able to follow circuit diagrams and to make and interpret tests with various instruments such as an oscilloscope and a multimeter.

Note that a strategy can be systematic but uninformed. For example, one could replace components of the test station one at a time until the bad component was found. This is inefficient because the circuit path involved in a test tends to include a little bit of each of a large number of components. However, the serial component-swapping approach is widespread among electronics technicians in general, even though it is usually impractical.

PRINCIPLES GUIDING SHERLOCK'S DEVELOPMENT

In this section, we discuss why SHERLOCK is the way it is. SHERLOCK is a practice environment; it affords opportunities to practice doing a task in a supported context. At the most abstract level, it is the cognitive version of earlier approaches to errorless learning (Terrace, 1964). With support from a computerized coach, the technician successfully completes problems of the complexity he wants to learn to handle on his own.

Pedagogical Principles

The Role of Practice

Rather than calling it a tutor, we refer to SHERLOCK as a supported or coached practice environment. The fundamental purpose of SHERLOCK is to provide an efficient artificial means of practicing, with support and feedback, a skill that cannot be practiced efficiently in its real application context. The routine activity of the manual avionics test station technician is to follow an essentially fixed procedure. Specific rules are read from a document and followed; there is little judgment required. On the other hand, when the test station fails, a strategy must be invented on the spot—a different strategy each time, because the failure is different each time. Verbal principles have to be mapped into richly varying situations in order to carry out this work. Practice is the means for making initially verbal knowledge stronger and more flexible (Anderson, 1983).

Making Practice Time Effective

For practice time to be effective, the following things are required. First, the proportion of time that involves the target cognitive activity should be maximized. If time is spent waiting for parts, dismantling components, and carrying out long sequences of performances that are already well learned, then that time is not available for practice of the decision process that is the core of troubleshooting facility. Second, cognitive (or working memory) overload should be controlled, a point also raised by Corbett & Anderson (this volume). In a complex cognitive performance like troubleshooting a test station failure, a trainee may simply forget what he has done so far or where he is in carrying out a plan. While trainees need ultimately to learn to handle this complexity, we assume that this virtuosity will come with practice. So we provide help when a trainee loses track of what he has done. This minimizes the experience of inadequacy and saves the time it would take to declare failure and begin another problem. Often, simply being reminded of what he has already done will be sufficient to enable a trainee to go on to work on a problem effectively. Third, advice should be available to overcome knowledge gaps. If the trainee simply does not know what to do or how to proceed, giving him a hint will both teach the missing knowledge and enable overall problem solving practice to continue. Fourth, performance should be coached beyond success toward optimality. Just as an athletic coach can watch a complete performance and then improve it by providing useful insights to an athlete, so a problem solving practice coach should provide critical insights that move the trainee toward more efficient performance.[3]

Refining the Environment Rather than Refining the Teacher

While coaching is an important aspect of SHERLOCK, primary emphasis is on the practice environment, not on the role of coach. This is a difference in nuance, not an absolute difference, but it means that we are focused primarily on having the environment reveal its structure rather than on having the coach know exactly what to say to a particular student. This approach includes certain biases. For example, the trainee is given much of the responsibility for learning. Very little feedback is provided other than that which the work environment normally provides.[4] Help must be requested explicitly. The assigned tasks, although at the limits of trainees' capabilities, are all completed;[5] support from the environment is available on demand. Fidelity to the work environment is emphasized, rather than tracking students' reasoning on a very detailed level.

Principles for Managing Complexity

The Problem Space Structure

We use the term problem space to refer to a graph structure in which nodes represent partial solution states and links represent next moves from one partial solution state to another (with the top node representing the complete solution). Often, the solution process for a problem can be split into several pieces, which we call subgoals (the overall goal is to solve the problem). We can impose partitionings on a problem space to generate a problem subgoal tree. (Actually, it is a subgoal lattice, reflecting the multiple paths toward problem solution.)

---

[3]SHERLOCK did not meet this fourth requirement. SHERLOCK II, its successor, does by providing broader experiences and a reflective follow-up or postmarker after each problem is solved.

[4]Dugdale (this volume) emphasizes also direct feedback from the working environment, although she *designs* artificial environments explicitly to provide good feedback, while SHERLOCK *replicates* the feedback of the real-world task environment.

[5]We have yet to encounter an instance in which the student failed to complete a problem, even though every problem is beyond the entering capabilities of most students.

Diagnosing a test station failure is a big problem because of the many components the station contains. Knowing what components are relevant reduces the problem, but it is still extremely complex. The problem spaces on which SHERLOCK's data structures are based are computationally manageable only because the following three techniques have been used to make them smaller (cf. Lesgold, Lajoie, Logan, & Eggan, in press). First, they do not contain all the theoretically possible combinations of actions. They contain only actions that tend to be taken by trainees or experts. A number of actions that might, in principle, be taken are left out simply because our experts assure us that they never occur. Second, a separate problem space is developed for each problem. While these spaces have a lot in common, the space for one problem is much smaller than the space of all possible test station failures, because only a small part of the test station is involved in a given test, and a system failure always occurs in the context of something the system was trying to do, some way the system was trying to configure itself. Third, we do not consider each of the test station's individual electrical components, of which there are thousands, nor each individual action that might be taken on those components. If we did this, just representing the possibility that each one of the thousands of parts could be broken (and therefore might need to be tested) would make the problem space unmanageably large. So, we abstract the test station structure to the level of replaceable modules, such as printed circuit boards, rather than representing each component on each board separately.

Our effective problem spaces have 50 to 60 nodes, rather than the thousands of nodes that a "complete" problem space for test station diagnosis would have. Figure 1 shows an example of part of one problem's effective problem space. The component nodes are in bold face and the broad action categories are in italic.

The leftmost node of the problem space represents the complete navigation of the problem from first attack to final solution. Branches to the right of any node in the space refer to the subgoals that must be achieved before that higher-level node can be achieved.

Our problem space is only partly elaborated, i.e., each subgoal still subsumes a lot of mental activity. SHERLOCK's representation of a problem, then, consists of an *effective problem space*, with the limitations described above.

An Object-oriented Approach

When working to diagnose station failures, a technician makes individual test measurements at specific points within a circuit board. Yet the nodes of the effective problem space correspond to complete boards or to broad sets of actions on a board. Information about components with a circuit board is handled by specialist miniprograms associated with a node of the effective problem space. Computer software designers call these specialist miniprograms objects. A generic object is first defined, and then each node's "personal" object is specified as a specialization of the generic template. Most of the specialization consists of data, not program: specific hinting information, test point values, etc.

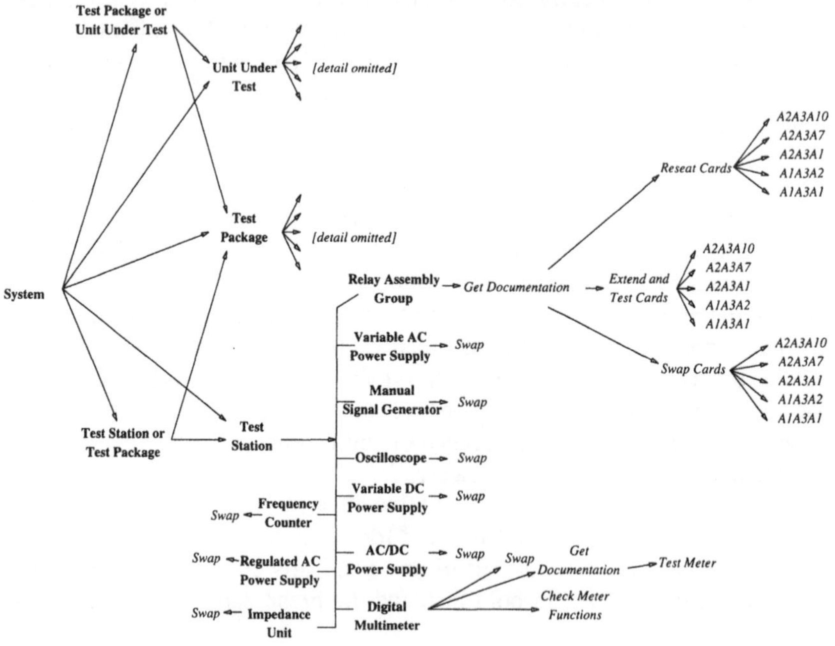

Figure 1: Part of a problem's effective problem space.

Substantial savings result from this combination of an abstracted effective problem space with specialized objects to connect problem space nodes to the details of the working environment. Rather than a network of separate problem space connections between every detail of one module and every detail of each of the others, there is only one path to or from each abstracted object. The approach is similar to the pattern of traffic in a large city. The effective problem space is like the network of main streets, and the objects are like small neighborhoods with their side streets. One gets from a neighborhood to a main street, takes the main street to another neighborhood, and then takes side streets to a specific address. Separate roads connecting every pair of addresses would be unthinkably more complex.

Goals of Training

SHERLOCK has three main sets of instructional goals: (a) troubleshooting strategy, (b) understanding test configurations that can be created with the test station, and (c) using test instruments to make measurements.

SHERLOCK is a holistic practice environment. What trainees do with SHERLOCK is to solve difficult test station diagnosis problems. Each problem exercises many of the needed skill components in the context of a complete, naturalistic performance. This is very different from many instructional activities, such as courses, where different sessions treat different instructional goals. In SHERLOCK, every session addresses almost every instructional goal. Nonetheless, SHERLOCK does have an explicit representation of its instructional goals.

Models of Students' Knowledge

Intelligent training systems generally maintain some form of or representation of the learner's current knowledge. Computer-implemented tutors that deal with constrained bodies of knowledge, like proofs of geometry theorems, model the student by trying to define a computer program that will behave just as the student behaves. A comparison between that program and a program that simulates an expert reveals what the student has not yet learned and is the basis for interactions with the student. (This is the central idea behind the tutors of Corbett & Anderson; Reiser et. al., Sack & Soloway; this volume). SHERLOCK does not use simulation techniques to model student performance. Its diagnoses are made in a simpler way, as follows.

SHERLOCK keeps two kinds of student models for each trainee. Its competence model is a notation of how well each instructional goal has been achieved. Its performance model, generated for each problem a student attempts to solve, indicates how well the student is expected to implement the knowledge associated with each node of the effective problem space. Both models are overlay models. That is, they involve a set of goals or actions for each of which an estimate of student capability is recorded.

The performance model for a particular problem is computed when a trainee begins work on the problem. For each node of the effective problem space, an estimate is made of how well he is expected to do at that node. The object associated with a node has a list of instructional goals that should be achieved before we can expect the trainee to be able to handle the problem solving activity required at that node. To estimate the student's likelihood of successful performance at a node, its object considers the competence-model entries for that node's associated instructional goals and makes a performance model prediction of *good, okay, or bad.* The performance model influences how SHERLOCK will provide explicit help at specific points in the course of problem solution.

The competence model is based on SHERLOCK's instructional goals. For each goal or subgoal, a notation is made concerning the level of capability the student is currently thought to have. This notation is updated after each problem to take account of how well the trainee performed at problem space nodes related to the given instructional goal. Four levels are used: *unlearned*, *perhaps*, *probably*, and *strong*. A capability at the *perhaps* level has been apparently manifested recently but is thought to be very fragile. If it fails to be manifested in the next few cases where it is appropriate, it will revert to the *unlearned* state. If it is remanifested, it will move to the *probably* state. If the capability is regularly and reliably manifested, it will move to the *strong* state. SHERLOCK also keeps the history of evidence used to determine the state of the competence model for each instructional subgoal.

After a problem is solved, any divergence of student performance from the predictions is used to update the student's competence model. So, if a student does better than expected at some point in a problem, this is prima facie evidence that he has improved on the instructional goals relevant to that point.

Hints as the Major Mechanism of Coaching

The coaching provided by SHERLOCK consists primarily of hints to the trainee as he tries to solve each fault isolation problem. Some hints are generated dynamically (especially the recapitulation hint described below), while most are "canned"— written in advance by the developers. Except in a few specific cases, hints are provided only in response to a trainee's request. The first kind of exception occurs when the student has finished taking an action in an effective problem space node and now wants to move to another point in the problem space that is definitely a wrong choice. On certain occasions, in the judgement of our expert consultants, certain choices were so clearly inappropriate that it makes sense to tell the trainee this rather than letting him discover it for himself. In these cases, making a bad choice of what to do next prompted a hint explaining why it was a bad choice.

The second kind of exception occurs when the trainee wants to redo a step that already has been explicitly taken, such as swapping a board again.[6] In such a case SHERLOCK will interrupt with a message that the proposed activity has already been completed. On the other hand, if the activity associated with a node in the effective problem space has been rendered redundant because some combination of other actions has logically ruled it out (e.g., several tests of other components might produce results that logically entail the correct function

---

[6]In SHERLOCK, all replacement components always work. This is not entirely realistic, but is part of the general strategy of focusing trainee time on activity deemed most likely to improve basic troubleshooting skill.

of a different board, which one would then have no reason to swap or test), then the trainee is still allowed to do the activity, but after he is done with it, he is advised that it was not necessary and is told why.

With these exceptions, the hints are provided in response to requests for help or pressing the *Panic* button. When the *Panic* button is pressed, the trainee is given an overview of the portions of the effective problem space that are still candidates for troubleshooting activity. Then, he is given the initial planning menu, essentially being allowed to start over again, from the top, on what is left of the problem. Our thought was that the one occasion on which we could probably get the trainee to step back from the details of tactics to look at strategy broadly was when he was completely at a loss for next actions.

When a hint is requested by clicking on the *Help* button, the system decides how to respond based on the performance model of the student for the subgoal node at which he is currently located and his activity status within the node. There are four categories of activity: *Action*, *Outcome*, *Conclusion*, and *Option*. *Action* refers to deciding which test to carry out and how that test is done. *Outcome* refers to getting the results of a test, perhaps by reading a meter. *Conclusion* refers to the determining the meaning of the results, and *Option* refers to deciding what to do next. So, for example, one might enter the node for testing a particular printed circuit board but not know what to measure on that board. Asking for help at that point would produce an Action hint. On the other hand, if one has just made an oscilloscope measurement, then presumably the needed help is in the area of Outcome or Conclusion. If one has already closed the page of schematic diagrams for the board and then asks for help, an Option hint is provided.

Several structural details help assure that an appropriate hint is provided. First, some stages of activity within a problem space node are easy to identify, especially the Action and the Option stages. Second, when available hints at one level are exhausted, hints for the next level can be provided. So, if one gets some Action hints and keeps asking for more help, eventually Outcome, Conclusion, and Option hints would also be provided. We planned a third approach, in which SHERLOCK was to put up a menu asking the trainee what kind of help was needed, but this plan was not implemented, due to scheduling urgencies.

Once the type of hint to be delivered is determined, then a decision must be made about how explicit a hint should be provided. Hints are classified from 1 to 5 on a scale of explicitness. Hint level 1 is always a recapitulation of what the trainee has done so far in trying to solve the problem.[7] Hint levels 2 to 5

---

[7]It differs from a Panic hint in that it is a structured account of the actions taken, while the Panic hint is a structured account of the problem space portions remaining to be searched.

are pre-written hints produced by our subject matter experts. There is not always a hint available for each level and each type.

The first time a trainee asks for help on a node, he gets a Level 1 recapitulation hint. The next time, he gets a hint determined by his expected performance on the node at which he is currently located. If the performance model expects him to do a *Good* job, he next gets a Level 2 hint. An *Okay* rating produces a Level 3 hint, and a *Bad* rating gets a Level 4 hint. Further requests result in progressively higher level hints till the appropriate set is exhausted, followed by hints from successive types (e.g., if SHERLOCK is out of Conclusion hints, it gives an Option hint).

EXAMPLES

The domain targeted by SHERLOCK and its mode of operation may become clearer through two examples. We first illustrate mental models of test configurations, both by an expert and by a novice learner. A mental model identifies what parts of the test station are involved in the failed test and, therefore, must be considered by the troubleshooting strategy. Second, we describe an interaction of a trainee with SHERLOCK.

Mental Models of a Circuit Test

One of our easier problems involves a situation in which, while a device from an airplane is being tested, an incorrect meter reading appears on the test station. The documentation available to the technician asserts that replacing a particular part of the device will result in restoration of the correct meter reading. When this replacement fails to eliminate the problem, the test station itself becomes a possible suspect. An expert will have a "model" of the test indicating exactly the small portion of the test station actually involved in the failed test. While the whole test station requires a few hundred pages of schematics (circuit diagrams) to capture all of its complexity, an expert's mental representation of the portions relevant to this problem would fit into one page,[8] shown as Figure 2.

We show mental models using the notation of schematic diagrams. These diagrams use symbols (like the boxes and lines) in Figure 2, to show how circuit elements are connected to each other. Schematics do not show how these objects are physically placed in the actual test station (i.e., the geometry of the circuit). They do show how they are connected (the topology of the circuit).

---

[8]An extensive task analysis (Lesgold, Lajoie et al., 1986) supported our assumptions concerning expert domain knowledge and performance as well as the ways in which more and less astute technicians handle test station troubleshooting tasks.

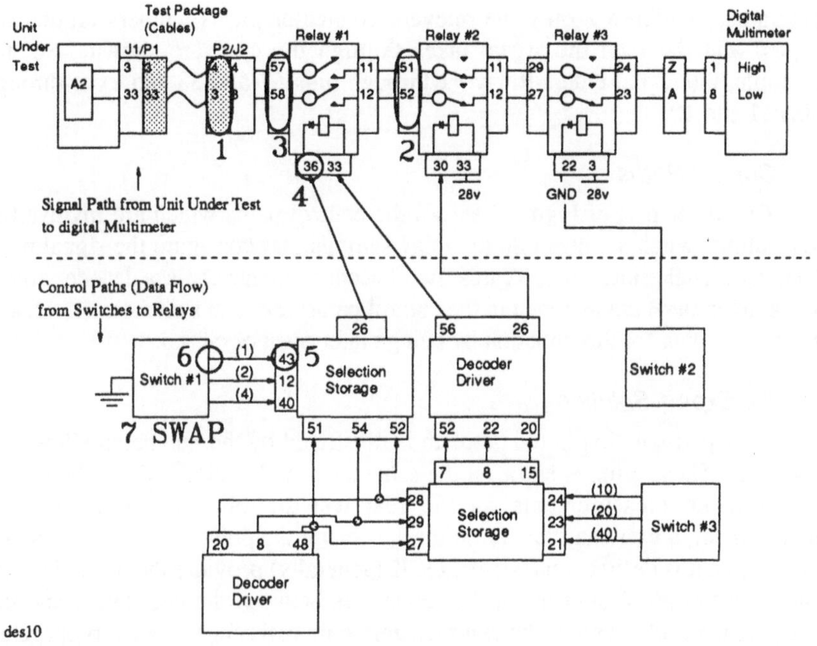

Figure 2: Expert's mental model.

Signal Path

From left to right across the top of the figure, the signal path is shown from the aircraft module that is being tested (the "unit under test") to the digital multimeter on the test station. The test that failed attempted to measure the resistance of a circuit in the unit under test that should have extremely low resistance (i.e., approximately zero ohms).[9] In order for the resistance measurement to be made, a path must be created from each end of the unit under test to the measurement device, a digital multimeter. This path passes from the unit under test through connectors (J1/P1) to a cable (the "test package") and then through additional connectors (P2/J2) to the test station. Everything else in the diagram is part of the test station. Upon entering the test station, the signal from the unit under test passes through three printed circuit boards (Relays #1,

[9]This test is particularly simple, since it involves a measurement that is made without any stimulus being applied to the device under test.

#2, and #3) before reaching the Digital Multimeter. Although each of the printed circuit cards is complex enough to require a page or more of schematic diagrams, in Figure 2 only the relevant connector pins (numbers around the edges) and the path the signal takes through the card are shown. So, for example, the signal enters Relay #1 through pins 57 and 58 and exits through pins 11 and 12.

Control Paths

The lower part of Figure 2 shows the control paths which are involved in translating switch settings into the relay settings that configure the signal path. Four additional printed circuit cards (two selection storage cards, a decoder driver, and a timer card) are involved in the control paths. Several switches, #1, #2, and #3, control data for this situation by being either open or closed.

An Expert Solution

An expert solution to the problem is illustrated by the numbered ellipses in Figure 2. These ellipses show on the schematic the locations where the expert would make measurements on the real test station. In SHERLOCK's environment, a user can identify on the schematic the point or points at which a measurement is desired, and SHERLOCK (generally) provides the desired value. The expert might first check at the connectors between the test station and the test package cable to see if the expected zero ohm resistance is being propagated from the unit under test to the test station [Step 1]. If it is, then he might check halfway between P2/J2 and the meter, at the inputs to Relay #2 [Step 2]. In this problem, the zero ohm resistance[10] is found at Step 1 and is missing at Step 2. This implicates Relay #1. The expert would verify the card's input at pins 57 and 58 [Step 3]. Since the signal is getting into Relay #1 but not getting into Relay #2, it is possible that the relay that switches the signal through Relay #1 is bad. Step 4 of the expert is to test that relay to see if the actuating voltage is passing through it.[11] When it turns out that the voltage is not passing through the relay, the expert traces through the control flow path and notes that the actuating voltage should be coming from a selection storage card, which decodes low-voltage control signals to determine which of its outputs should be relay-actuating voltage levels. He then checks to see if the correct control voltages are reaching that card [Step 5]. They are not. So, he tests to see if the switch that connects those control voltages to the selection storage card is working [Step 6].

---

[10] This value would appear on the dial of an appropriate meter applied to these points.

[11] What really happens is more complex, but not necessary to this exposition. Ordinarily, when the relay is to be open, there is 28V relative to ground on both sides of the relay coil. The selection storage card operates by grounding one side of the coil, creating a voltage drop through it and thereby a magnetic field to actuate the relay.

The expert's measurement shows a defect in the switch, so he swaps the switch [Step 7], and this solves the problem.

This activity involves perhaps a total of a square yard of complex schematic diagrams (and a comparably large amount of circuitry in the test station), so it is non-trivial. Figure 2 shows just those elements the expert identifies as relevant to the problem. In fact, our trainees generally were far less facile than the experts in solving this problem. For example, while our expert solved it in seven steps, one trainee took 14 steps and another took 20 (the others were similar).

A Trainee Solution

The 14 numbers in Figure 3 show the activity of the trainee who took 14 steps. Superficially, it is apparent that he tended to trace through circuit paths from one end to the other (e.g., Steps 1-4) rather than trying to make measurements in the center of the path so as to isolate the problem to one half or the other. In contrast, the expert used a strategy called "space splitting;" performing a test to rule out a large group of elements as possible sources of the problem. The trainee also tried to make a few measurements (10, 11, 12) that could not logically be involved in the failure. Since the component that was tested had already been replaced in Step 9, no measurements on that component were likely to be helpful. The actual measurements made were on a part of the component not involved in the circuit path at all. Some redundant tests were also done (e.g., steps 6 and 8 test the same point on the circuit, although they are somewhat separated on the descriptive schematic diagram). Finally, three unnecessary swaps were made (the unit under test, the test package, and the selection storage card). However, he did solve the problem.

Interaction of a Trainee with SHERLOCK

While performing tests on Relay #1, our example trainee asked for help several times. First he was just given an overview of what he had done so far. Asking for additional help, he was told by SHERLOCK:

"You need to determine if the 0.0 ohms from the unit under test is getting to this card.[12] If there is an input you need to test the output. If there is no output you need to determine why the 0.0 ohms signal is not getting through this card."

---

[12]This wording may annoy the physicist. However, it is an example of our efforts to situate the work environment and coaching in the world of the trainee. Technicians use such language, and we tend to follow their usage except when we have an important point to make that is obscured by technician parlance.

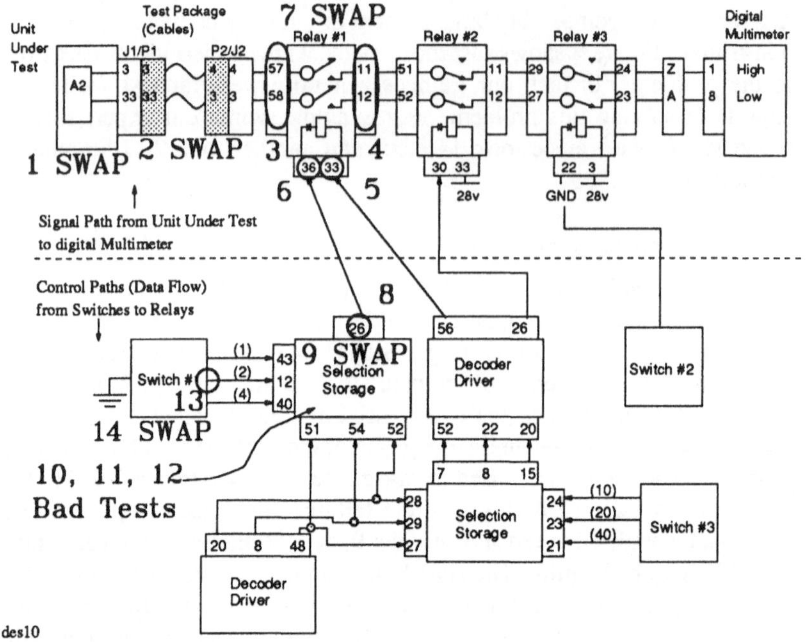

Figure 3: Trainee's mental model.

Asking for even more help, he was given more specific information about which pins on the card were relevant. After doing the required measurements, if he had asked for more help, he might have been told:

"The input to Relay #1[13] is good. The output from Relay #1 is bad. If there's no output from this card, then you should conclude that this card, or the data to this card which sets the relays, is the cause of the problem. Since Relay Card #1, Pin 36 reads +28VDC[14], when it should read 0VDC if the relay is to be set, SHERLOCK suspects that you should investigate the selection storage card connected to Pin 36." [The failure was in a switch, but the selection storage card is the next sensible place to look at this point in the problem.]

13The actual wording of the hint uses the technical labels for cards, in this case A1A3A2. To simplify exposition, we have modified hint text to match the simplified labeling of Figures 1 and 2.

14This is the value obtained by the trainee by applying a meter to Pin 36 in the schematic in Figure 3.

The trainee in this example tried, on about a half dozen occasions, to take an unsafe step, usually removing a card without first turning off power to it. In real life, this could damage the equipment or even shock the trainee. Whenever this happened, he received an appropriate warning. He also tried to make some measurements with the meter set incorrectly and got feedback about that problem.

Note that an important property of SHERLOCK is that it affords opportunities for practice of the complex skill and that it speaks primarily when spoken to. In certain respects it is a rich environment, and the student, not the computer, is the teacher and is in control. SHERLOCK exerts control where the environment would, on issues of safety or impossibility. It also tries to cut off long ventures down dead ends, but for the most part the trainee decides what steps to take, when to seek advice, etc. We think this promotes active, conscious learning, and trainees have been willing to take the responsibilities that SHERLOCK implicitly assigns to them.

IMPLEMENTATION OF THE SYSTEM

Overview of the Design Approach

SHERLOCK's knowledge base has three components: the work environment, the effective problem space for each problem, and the instructional goal. The instructional goals (troubleshooting strategies, mental models of test configurations, and the use of test instruments to make measurements) are taught through practice and a rich hinting mechanism.

The Work Environment

SHERLOCK presents a partial simulation of the work environment in which the skills it teaches are ordinarily exercised. The controls of the test station are shown and are manipulable, and control settings are monitored so that unsafe or inappropriate actions can be pointed out and blocked. The basic data-gathering action of troubleshooting the test station is to measure electrical properties at various points in the circuitry. SHERLOCK therefore allows trainees to make measurements by pointing, in schematic displays (like those in Figures 2 and 3), to locations at which meter probes should be placed.[15] The measurement devices include those built into the test station, and also a hand

---

[15] As will be discussed below, not all test values are available. That is, our work environment simulation is not as complete as it could be (compare to SOPHIE [Brown, Burton, & De Kleer, 1982], for example). The strategy for deciding which data values should be available is a subject of continued research on our part.

held multimeter. A wire is also available and may be connected to two points in a schematic. This is because many tests can be performed by connecting (or "shorting") two points and observing the effects on overall test station function. The schematic diagrams are taken from the Technical Orders, printed manuals used by technicians in their everyday work.[16]

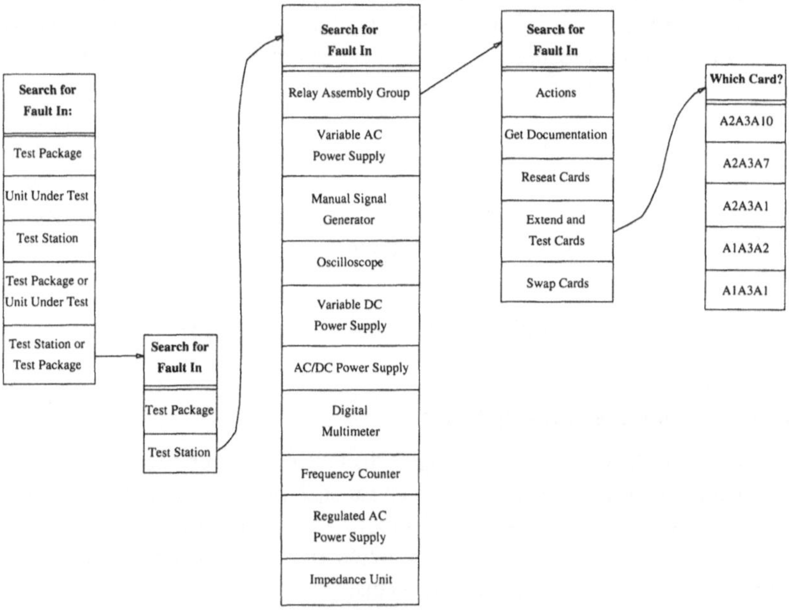

Figure 4: Menus corresponding to the effective problem space structure shown in Figure 1.

The Effective Problem Space

At any given moment the trainee can, by use of an action menu, move through the effective problem space. Figure 4 shows some of the menu hierarchy associated with the effective problem space shown in Figure 1. Actual

[16]There are, of course, other components to the Technical Orders besides the schematic diagrams, including indexing of the schematics by test point and componential structure. There are also extensive troubleshooting procedures, for diagnosis of units from the aircraft using the test station and for diagnosis of the test station itself (including the "test package" that connects units to the test station).

menus were determined in a slightly more complex manner and included items that were frequently requested even if they were not associated with the particular part of the problem space from which the menu was derived. The data structures to support this are feasible only because, by the means described earlier, we have been able to specify a sufficiently compact effective problem space. These menus let the trainee perform actions associated with the effective problem space (e.g., tightening connections, swapping boards, and replacing specific components). Additionally, interaction with these menus allows SHERLOCK to infer aspects of the trainee's strategy. We have found the idea of an effective problem space to be workable, and we expect that extensions to the approach will not require a major change.

Instructional Goals

As described earlier, SHERLOCK has three main areas of instructional goals: (a) troubleshooting strategy, (b) mental models of test configurations that can be created with the test station, and (c) using test instruments to make measurements. A mental model identifies what parts of the test station are involved in the failed test and, therefore, must be considered by the troubleshooting strategy.

Connections between the Effective Problem Space, the Work Environment, and the Instructional Goals

The connection between the instructional goals and the nodes of the effective problem space provides the primary means of individualized coaching in SHERLOCK — a rich hinting mechanism. Individualization is possible because the computational object associated with each node of the effective problem space knows which instructional goals must be accomplished before a trainee can handle the part of the problem space it represents. As noted above, this allows the object to compute an expectation of the level of trainee capability for its part of the problem space, using the instructional-goal-based competence model for that trainee. Each node also knows about a variety of hints, both prepared hints and ones that can be constructed for the specific occasion. The choice among hints is determined partly by the specifics of the student's recent activity and partly by the node's performance expectation for the student.

In the current version of the tutor, each student encounters the same 34 problems, each of which takes an average of 35 minutes to solve. The primary mode of individualization over the average 20 hours of coached practice is the hints. The average student sees about 95 hints during the 20 hours, and these are highly particularized according to where in the course of problem solution he was when a hint was requested and how well the object corresponding to that point in the effective problem space expected him to perform the next required step.

Connections between the effective problem space and the work environment have to do with individual measurements the airman may want to carry out, by pointing to various points in schematic diagrams. In these interactions with the work environment, the airman is taking active problem solving steps, which must in some way be communicated to the effective problem space. This would be easy if the step taken by the airman was always exclusively a sensible next step in his troubleshooting plan. However, it is quite possible for a trainee to make additional measurements on a particular board just because he has current access to it. We couple the work environment to the effective problem space by means of small flexible programs tied to each work environment unit (each schematic circuit diagram). When the airman finishes work on a schematic, its program runs and notifies effective problem space nodes of information relevant to them.

The following paragraphs discuss in more detail the implementation of each of the three major components of SHERLOCK (the effective problem space, the instructional goals, and the work environment).

Implementation of the Main Components

The Effective Problem Space

As noted above, the trainee's problem solving activity on SHERLOCK is monitored and guided by an effective problem space for the problem currently being solved. This structure reflects a range of both situation-specific and more general knowledge, including the architecture for the test station, the function of the tests that can be carried out with the test station, and various testing strategies.

Instructional Goals

The Structural Model of the Test Station

The work environment consists of simulations of the the test station, the unit from the aircraft that is currently being tested, and a test package which connects that unit to the test station. Within the test station, there are twelve large drawers (power supplies, signal generators, switches, and measurement devices) containing the various components that enable testing of aircraft units. Figure 5 shows how this structure is represented on the computer screen in SHERLOCK. The array of rectangles represent drawers of electronic circuit boards. The labels indicate their content, but the meaning of these labels is not important to understanding this figure.

To a large extent, the drawers represent a first cut on a functional decomposition of the test station. If one were told only that the test station contained a defect, a reasonable strategy might be to try to localize the defect first to a specific drawer and then to a specific circuit board or other component (e.g., transformer) within the drawer, just as a physician's first effort to narrow down a diagnosis might be to decide if it is a problem of the cardiovascular system, or the digestive system, or some other system, each of which is in somewhat sequestered anatomy.

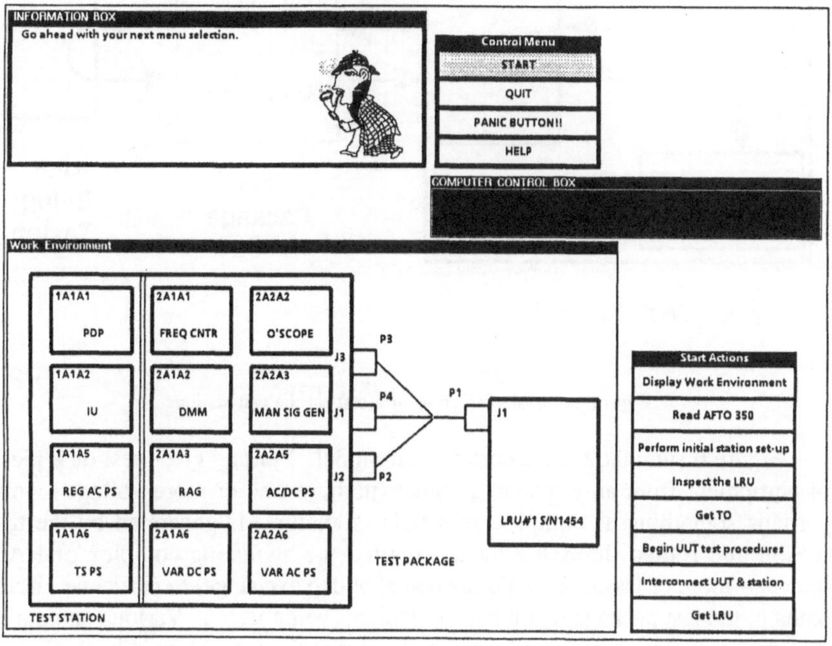

Figure 5: SHERLOCK basic screen.

The Mental Model of a Test

In fact, though, the real diagnostic situation is constrained by factors beyond the obvious physical layout. Test station failures become manifest when the test station is used for a purpose and that purpose cannot be achieved. We have designed SHERLOCK to emphasize a fundamental mental model of, or way of thinking about, an electronic test. In its generic form, a test consists of three components: a stimulus, a device being tested, and a measurement device. The stimulus is a source of patterned energy that passes through the device being tested to the measurement device.[17]

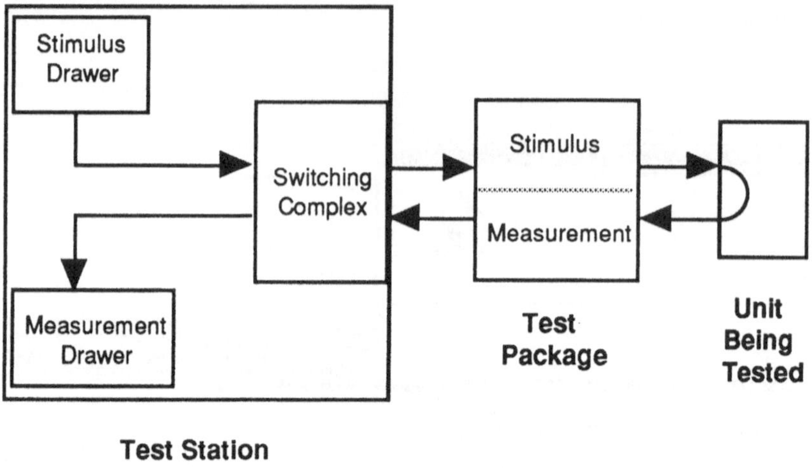

Figure 6: Basic Structure of a test on the test station.

Figure 6 summarizes the core mental model. For any given test on a piece of equipment from an airplane, a signal (perhaps one or more voltage levels, perhaps something as complex as a radar signature) is generated by the test station and routed through a switch (called the switching complex or RAG drawer—more or less like an old fashioned phone exchange) to particular circuit paths in the test package and thence to the unit being tested. Various outputs of the unit being tested are routed through the test package to the switch which then routes them to a measurement device in the test station. Additional control logic, not shown in Figure 6, causes the test station to make the right signal connection for a given test.

The idea is that the test station configures itself to carry out tests. When it fails, it fails in the course of carrying out a test. The failure must be somewhere in the particular configuration of the components of the test (stimulus, device being tested, and measurement device) or in the paths between them.

Consequently, efficient troubleshooting should be organized, in part, as an effort to identify the parts of the test station that are filling the roles in the test that failed, to identify the pathways in the test station that connect those

[17]Sometimes, extra circuitry, called a load, is added to dissipate excess energy or to transform the output signal into a pattern within measurable range.

components, and then to split the space of those identified components into subspaces that can be efficiently determined to either include or not include the system fault. Further complexity arises because the test station also includes switching devices that implement connections among particular components to realize a particular test.

That is, the paths between the components of a test are created by other test station components, namely the switching logic (or the control path). (See Figures 2 and 3.)

Troubleshooting strategies

Finally, the effective problem space and the instruction it supports have to take account of the troubleshooting strategies that novices and experts will employ in trying to find a fault. Two types of strategies are *space splitting* and *generic cures.* Space splitting, as described earlier, means systematically choosing tests to rule out groups of elements as possible sources of the problem. By a generic cure we mean a step one can take when no systematic plan is in hand or apparently productive. For example, sometimes a connection will loosen. So, tightening a number of connections will sometimes fix a test station. Tightening a set of connections would be considered a generic cure if it was done without being motivated by the process of searching the problem subgoal space systematically for a solution but rather as a default. This has some chance of fixing the problem. However, generic moves often are a form of thrashing around by novices who do not know what to do.

More interesting are the space splitting variations. In our samples of airmen who have been through electronics training and who were selected to have high promise of being able to do their jobs, almost all try to be systematic either by space splitting or by moving sequentially through a circuit. What differs with expertise is the space that is split when space splitting strategies are employed. Some split the physical space of swappable drawers, printed-circuit cards, and other components. Others split the conceptual space of functional subdivisions of either the test station in general or the specific test configuration that failed.

We do not completely capture these strategy considerations in our tutoring, but our effective problem spaces seem sufficient to allow them to occur and to be captured in SHERLOCK's student models. We see little evidence that there were airmen who could not try what they wanted to try in problem solving because of some missing pieces of the problem subgoal structure. This is partly because the mechanisms that allow specific tests to be done on particular test points of a particular printed circuit board are part of the work environment simulation and not part of the effective problem space. At the more microscopic level of placing meter probes anywhere on any of our 50 pages of schematic diagrams, there were occasional cases in which SHERLOCK could not provide a potentially relevant test measurement result. Future versions of SHERLOCK will avoid this problem by deeper representation of the circuit paths that are part of an expert's mental model.

The Work Environment

Components of the Work Environment

The work environment has three components: a simulation of the external work environment (panels of the test station), a set of schematic circuit diagrams, and devices for measurement.

Simulation of the External Work Environment

This simulation includes the front panels of the test station, the test package, and the unit from the airplane that is being tested on the test station. When the display shown in Figure 5 is on the screen, the front panel of any of the twelve major test station components can be accessed by selecting (with a mouse) the appropriate one of the twelve boxes shown inside the test station representation. For example, Figure 7 shows the front panel display for the oscilloscope drawer. Each of the knobs and switches is manipulable. Mousing[18] alongside any knob or switch causes it to reset to the position indicated by the mouse. The effects of the change are propagated to all displays immediately. So, for example, the Channel 1 Volts/Division display in the top center of Figure 7 could be changed from 1 V/Div to 2 V/Div by mousing the 2 just below the present setting of 1. The result of doing this would be to change the scale of the display, causing the waveform shown on the left to shrink to half its current size.

Schematic Circuit Diagrams

A second part of the work environment simulation consists of schematic circuit diagrams for many, but not all, portions of the test station and test package. These diagrams are also available to the trainee in printed form in a booklet that is at the computer workstation for use during practice sessions on SHERLOCK. The reason for putting them on the screen is to provide a highly real-world-situated environment for practice. Trainees make measurements on the test station by calling up a schematic and pointing to the locations in the schematic at which meter probes should be applied.

---

[18]By mousing, we mean pointing to an object and then pressing a button on the top of the mouse (pointing device).

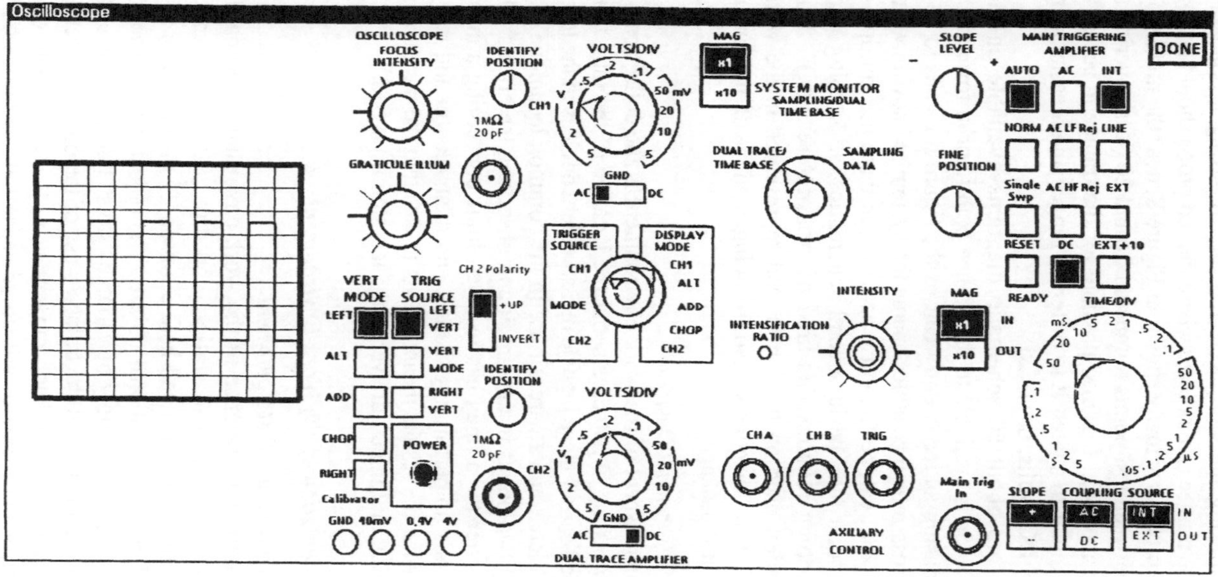

Figure 7: Oscilloscope front panel display.

Figure 8 shows part of the screen during such a test. The hand-held Simpson™ multimeter is indicated in icon form on the upper left of the figure. By first mousing the word Red and then mousing a point in the schematic diagram, the trainee can indicate where the red probe should be applied. The icon for the red probe is actually shown in Figure 8, near the middle of the schematic diagram, between test points numbered 52 and 20 (it is covering the test point to which it is applied). It is also possible for the trainee to access the front of the hand-held meter to switch it to different ranges and measurement types (ohms, DC+ volts, DC- volts, or amps).

There are about 60 schematic diagrams available on the screen. An extensive index is available to the trainee both in print form and actively on the screen (mousing an index entry causes the figure it names to be displayed). In addition, cross-reference tables enable the system to know in which schematics a given test point can be found (in some cases there are multiple views, and the same test point may be in several schematics, so keeping track of what the trainee is doing requires this kind of cross-referencing). Thus, the printed documentation used on the job is well represented in the work environment simulation, simultaneously also allowing a view of the innards of the test station and test package.

Measurement Devices

The final aspect of the work environment is the collection of measurement devices for testing hypotheses about the location of the fault in the test station. As described earlier these include measurement devices in the test station itself, a hand-held meter, and a wire for use in the common technique of connecting (or "shorting") two points in the circuit and observing the effects. Figure 9 shows the screen after the airman has received hints concerning a move that uses the wire—he ends up performing the test and then asks for and receives additional advice on what the results mean: "This means that the measurement path to the DMM [digital multimeter drawer of the test station] is bad."

Implementation of the Work Environment

Drawers and Test Equipment

The external appearance of the work environment primarily involves the front panels of the test station and the test equipment available for troubleshooting (e.g., the hand-held Simpson™ meter). Each of those panels is represented as a computational object. The object for a drawer or piece of test equipment contains a variety of variable "slots" that store the state of the object and also information about the trainee's use of the object (currently, we store the time and nature of every knob movement in the appropriate object; tests, i.e., placements of meter probes are stored separately, as discussed below). Other

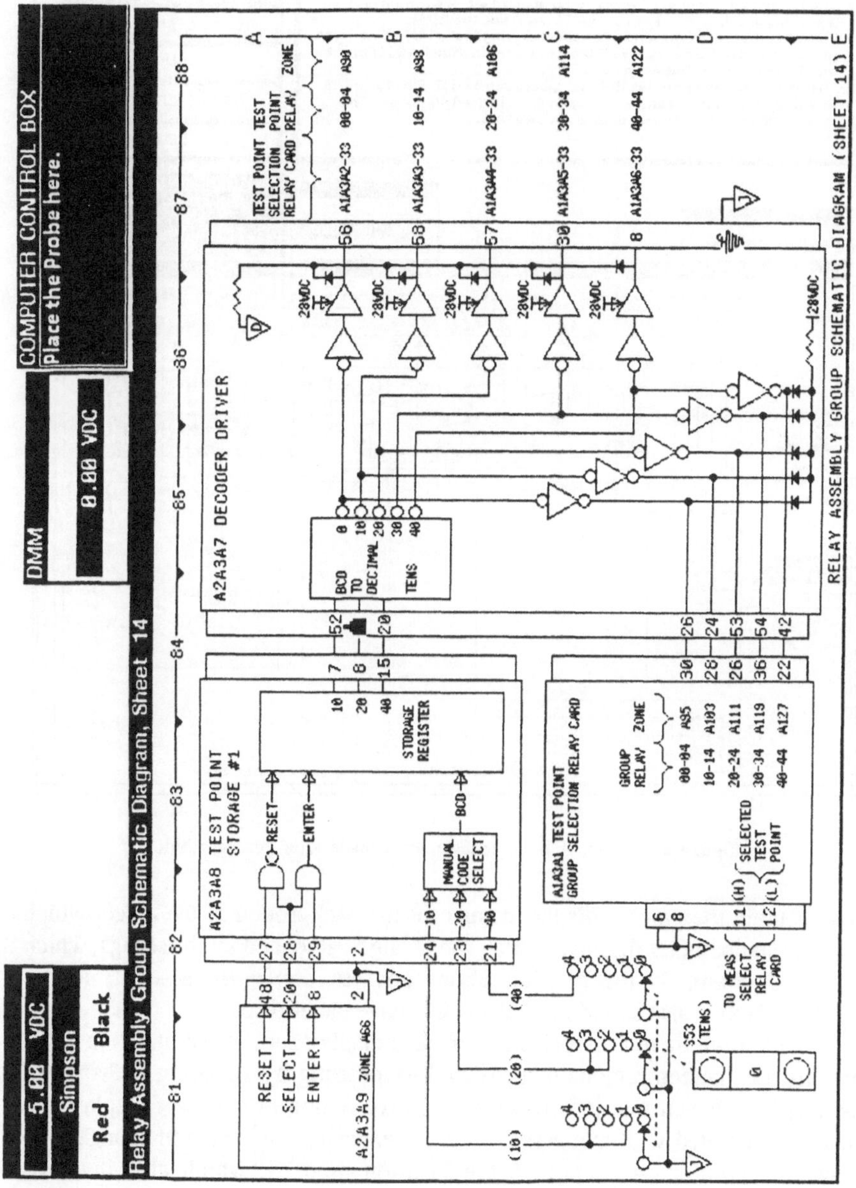

Figure 8: Making a test on a schematic.

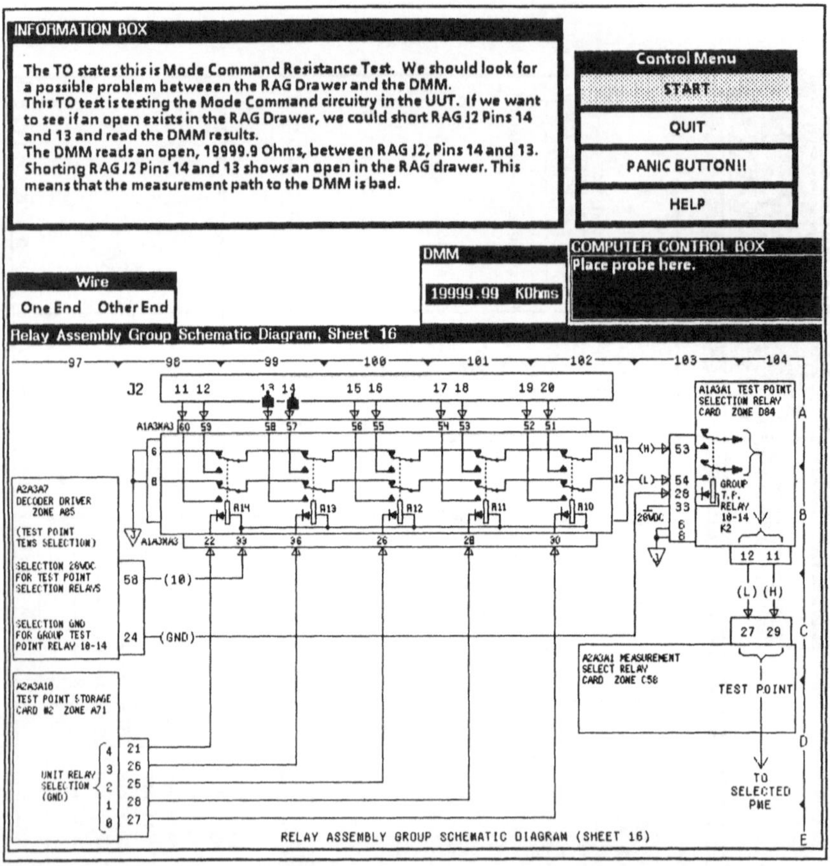

Figure 9: Screen showing measurement made after getting a hint.

slots contain the graphic display details for the background of the object which remains static; meter displays, which can change value; and knob settings, which can also change. Information about how to configure a small iconic representation is also stored for drawers that have meter displays.

In addition, there is associated with each display panel a list of active value regions, i.e., screen regions that respond to mousing by signaling a change to the display. When a trainee mouses an active region in a drawer display, the change associated with that active region is executed. A common change is to move the pointer on a knob to the location moused, which also involves propagating the new knob setting value to other display components that might be affected by it (e.g., turning the knob that sets the scale of the oscilloscope requires not only changing the knob display but also updating the oscilloscope waveform display).

Each drawer or test equipment object contains methods for carrying out certain procedures. These include methods for updating knob settings and display dials, building the original display of the drawer, and building and updating the smaller iconic display. While the overall program is quite large, each individual updating function is quite compact and manageable.

The Schematic Diagrams

Another critical part of the test station work environment representation is the set of schematic diagrams. In the real work environment, these schematics are part of the Technical Orders, a multi-volume documentation set. In our task analyses, there was some indication that finding material in the Technical Orders was difficult for some first-term airmen, so we wanted to capture the access problem in our work environment simulation. We did this by providing an indexing scheme for screen-based Technical Orders pages that corresponds closely to the indexing scheme in the printed Technical Orders.

There are two important characteristics of the Technical Orders that should be noted. First, we made paper copies of SHERLOCK's Technical Orders available to airmen while they used the system. Schematic diagrams are very detailed, and the higher resolution of the print medium makes them easier to examine in that form. The reason for also having the schematics available on the computer is that they were the means by which the airman indicated the points to which he wanted to attach meter probes to make measurements. Second, we developed our own slightly simplified Technical Orders for the tutor. We did this for logistical reasons—the complete real ones did not become available quickly enough. In retrospect, this may not have been an ideal arrangement, but the success of SHERLOCK has been demonstrated with post-training criterion tasks that used the real Technical Orders, so not much has been lost due to our simplifications.

Two kinds of indexing were involved in managing Technical Orders content in SHERLOCK. First, there was a reproduction of the index scheme found in real printed Technical Orders. In any page of this index that appeared on the screen, one could access an index entry by mousing its page number. Second, because of the complexity of the schematics and their partial redundancy,[19] it was necessary for SHERLOCK to have an index of test points. This index made it possible for airmen to determine which page(s) of schematics they should consult in order to access any given test point on any given circuit card.

---

[19]A given point in the circuitry may appear on more than one page of the schematic diagrams.

Carrying out Tests

To carry out tests, then, the airman would first indicate in the planning menu that he wanted to test a particular printed circuit board or other component (e.g., a switch). Sometimes, the desired component first had to be manipulated to make test points accessible.[20] Then, in most cases, he would need to set the controls on a hand-held multimeter, the most common piece of test equipment. The hand-held meter display is another front panel knob-and-dial simulation of the sort shown in Figure 7. After making the appropriate settings, the airman would then call up the appropriate page of schematics, the page on which he could indicate where the meter probes should be placed. The hand-held meter then appears above the schematic diagram in iconic form, as shown in Figure 8.

If the requested test has a result that SHERLOCK knows about, the appropriate information is displayed in the meter icon, as shown in Figure 8. If not, then the airman is informed that the measurement is not available. SHERLOCK is also able to note cases where the meter is set inappropriately. For example, there may be a spot where one can appropriately measure resistance but where a voltage value might be meaningless, or the meter might be set for DC+ Volts and the probes placed to produce a negative voltage reading. In this case, appropriate comments are offered by SHERLOCK, so that the airman doesn't think his decision about where to measure was wrong.

Training in Testing Strategy and Technique

In the current version, we relied on expert guidance concerning which test values SHERLOCK should know about. We provided all test values that our experts believed would be used by experts, along with a number of additional test points that the experts expected trainees to request. Some test points were intentionally omitted, in order to force the trainee to ask for help rather than succeed with an inefficient strategy. For example, it may be possible to find a gap in a lengthy circuit path by exhaustive point-to-point continuity testing starting at one end of the path and working toward the other. In order to avoid having the trainee successfully solve the problem in this way, some test values consistent with the sequential strategy but inconsistent with a space splitting strategy were omitted, making the strategy unworkable.

While this approach was generally successful, some trainees who used the tutor complained about "missing" test points (sometimes because they felt that a purely sequential testing strategy was appropriate), and indeed a small number of reasonably requested test values were not available. We now believe that the key to improving this part of SHERLOCK is to split the test value problem into two parts. First, all potentially relevant test values should be included. Second,

[20]Ordinarily circuit cards plug into the back of a drawer, making test prints inaccessible. To do most tests, an extender card must be inserted between the circuit card and the slot into which it ordinarily would be plugged.

intelligent coaching should be provided in cases where the pattern of tests shows successful but inefficient testing.

The procedure we hope to use in our next version for generating test point values will be based on the notion of a circuit path that is active in a given test station configuration. When the test station is being used to perform a given test on the unit from the aircraft, a path is switched into place involving a stimulus source, the unit, a measurement device, and the signal paths connecting them. All of the measurements between consecutive test points in that path should be provided, we now think. Further, if the switching logic is bad or the controls for it are bad, then measurements of all points in the paths controlling the point at which the primary test circuit is disrupted must also be included in the collection of known test values. Similarly, paths involving power sources for devices in the primary path must be included if implicated. This would have the effect of making the absence of a test value an indication that it was not relevant to a reasonable model of the test station as configured at the time of failure. Currently, the absence of a test value indicates that it is not relevant to an efficient diagnostic strategy.

To supply intelligent coaching for inefficient testing sequences, we will need to include an assessment of testing efficiency in a wrap-up discussion that we would like to add to SHERLOCK. An intelligent coach might consider the length of the trainee's testing sequence, compare it to the length of an expert sequence, and then comment on the difference if it is large. Similarly, a lucky guess, which now produces only positive feedback, might be labeled as such in a wrap-up commentary.

Connecting the Work Environment to the Coach

We have described two levels of function in SHERLOCK. The *effective problem space* level is a hierarchy of plans and actions down to the level of actions involving replaceable components: boards, switches, etc. Most of the hinting and virtually all of the student modeling is driven from this level. The *work environment* represents a more detailed level, the level of individual tests of small aspects of the replaceable components. At this level, coaching must be more generic or must be the result of data sent back to the effective problem space. We now turn to the manner in which the two levels are linked.

At the start of a problem, the student is following the Technical Orders, doing specific tests of the unit from the aircraft by setting controls on the test station and recording meter readings from it. He continues doing this until he finds a test value that is outside the acceptable range, after which he comes under the control of the coach. The tests are conducted using a printed set of Technical Orders which specify which switches must be set on the test station and what the appropriate test values are. Each test in the Technical Orders is represented by a specialized object that knows what settings are required on the test station, what value should be displayed on which device to indicate the outcome of the test, what button on the test station must be pushed to produce the reading, whether it is in bounds or not (i.e., whether the test is passed by the aircraft unit or not), how the student has performed on this test if he has already done it before,[21] and a few other details. The object knows how to decide whether doing the test is currently appropriate, how to let the student conduct the test, how to comment if steps are left out or an unsafe condition created, and how to provide a resultant meter reading.

When a fault is first evidenced,[22] the trainee begins interacting with a wider-ranging menu structure that permits him to express plans and take high-level actions, swap replaceable units, check that the boards are firmly in place, etc. Once he proposes to test a board or similar unit, he is permitted to call up the relevant schematic diagrams and choose a measurement device. He then comes under the control of the work environment simulation, doing tests and receiving feedback (but still having access to hints). He continues doing tests as long as he likes, eventually indicating that he is done by mousing a "Done" box on the screen.

At this point, as summarized earlier, the work environment executes a small program that updates the effective problem space structure by marking any nodes that have been ruled out by any combination of subgoals satisfied and work environment tests carried out earlier. Not only are the nodes that are ruled out marked as such, but a message concerning why they are ruled out is sent to them so that they have it available to provide later explanations. Thus, if a trainee later tries to search a ruled-out portion of the problem space, he will receive a message telling him how the proposed action has already been ruled out. Currently, this message is provided after the action is taken, just to advise that it wasn't really necessary. For example, in one of our problems, one trainee did some tests that ruled out the unit from the aircraft as the source of a fault. Later, if he had swapped a card in that unit, this would have been permitted, but he then would have received the message: "You took a voltage reading at A2A3A7 Pin 58 with respect to ground. The result of that measurement ruled out this unit."

The small programs linking the work environment to the effective problem space together constitute an *expert system.* That is, they contain only the rules experts give us, since deep reasoning at the level of individual circuit values is an intractable task for a system as complex as the test station for which our tutor is designed.

---

[21]Normally, a test is repeated after a swap, to be sure that the system has been fixed, so multiple records of student performance on a test may be recorded.

[22]The trainee actually starts in the mode of using the test station to diagnose parts from an aircraft. This part of SHERLOCK will be described below. We are concerned in the present section with what happens once a fault is evidenced.

Functionality of the Decomposition into an Effective Problem Space and a Work Environment

What does an effective problem space look like?

Figure 1 shows a graphical representation of the effective problem space for one of our problems. Each label represents a node in the structure, and the lines represent hierarchical relationships; nodes on the left subsume nodes on the right to which they are connected. That is, the nodes branching off to the right of a given node represent the wherewithal for completing the purpose of their "parent." This does not mean that every "offspring" of a node must be exercised before that "parent" is completed. Sometimes the actions and outcomes associated with a single "offspring" make it clear that a whole region of the problem space can be discounted. Also, trainees will not always carry out all components of a plan; the effective problem space is in the computer but not (yet) in the trainee's mind. Table 1 outlines what one of our typical effective problem space objects looks like.

Why have a separate effective problem space and work environment?

As one would suspect, and our data (Gitomer, 1984; Lesgold et. al., 1986) appear to confirm this, there is much more idiosyncrasy at the higher level of individual electronic tests or measurements than at the level of the replaceable components such as printed circuit cards. Thus, the design approach of building individual problems around an effective problem space but situating the activity of the trainee in the work environment, has important practical advantages. For the level of detail at which we have good understanding of expert and novice behaviors, we can work from a problem space and plan for how we will want to coach performance, attending to both global and more local details of expert problem solving within the domain. At this level, coaching can be an intelligent process. For the microscopic level at which our incomplete understanding and combinatorial complexity make this less possible, we can still provide a rich device simulation and a more symptom-driven and preprogrammed level of coaching. With this two-prong strategy, we feel that we can provide a very cost-effective approach to tutor design, including intelligent coaching where this is feasible, and can retain maximal situated detail to insure transfer to the real job environment.

Table 1:
Components of an Effective Problem Space Object

Local Node Information	
InstanceName	What this subgoal will be called in action menus and submenus.
Message	Printed in the Concept Window when the student enters the node. If this subgoal is a part of the subgoal tree that it no longer makes sense to search, this message may amount to a hint that this is the wrong place to look.
Display	Which view of the work environment should be displayed when this subgoal is entered; defaults to leaving current display in window.
Relation to Other Nodes	
Preconditions	Conditions to be met upon entry to the subgoal (for example, if this subgoal represents swapping a drawer of the test station, that drawer must be turned off before the swap can occur).
Options	List of subgoals to be included in the actions menu for this subgoal; i.e., what can come next?
Parents	Backward pointers to the goal of which the present node is a subgoal.
Children	Forward pointers, to subsubgoals.
Instructional Goals	
Curriculum-SubGoals	List of relevant curriculum issues for this subgoal. These issues are used to calculate the student performance expectation for the subgoal and therefore control the hints that the student gets.
Marker	Indicates whether the trainee completed the actions subsumed by this subgoal. Can also contain additional information about circumstances in which this subgoal is nonproductive or inappropriate, including messages for display in those circumstances.
Hints	Hints for this subgoal (prewritten hints; additional hinting is generated dynamically). In a plan subgoal, this is a simple list of hints which are presented in turn to the student. In an action subgoal, there are four categories of hints and as many as four hints for each category.
Outcome	PASS, FAIL, or for some subgoals, a list of conditions which determine outcome of measurement/test actions subsumed by this subgoal.
Hints	
NumberOfHints-Used	Keeps track of the number of hints presented while the student has been working on this subgoal (in action subgoals, counts are kept of each hint type used).
LastHintUsed	The number of the last hint used (in action subgoals, by category).

Table 1: (continued)

Student Models	
WhoCalledMe	Subgoal the trainee entered from.
WhereDidIGo	Subgoal the trainee exits to.
NodeHistory	List of student actions while pursuing this subgoal, with time stamps.
StudentPerf-Rating	Actual (as opposed to predicted) student performance rating for this subgoal.
StudentPerfExp	Expected student performance on this subgoal.
LevelInNode	Controls the category of hint given (e.g., taking measurement actions, interpreting outcomes, and deciding what to do next).
RunTOTestFlg	TRUE if the student needs to rerun the Technical Orders test (the activity of the test station that failed because the test station was broken) before completing this subgoal.
SequenceNumber	Sequence number for order of subgoals pursued by trainee.

SOME PEDAGOGICAL ISSUES

Situated learning

The ideal of "situated learning" is currently fashionable, especially in informal discussions of instructional systems by their designers. It has been noted (Rogoff & Lave, 1984; Jordan, 1987) that in simpler, more unified and coherent cultures, much of learning is socially supported by groups of people in direct contact with the parts of the environment in which the knowledge will be needed. People learn about details of agriculture by watching planting, cultivating, and other processes and helping with them. Tailors learn to make clothes in an apprenticeship. Often, children follow in their parents' footsteps, and many jobs are done at home or otherwise with children present, so one lives in the environment one will act in, watching and helping with expert actions. Learning does not seem to be a problem when all of these conditions are met.

Life in a large, pluralistic, high-technology society tends to lack all of the characteristics just listed, and there have been proposals for forms of "cognitive apprenticeship" that attempt to provide some of the support that is automatically present in more primitive societies (cf. Collins, Brown, & Newman, in press). We have tried to design SHERLOCK with these ideas in mind; so, for example, the forms of work match those on the real job. Each front panel with knobs and dials looks like the panel in the real work environment. The schematic diagrams, instructions for testing units from aircraft, and other documentation, while slightly simplified, retain many aspects of those used in the real job: the symbols in diagrams are the same, the layout of testing algorithms is the same, the indexing schemes are the same, etc.

What is not yet evident is whether this approach matters. The experiments have not yet been done to compare our approach to alternatives. There are broad alternatives, such as componential rather than holistic training. In addition, there are a number of details of realism or abstraction that might or might not be important. For example, tests might be requested via a menu or calculator keypad in which test point numbers and measurement details (volts vs. ohms, etc.) were requested. We might not require people to put the simulated test station into a safe condition via knob settings before making measurements. We might even go to diagnosis of arbitrary circuits different from those used on the job. Transfer studies will have to be conducted to fully justify our approach. For now, all we know is that, in general terms, it works very well and that airmen are able to start using SHERLOCK with minimal introduction and without having to invest much thinking capacity into figuring out how to talk to it.

Individualized coaching

A second area worthy of comment is individualization. In most individualized instruction systems, and even in the early plans for ours, what is individualized is the rate of progress through a curriculum. There is an implicit ranked listing of learning tasks, and people are passed over various of these as a function of the system's knowledge of their competence. We took a different tack. All of our trainees get the same series of problems. What differs with differing competence levels is the specificity of support (through hinting) that they receive. A fast learner will characteristically be given very general and sketchy help unless he keeps asking for more, while a slow learner, at points where he is out of his league, will almost be walked through the problem solving process.

This approach arose after one of us spent a week evaluating uses of individualized print and computer technology at schools in Israel.[23] He observed schools in which there were three different sets of reading material, but all with the same stories in them. The fast track received versions of the stories that were longer and more detailed, and the corresponding workbook assignments were also more sophisticated and demanding. At the slow end the stories were mostly gist, with simpler words and simpler workbook tasks. Nonetheless, in class discussions, the whole class could talk about the same story and its implications.

---

[23] AL was on an enquiry commission of the Rothschild Foundation and the Ministry of Education and made the observations reported while looking at a printed reading curriculum developed by the Center for Educational Technology in Ramat Aviv, to whom he is now an advisor.

We similarly thought that one way to leverage the training provided by SHERLOCK was to provide common experiences, so that discussions at the end of the day could be about problems and how they were solved rather than about who was ahead of whom. We do know that SHERLOCK generated a lot of excitement at the bases where it was tested, and we like to think (a) that excitement is important to effective learning and training; and (b) that our individualization approach contributed to that excitement. However, further analysis of the data from our field tests and possibly further experimentation will be required to confirm our views.

On deciding what works

Where we now stand is that we have a coached practice environment that produces effects of clear economic importance. However, it will take considerable study to determine which of the features of our design worked, which were exercised often enough to even have a chance of being influential, and which, while possibly important in our thinking, need further and more direct demonstration and evaluation. This is the nature of any artifice with utility. It reflects our hypotheses and provides preliminary pilot testing of the validity of those hypotheses. It is, in consequence, both more and less than the theory that motivated it.

ACKNOWLEDGEMENTS

SHERLOCK was a massive undertaking. It took a lot of work from a lot of people. It was, as a real-world applied activity in a setting with real work that could not be halted, a test not only of ingenuity and hard work but also of courage, patience, tolerance, perseverance, and the love and respect of many players for each other. Joining us in the effort at one point or another were Jaya Bajpayee, Jeffrey Bonar, Lloyd Bond, James Collins, Keith Curran, Richard Eastman, Drew Gitomer, Robert Glaser, Bruce Glymour, Linda Greenberg, Denise Lensky, Debra Logan, Maria Magone, Tom McGinnis, Valerie Shalin, Cassandra Stanley, Arlene Weiner, Richard Wolf, and Laurie Yengo. Equally important were Sherrie Gott and the many people who worked with her at the Air Force Human Resources Laboratory, Dennis Collins, and other Air Force subject matter experts who helped us when we needed it most, and the officers and personnel of the 1st and 33rd Tactical Fighter Wings, at Langley and Eglin Air Force Bases, especially those in the Component Repair Squadrons, who made room in their worlds for SHERLOCK and his many retainers.

The work was done as part of subcontracts with HumRRO and Universal Energy Systems, who were prime contractors with the Air Force Human Resources Laboratory. Many of the tools and much of the infrastructure that permitted us to efficiently conduct this project were put in place by earlier efforts and the foresight of the Office of Naval Research, where Henry Halff, Susan Chipman, Marshall Farr, and Michael Shafto patiently invested in a future that took a number of years to unfold.

REFERENCES

Anderson, J. R. (1983). *The architecture of cognition.* Cambridge, MA: Harvard University Press.

Brown, J. S., Burton, R. R., & De Kleer, J. (1982). Pedagogical, natural language and knowledge engineering techniques in SOPHIE I, II and III. In D. Sleeman & J. S. Brown (Eds.), *Intelligent tutoring systems.* London: Academic Press.

Collins, A., Brown, J. S., & Newman, S. E. (1988). Cognitive apprenticeship: Teaching the craft of reading, writing, and mathematics. In L. B. Resnick (Ed.), *Knowing and learning: Issues for a cognitive science of instruction.* Hillsdale, NJ: Lawrence Erlbaum Associates.

Gitomer, D.H. (1984). *A cognitive analysis of a complex troubleshooting task.* Unpublished doctoral dissertation, University of Pittsburgh

Jordan, B. (1987). *Modes of teaching and learning: Questions raised by the training of birth attendants.* Technical Report #004. Palo Alto, CA: Institute for Research on Learning.

Lesgold, A., Lajoie, S., Logan, D., & Eggan, G. (1990). Applying cognitive task analysis and research methods to assessment. In N. Frederiksen, R. Glaser ,A. M. Lesgold & M. Shafto (Eds.), *Diagnostic monitoring of skill and knowledge acquisition.* Hillsdale, NJ: Lawrence Erlbaum Associates, **325-350**.

Lesgold, A. M., Lajoie, S. P., et al. (April, 1986). *Cognitive task analysis to enhance technical skills training and assessment.* Technical Report. University of Pittsburgh, the Learning Research and Development Center.

Nichols, P., Pokorny, R., Jones, G., Gott, S. P., & Alley, W. E. (In press). *Evaluations of an avionics troubleshooting tutoring system.* Special report. Brooks AFB, TX: Air Force Human Resources Laboratory.

Rogoff, B., & Lave, J. (Eds.). (1984). *Everyday cognition: Its development in social context.* Cambridge, MA: Harvard University Press.

Terrace, H. S. (1964). Wavelength generalization after discrimination learning with and without errors. *Science, 144*, 78-80.

8 From PROUST to CHIRON: ITS Design as Iterative Engineering; Intermediate Results are Important!

Warren Sack and Elliot Soloway
Université de Paris 8, Département d'Informatique and University of Michigan

INTRODUCTION: MOTIVATIONS AND GOALS

For the past few years our group has worked on systems for automatic diagnosis of non-syntactic errors in novices' computer programs (Soloway, et al., 1983; Johnson, 1986; Sack, in press). Such errors (or "bugs") go beyond simple mistakes in the language syntax; they reflect deeper misunderstandings of how an algorithm works and how it should be implemented in that language. Our automatic debuggers are on-line help facilities designed to find such errors in students' programs. To be effective, an automatic program debugger must have methods allowing it to both:

- *Identify* errors in computer programs, and
- *Explain* to the student the errors it has found.

Like many other problems tackled by researchers in Artificial Intelligence (AI), the problems of bug identification and bug explanation are open ended: no parsimonious, general solutions exist for them. Our scientific aesthetic motivates us to search for economical, non-idiosyncratic solutions to the problems of bug identification and explanation, but the methods we use to find such solutions look more like those of engineering than of science. We iteratively refine our solutions by constructing working programs that incorporate our current ideas about bug identification and explanation. We submit our working systems to measures of performance, by trying them out with real students. Finally, we build a successor that we hope will measure up better than the previous debugger.

This paper is an attempt to make explicit some of the evaluative decision making that goes into the patching and redesign of our automatic debuggers. Specifically, this paper is a description of the performance tests to which we submitted the instructional debugger, PROUST, the results of those tests, and a discussion of what we believe are the design implications of the test results. We want to describe how CHIRON (our newest debugger) was born out of the ashes of the earlier PROUST.

The approach we follow has many precedents in the AI literature. R1 (McDermott, 1982) became new-XCON (Bachant and Soloway, 1989); EMYCIN (Clancey, 1982) was distilled out of MYCIN (Shortliffe, 1974) as the Truth Maintenance System (Doyle, 1977) was isolated from EL (Stallman and Sussman, 1977); GPS (Newell and Simon, 1972) begat STRIPS (Fikes and Nilsson, 1971) begat ABSTRIPS (Sacerdoti, 1974) begat NOAH, (Sacerdoti, 1975); and SOPHIE I grew into SOPHIE II and then SOPHIE III (Brown, Burton, and de Kleer, 1982). Typically, improvements included in a sequel system are responses to either anecdotal evidence that the old design needs fixing (e.g., "Spade-0 does not use information in the problem description. This severely restricts its range of planning advice and debugging assistance ... To address this difficulty, we have designed and are now implementing Spade-1, an improved environment, ..." (Miller, 1982, p.130)) or to common sense arguments that the old design is fundamentally flawed, e.g., PAM (Wilensky, 1978) was developed after SAM (Cullingford, 1978) "Since people can understand situations that they have not experienced, they must have an understanding ability beyond that obtainable from simple script or frame application." (Wilensky, 1981, p. 136). Anecdotal evidence and common sense arguments are necessary ammunition to attack a previous AI design, but we think more is needed to make substantial improvements to an Intelligent Tutoring System (ITS) like our last debugger, PROUST.

The acid test of an ITS is "Can it teach students what it is supposed to teach them?" An ITS stands or falls upon its ability to perform in the face of the day-to-day, pragmatic challenges of the classroom. Consequently, the feedback central to developing an ITS is *data* that documents its performance in instructing students.

We begin our critique of PROUST by asking, "Can PROUST teach students what it's supposed to teach them?" More specifically:

1. Does PROUST globally improve programming performance on an exam?
2. Does PROUST, as an on-line aid, help students to find and correct bugs?
3. Does correcting bugs in homework improve subsequent ability to correct bugs?

We continue by describing an investigation designed to measure PROUST's bug-finding skills, addressing the question:

4. Can PROUST perform the task it teaches? How accurate is PROUST in identifying errors in student computer programs?

In this chapter, our tests of PROUST are sandwiched between an introductory section on what PROUST is and how it works and a wrap-up section on our newest debugger CHIRON. CHIRON embodies some (as yet unevaluated) answers to questions that have appeared as a result of tests performed on PROUST. In the conclusion section we summarize the benefits we have gathered from testing PROUST.

DESCRIPTION OF PROUST

What PROUST Does

PROUST has been used by novice Pascal programmers as an on-line debugging aid. Normally, students use a text editor to create their programs and then invoke PROUST by typing a command like

```
proust <program filename> <output filename>
```

from their top-level environment (e.g., cshell in UNIX). PROUST analyzes the student program, and then it writes into an output file specified by the student a description of the errors found. The student then returns to the text editor to make changes in the program and is able to invoke PROUST again.

> Write a Pascal program that will prompt the user to input numbers from the terminal. Each input stands for the amount of rainfall in New Haven for a day. Note: since rainfall cannot be negative, the program should reject negative input. Your program should compute the following statistics from this data:
>
> 1. the average rainfall per day
> 2. the number of rainy days
> 3. the number of valid inputs (excluding any invalid data that might have been read in)
> 4. the maximum amount of rain that fell on any one day.
>
> The program should read until the user types 99999. This is a sentinel value signaling the end of the input. Do not include the 99999 in the calculations. Assume that if the input value is non-negative and not equal to 99999, then it is valid input data.

Figure 1: The Rainfall Problem.

PROUST first checks the student program for syntax errors. If it finds any, PROUST simply informs the student that there *are* syntax errors and terminates its analysis, leaving the student to correct errors of this kind. Only when the syntax is correct does PROUST begin its main analysis. Currently, PROUST analyzes programs written to solve two programming assignments, including the Rainfall Problem shown in Figure 1. All data examined in this paper come from this problem.

The Rainfall Problem requires students to generate a moderately complex program of between 30 and 50 lines. Mental execution of a program for this problem is not trivial, nor are the data flow relations. The student must also remember a myriad of small details (such as whether a test should use the predicate <and> or the predicate <or>).

This description of PROUST's performance is organized around a sample buggy program segment (Figure 2) written for the Rainfall Problem, PROUST's resulting bug report (Figure 3), and code correcting these bugs (Figure 4).

This buggy program segment in Figure 2 follows a segment in which a user's input is accepted and VALIDDAYS, TOTALRAINFALL, and MAXIMUM are computed. The following three bugs occur in the program segment:

```
.....
AVERAGE   := TOTALRAINFALL/VALIDDAYS;
     (*Missing Divide-By-Zero Guard*)
Writeln ('Average = ', AVERAGE) ;
     (*Missing Output Guard on Average*)
Writeln ( 'Maximum = ', MAXIMUM) ;
     (*Missing Output Guard on Maximum*)
.....
```

Figure 2: Sample buggy program segment.

Missing Divide-By-Zero Guard: If the user inputs no valid days, the average (which is the total amount of rain that fell divided by the number of valid days input) should not be computed because the computation will result in a divide-by-zero error.

Missing Output Guard on Average: Similarly, if the average is not calculated it should not be output.

Missing Output Guard on Maximum: If the user entered zero valid days, no maximum amount of rainfall that fell on some given day can be computed. Therefore, the maximum should not be output.

After identifying the three bugs shown in Figure 2, PROUST outputs the bug report shown in Figure 3.

```
Starting bug analysis, please wait

NOW BEGINNING BUG REPORT

>>> Now Reporting CRITICAL Bugs in the OUTPUT part
of your program

BUG 1:  You need a test to check that at least one
valid data point has been input before line 2 is
executed.  The average will bomb when there is no
input.

>>> Now Reporting MINOR Bugs in the OUTPUT part of
your program

BUG 2:  The average is undefined if there is no
input.  But line 3 outputs it anyway.  You should
output the average only when there is something to
compute the average of.

Bug 3:  The maximum is undefined if there is not
input.  But line 4 outputs it anyway.  You should
output the maximum only when there is something to
compute the maximum of.

BUG REPORT NOW COMPLETE
```

Figure 3: PROUST bug report.

```
. . .
    If (VALIDDAYS > 0)
        Then Begin
            AVERAGE := TOTALRAINFALL/VALIDDAYS;
            Writeln('Average = ', AVERAGE);
            Writeln('Maximum = ', MAXIMUM);
        End;
 . . .
```

Figure 4: Program segment correcting the bugs identified in PROUST's report.

All three of these bugs can be fixed with one correction: surrounding the three lines in the original program segment with one appropriate guard (see Figure 4). Nevertheless, PROUST reports them as three errors. The reasons are first that PROUST finds each of them separately: Bug 1 is found when PROUST is checking to see how the average is computed, Bug 2 is found when

PROUST is checking to see how the average is output, and Bug 3 is found when PROUST is checking to see how the maximum is output. Second, PROUST does not correct bugs for students. Rather, it is up to the student to figure out that all three bugs can be eliminated with one guard.

As we shall see, interactions with PROUST like that shown in Figure 3 do help students to find bugs, and to become more effective debuggers. However, the nature of the interaction is almost certainly not optimal, and we will suggest ways in which it might be improved.

How PROUST Works

PROUST's internal libraries contain four kinds of information, illustrated in Figures 5-9. *Problem specifications* (Figure 5) describe the objects in the problem and the goals that constitute a problem solution. *Goals* (Figure 6) reflect standardized parts of program code. *Plans* (Figure 7) are stereotypical methods for realizing typical programming goals. Several alternate plans may provide alternate means of implementing a single goal.

Plan-difference rules relate PROUST's plans to possible plan variants in students' code. These rules (a type of production rule) have a test pattern that is matched against the student's code and an action that transforms the student's code into a plan in PROUST's library. Plan-difference rules include *transformation rules* (Figure 8) which match correct plan variants and *bug rules* (Figure 9) which match incorrect plan variants.

In all of these figures, PROUST's code is in normal type, with explanatory comments in italics.

PROUST uses the following steps to identify bugs in a student's program.

1. PROUST is given a problem specification and the name of the file containing a student's Pascal program. After PROUST has scanned the problem specification to determine which goals should be implemented in the student program, it selects an initial goal set to consider and gives it to the interpretation manager.
2. The interpretation manager accepts the initial goal set, orders them, and puts them onto the goal agenda. The first goal on the agenda is selected, and PROUST fetches all plans that implement this goal. This list of plans is given to the plan matcher.
3. The plan matcher tries to match plans on the list against the code in the student program stopping with a successful match. A plan usually contains many segments, and is matched segment-by-segment. Plans also can contain sub-goals. If the plan matcher encounters a plan with subgoal, it adds the subgoals of the plan to the goal agenda and works on matching the subgoals before returning to work on the plan that spawned the subgoals. If a segment of a plan cannot be matched then

that plan match is suspended. If the current plan is suspended, PROUST tries to match the next plan on the list for the current goal, until a successful match is found. If one or more plans are matched successfully, then processing proceeds with step 5. Otherwise all of the suspended plans are processed by the plan difference rules. A suspended plan can be reactivated if the unmatched segment can be matched using plan difference rules.

4. Plan difference rules seek to identify the student code as a variant (correct or buggy) of a plan that PROUST knows. If the plan difference rules are able to explain all of the current match errors for a given plan, then that plan is sent back to the plan matcher.

Rainfall is the problem. The resulting program must process a sequence of inputs, DailyRain, that are of the ObjectClass ScalarMeasurement.

```
DefObject ?Rainfall:DailyRain ObjectClass
ScalarMeasurement
```

Input a sequence of values and terminate when the sentinel value 99999 is read in.

```
DefGoal Sentinel-Controlled Input Sequence
(?Rainfall:DailyRain, 99999)
```

Make sure that none of the values read in are less than zero.

```
DefGoal Loop Input Validation
(?Rainfall:DailyRain, ?Rainfall:DailyRain<0 )
```

Calculate the average of the values read in, and output the computed average.

```
DefGoal Output ( Average (?Rainfall:DailyRain) )
```

Count the number of values read in, and output the count.

```
DefGoal Output ( Count (?Rainfall:DailyRain) )
```

Count the number of values read in that were greater than zero, and output the count.

```
DefGoal Output ( Guarded Count
(?Rainfall:DailyRain, ?Rainfall:DailyRain>0) )
```

Find the maximum value read in, and output the maximum.

```
DefGoal Output ( Maximum (?Rainfall:DailyRain) )
```

Figure 5: **PROUST** problem specification.

A count goal has two main parameters: the sequence of values being counted, and the variable that holds the current value of the count.

```
Form: Count ( ?New, ?Count)
```

The variable that holds the current value of the sequence being counted is referred to as ?New.

```
SequenceVariable: ?New
```

The variable that holds the current value of the count is referred to as ?Count.

```
ResultVariable: ?Count
```

The central part of a counter plan is its Update: segment.

```
MainSegment: Update:
```

A count goal should be called a "counter" when generating comments to be read by students.

```
NamePhrase: counter
```

A count goal can be fulfilled with either of two plans:

(1) a Counter Plan, which initializes ?Count, and then updates it every time the next value of ?New is encountered, or

(2) a Split Counter Plan, which separates the values to be counted into two or more sets (e.g. values greater than zero and values less than or equal to zero), counts the sets separately, and then adds the results together to get the final value of ?Count.

```
Instances: Counter Plan
           SplitCounter Plan
```

Figure 6: A PROUST goal.

One variable is used in the counter plan; it is called ?Count.

```
Variables: ?Count
```

A counter plan's template has two parts to it:

(1) the initialization sets the value of ?Count to zero, and

(2) the update increments the value of ?Count by 1 every time the next value is encountered of the sequence of values being counted.

```
Template:
Init: ?Count := 0
Update: ?Count := (?Count + 1)
```

Figure 7: A PROUST plan.

IF a statement in a plan must always be executed
THEN
  IF the student has used a series of guard statements
  (e.g. IF statements and CASE statements)
  AND
  the body of at least one of the guard statements will
  always be executed
  THEN the statement can be replicated and embedded in
  each of the guard statements
  ELSE a single copy of the statement, outside of all of the
  guard statements, can be used for the plan.

Figure 8: A PROUST transformation rule.

5. If a plan is matched successfully to the student code, i.e., if all of the segments of a plan have been matched (with or without the aid of plan difference rules), then PROUST stores it (along with the goal it implements) in the current interpretation for the student program. If more than one plan matched successfully, the interpretation manager applies some heuristics to select which one is the best plan. If the current plan is not a successful match, PROUST tries to match the next plan on the list for the current goal, until a successful match is found.

IF the goal is Guard Exception
  AND
  the statement is a While statement
    OR
    an If statement
    OR
    a Case Statement
  AND
  the test is >= instead of >
    OR
    <= instead of <
    OR
    < instead of <=
    OR
    <= instead of <
THEN the mismatch is due to a Sloppy Guard bug

Figure 9: A PROUST bug rule.

6. The next goal is then selected by the interpretation manager. PROUST works to successfully match a plan for this goal.
7. At the end of an analysis, the interpretation assessor assigns one of the following confidence ratings:
   - In a *full* interpretation every piece of student code matches a programming plan.
   - In a *partial* interpretation some of the code matches PROUST's plans. PROUST outputs comments on each line of code it did not understand.
   - In an *incomplete* interpretation, most of the student code does not match PROUST's programming plans, and there is no coherent analysis of what the student is trying to do.
8. The bug reporter generates a bug report based on the interpretation and the confidence rating.

Implementation

PROUST is 15,000 lines in length and is written in T, Yale's dialect of LISP. It takes about 0.5 - 1.0 minute to execute and runs on a DEC VAX 11/750 with 4 megabytes of memory. PROUST's knowledge base contains about 37 goals, 55 plans, and 70 bug rules.

CAN PROUST TEACH WHAT IT'S SUPPOSED TO TEACH?

Having described the workings of PROUST, we turn now to the central purpose of this paper—to examine PROUST's performance and what we can learn from it.

We examined performance (students' and PROUST's) on the three bugs shown in Figure 2. These bugs have the following desirable properties for answering our questions:

High-Frequency: we needed to find bugs that were made by a sufficiently large number of students to allow us to carry out statistical tests. Moreover, we wanted bugs that were seen both in the homework assignments and on the midterm. These constraints significantly limited the bugs that we could use in our analyses: the three bugs in Figure 2 are essentially the only ones that met these constraints. Of the 80 students in the study, 60 (75%) of them made one or more of these three Missing Guard bugs.

Representativeness: The Missing Divide-By-Zero Guard is what we call a *common* bug. No programming knowledge is required to avoid or find this bug because underlying knowledge comes from basic algebra: a divisor must never be zero. In contrast Missing Output Guard on Average and Missing Output Guard on Maximum are what we call *idiosyncratic* bugs because finding and correcting them requires knowledge specific to programming: it is a generally accepted programming convention that variables are only output if they hold meaningful information. In the Rainfall problem, the variables `VALIDDAYS` and `MAXIMUM` hold meaningful information only if there has been some user input of valid rainfall values. The Missing Output Guards protect against outputting these variables unless they actually contain meaningful information.

We do not claim that the distinction between *common* and *idiosyncratic* bugs constitutes any great leap forward in student modelling; nevertheless, it is a common-sense, knowledge-based, student-oriented distinction that we, at the time, felt would enhance our understanding of the data. Since the data analyses for this paper were performed, members of our group have made much progress in the areas of student errors and student modelling in the programming domain (Spohrer, 1989), and bug explanation and tutorial dialog in the programming domain (Littman, in preparation).

With respect to these bugs, we examined PROUST's educational effectiveness by asking (a) whether PROUST globally improves programming performance on an exam, (b) whether PROUST helps students to find and correct bugs, and (c) whether correcting bugs in homework improves subsequent ability to correct bugs. The following sections describe experiments addressing these questions.

Does PROUST globally improve programming performance on an exam?

To address this question, we designed a midterm exam, which was taken about one week after the Rainfall homework problem, and which required students to identify and repair bugs in three programs.

Student Groups

In the spring of 1985 at Yale University, the following two sections of the introductory Pascal programming course intended for humanities students were created by random assignment:

ACCESS Group (39 students): As they were developing their solution to the Rainfall Problem (Figure 1), students in this section had access to PROUST, and thus could run PROUST and receive PROUST's analysis of the programs they wrote for their homework assignments. They used PROUST on the Rainfall problem only.

NO ACCESS Group (41 students): Students in this section did not have access to PROUST.

The two sections met at different times, but they both had the same instructor, received the same instruction, used the same textbooks, took the same examinations, and did the same homework assignments.

Results and Discussion

On the midterm examination, the mean score of the ACCESS Group was higher than that of the NO ACCESS Group. Controlling for SAT scores in the two groups, an analysis of covariance showed that 16% (Baker, private communication) of that difference was accountable for by PROUST. Though this performance difference did not quite attain conventional levels of statistical significance, a single exposure to PROUST had an observable effect on students' programming skills tested one week later in a different setting.

In analyzing the effect of an instructional innovation like PROUST, one would like to take into account all of the possible variables that might influence the result. Pragmatically, it is impossible to enumerate, much less gather information about all of the variables that might effect the overall result. (Background education in mathematics and computers seem relevant, but so do "small" details like the percentage of the hours of classroom lecture that a given student attended prior to working on the Rainfall Problem.)

In our analysis, we only took into account the SAT scores of the two groups. However, the SAT scores played a large role in measuring the effects of PROUST: without taking SAT scores into account the ACCESS group did *much* better than the NO ACCESS group. This observation indicates the crucial importance of considering the setting in which an instructional tool is used. We could have made PROUST look considerably better had we omitted this consideration.

If our purpose were simply to give a global evaluation of PROUST's educational benefits, we could stop here. The answer to "Can PROUST teach debugging?" seems to be "yes," (if not a statistically resounding YES!!) under demanding conditions (one week delay, different problems, and limited exposure to PROUST), and with serious attention to differences in student abilities (SAT scores).

The following sections explore the nature of learning with PROUST.

Does PROUST help students find and correct bugs?

Does PROUST, as an on-line aid, help students identify and repair bugs? To answer this question, we collected copies of each syntactically correct version of a student's program, along with the output provided by PROUST for those in the ACCESS Group.

Student Groups

GOOD ADVICE group: This group is a subset of students with access to PROUST identified as follows. We examined the programs collected, together with any output given from PROUST. For each of the three bugs we identified a group of students who (a) introduced the bug into their programs, and (b) turned on PROUST and got correct advice at least once.

NO ADVICE group: These are the students in the section without access to PROUST.

Because the GOOD ADVICE group is a non-random subset of the ACCESS group, we checked the comparability of the GOOD- and NO-ADVICE groups with respect to SAT scores and quality of the homework programs as ranked on a 3-point scale by two expert programming tutors. The experts achieved an 85.4% agreement rate on all programs. There were no significant differences on either measure.

For each of these groups, we categorized in the following way what the student did about each missing-guard bug appearing in their program:

FIX: The bug was correctly fixed in the last version of the program.

NO FIX: The bug still appeared in the last version of the program.

Results

Figure 10 shows that students with good advice from PROUST were more likely to fix the two output guard bugs (see Figure 2) than were students with no advice from PROUST. But there was no such difference for the Divide-by-zero bug.

		Bug (Guard Omitted)					
		Divide-by-zero		Output, average		Output, maximum	
	Bug Fixed?	Yes	No	Yes	No	Yes	No
Advice:	Good	6	5	9	9	7	11
	None	7	10	5	25	4	29
		($p<0.24$)		($p<0.05$)		($p<0.01$)	

Figure 10: For each bug, the number of students with good or no advice who ultimately fixed, or did not fix, the bug in the Rainfall homework problem. (Statistical significance was calculated by Fisher's exact p test.)

The differential effectiveness across bugs corresponds to our distinction between bugs correctable by common knowledge (missing divide-by-zero guard), and bugs requiring programming knowledge (the missing-output guards). Novice programmers are not familiar with programming conventions. Consequently, they can't identify bugs based on such knowledge until they are explicitly told the relevant information, here that a variable should not be output unless it holds meaningful information. PROUST can explicitly point out this programming convention to students as it does in Figure 3.

Discussion

The results of this analysis are not clear cut recommendations for modifying PROUST, nor do they make transparent the cognitive activities of the students. Nevertheless, these results do cast some light on students' and PROUST's (in)abilities to provide students with on-line debugging help. The fact that PROUST was not very useful to students in helping them fix *common* bugs could be interpreted in at least three different ways.

With respect to PROUST's construction: PROUST's knowledge about domains other than programming is shallow. Perhaps PROUST's common-knowledge should be increased to allow PROUST to better explain *common* bugs to students.

With respect to students' cognitive make-up: On the other hand, perhaps, filling out PROUST's common knowledge wouldn't improve PROUST's performance in explaining common bugs to students. Perhaps, since knowledge like "*The number 0 should never be used as a divisor*" is so ubiquitous, students may tend to ignore simple repetitions of this information. If this is the case, then PROUST's advice with respect to common bugs would only be useful if PROUST were able to state its advice in a novel manner.

With respect to PROUST's communication ability: PROUST might produce better results for common bugs if it more directly stated the relevant common knowledge. PROUST's bug report in Figure 3 does not, for example, explicitly state that the number 0 should never be used as a divisor.

Does correcting bugs in homework improve subsequent ability to correct bugs?

As part of their midterm examination students were asked to identify and repair the bugs in programs. Points were awarded separately for identification and repair. One of the buggy programs was structurally identical to the Rainfall Problem. Specifically, the Rainfall Problem required the processing (average, maximum, etc.) of integers that represented inches of rainfall per day, and the midterm exam program required the processing of integers that represented insurance claims. This program was seeded with the three missing-guard bugs shown in Figure 2. Thus, we were able to compare how well students did at fixing bugs in their own programs with how well students did at fixing the same bugs in the program on the midterm.

Student Groups

The students included in this analysis had made all three MISSING GUARD bugs in their own Rainfall programs. The students classified as FIX ALL were those who fixed all three of the MISSING GUARD bugs in their own Rainfall programs. The remaining students were classified as NOT FIX ALL. We found no significant differences between the two groups with respect to their mean SAT scores.

Here we drop distinctions between the nature of PROUST advice (accurate and inaccurate). Maintaining this distinction along with the FIX ALL/NOT FIX ALL distinction would have made our sample sizes too small for reasonable analyses. Because of this grouping, the following results indicate the effect of successful bug-fixing experience on later ability to identify and repair similar bugs, but they do not directly indicate effects of PROUST.

Results

On the midterm, there were six possible points awarded for correctly *identifying* all three MISSING GUARD bugs and four awarded for correctly *repairing* them. Figure 11 summarizes the performance of the two student groups. Although t-test comparison of the identification scores for the FIX ALL and NOT FIX ALL student groups did not quite attain the conventional 0.05 level of significance for identification, there is an indication that those students who fix all three bugs are superior at bug identification. As shown in Figure 11, those students who made and fixed all three bugs in their own programs did score significantly higher on bug repair on the midterm than those who did not fix all bugs.

Midterm:		IDENTIFY		REPAIR	
	N	mean	SD	mean	SD
Homework:					
NOT FIX ALL	26	2.8	2.9	1.3	1.8
FIX ALL	8	4.5	2.8	3.0	1.8
		t=1.4 (0.05<p<0.10)		t=22 (p<0.025)	

Figure 11: Mean number of points awarded for identification and repair of MISSING GUARD bugs on the midterm exam for students who did and did not fix all bugs on their homework. (p values are for one-tailed t tests.)

Discussion

In sum, students in the FIX ALL group are better able both to *identify* and to *repair* the missing-guard bugs on the midterm. On the one hand these results are not counter intuitive: one would expect that those who do their homework will score better on tests. On the other hand, however, what is interesting and rather non-intuitive about these findings is their particularity. We have pinpointed exactly what homework (fixing all three missing-guard bugs) correlates with a better score on a specific part of a midterm exam (the part that contains the missing-guard bugs). This micro analysis allows us to identify specific bugs where PROUST's identification assistance is most helpful.

Summary of PROUST's Educational Effectiveness

Students who had access to PROUST's bug identification reports while doing programming assignments performed better on a midterm examination specifically designed to exercise bug identification and repair skills. This macro effect is all the more impressive because the improvement in midterm performance is due entirely to using PROUST on a single homework assignment.

Students who had the benefit of accurate bug reports from PROUST were significantly better at fixing bugs on their programming assignments than students who did not have such reports.

Students who succeeded in fixing particular bugs on their programming assignments (with or without accurate advice from PROUST) were significantly better at repairing similar bugs on the midterm examination. Thus debugging help such as that provided by PROUST could *potentially* produce improved debugging ability.

CAN PROUST PERFORM THE TASK IT TEACHES?

How accurate is PROUST in identifying bugs in computer programs?

Program debugging is still more of an art than a science. Our purpose in building automatic debuggers has been in the interest of helping and instructing students in the process of debugging. However, by building automatic debuggers we have also had to carefully define what we think the process and skills of debugging are *irrespective* of how debugging can be taught to students. PROUST's debugging knowledge and skills are its domain intelligence, what Anderson (1988) calls "...the backbone of any ITS." The importance of this domain intelligence, the skills and knowledge of debugging, and its current status as an art make it a research area unto itself.

In this section we make explicit some of the strengths and weaknesses of the model of debugging embodied in PROUST. We hope that this analysis will uncover some of the knowledge and processes that must be coded into any effective automatic program debugger. And, we hope that this analysis of PROUST's debugging skills will give us better insight into what skills novice programmers must be taught in order to be able to debug programs.

Experimental Design and Description of the Data

To quantify PROUST's debugging behavior we tested PROUST using Rainfall programs written by 39 students in an introductory programming course offered at Yale in the spring of 1985. This programming course is offered every year at Yale. Student programs from this course in 1982 and 1983 were used as training data during PROUST's construction. Johnson (1986) tested PROUST's accuracy on student programs written for this course in 1984.

As test data, we used the first syntactically correct program version written by each student. These first versions usually contain more bugs than do subsequent versions and, so, are a more rigorous test of PROUST's diagnostic power. The student programs were collected by modifying the operating system so that every version of a program saved by the student is copied and saved into a permanent file. We also counted the number of versions of the program each student saved and counted the number of bugs in both the first syntactically correct version and the last version saved by the student (i.e., the version that the student handed in for a grade). None of these 39 programs were seen by the author of PROUST (Johnson, 1986).

Four expert graders independently identified the bugs in the student programs. They met to discuss their independent results, work out disagreements, and finally agree upon one set of results. The bugs listed in Figure 12 and discussed below were identified by this procedure.

Number of Programs	Bug Type
30	missing guard on average output
28	missing guard on maximum output
21	missing guard on average calculation
13	malformed loop termination test
12	missing re-input inside of loop
12	missing guard after rainfall is re-input
6	missing maximum initialization
6	missing maximum output
5	malformed average calculation
5	missing rainfall input initialization
5	missing maximum update
4	missing rainy day initialization
4	missing rainy day update
4	missing total rainfall initialization
4	missing day count initialization
3	average declared integer
3	"DIV" used in average calculation instead of "/"
3	malformed total rainfall update statement
3	missing day count output
3	spurious average initialization
3	spurious guard on day count update
3	spurious initialization
1-2	(38 other bugs)

Figure 12: Most common bug types and number of programs in which each was found.

The diversity of these data on which we tested PROUST is considerable. PROUST's average run time to diagnose bugs in the first program versions ranged between 10 and 60 seconds, with a mean of 33.3 sec. The number of bugs in students' first programs ranged from 1 to 14, with a mean of 6.1 and from 0 to 9 with a mean of 2.8 in the final version. The students' persistence in pursuing the assignment to completion also varied widely, from 1 to 29 versions written with a mean of 7.9. We also counted the number of versions of the program each student saved and counted the number of bugs in both the first syntactically correct version and the last version saved by the student (i.e., the version that the student handed in for a grade). There were 67 unique bug types and 236 instances of bug occurrence. Figure 12 shows in how many initial programs each of the 67 unique bug types appeared. A few bug types accounted for the vast majority of the bug instances. The five most common bugs account for 116, or about half of the bug occurrences. Thirty four bug types appear in just one program.

PROUST's Accuracy in Identifying Bugs

To evaluate PROUST's ability to identify bugs in students' programs we compared PROUST's bug diagnoses with those of expert human coders. Out of the 236 bug instances found by human coders in 39 programs, PROUST found 100 (42.3%), missed the remaining 136 (57.7%), and produced 38 false-alarm bugs (i.e., inaccurately identified correct code as buggy code.).

42.3% seems like a surprisingly low rate for recognizing bugs, especially since we know that PROUST is able to improve students' debugging. In the following sections we provide some micro-analyses of this result in order to better understand what this 42.3% accuracy rate means.

When is PROUST inaccurate?

We explained previously how, after completing an interpretation of a student program, PROUST rates its interpretation according to how confident it is of the interpretation's validity. A *full* interpretation occurs when PROUST is able to match every piece of code to a programming plan. A *partial* interpretation occurs when PROUST is only able to match some of the code to plans. PROUST's output after a partial interpretation consists of a set of comments about the code it did understand plus a listing of the lines of code it did not understand. PROUST labels an interpretation *incomplete* when it hasn't matched enough of the code to produce a coherent analysis of what the student is trying to do.

Figure 13 shows, for each level of interpretation, the number of bugs found by PROUST and the human coders, the number found by the human coders and missed by PROUST, and the number of false bugs PROUST "found," which were not judged bugs by the human coders.

	Bugs Identified: True Bugs	Bugs Identified: False Bugs	Bugs Missed:
Interpretation:			
Full (16 programs)	69	13	12
Partial (14 programs)	31	24	55
Incomplete (9 programs)	0		69
Found by Human Coders:	100	38	136

Figure 13: Bugs identified and missed by PROUST and by human coders.

These results show that PROUST is usually correct when it thinks that it is correct (i.e., when PROUST rates its interpretation *full*). This micro-analysis points out a feature of PROUST that should be incorporated into our next debugger: the debugger should rate its confidence in an interpretation so that students can accept the debugger's advice with a grain of salt if the debugger is less than certain about its interpretation of a given student's program.

Could tweaking PROUST make it a lot more accurate?

We noticed a few cases in which very minor glitches with PROUST resulted in exceedingly poor performance. Consequently, we were attracted by the idea that perhaps, in principle, PROUST was very accurate at correctly identifying bugs in student programs. Perhaps, if PROUST could be tweaked a little it would show its true colors. We discovered this hypothesis to have some truth to it, reanalyzing the same data as used above.

We made four minor revisions to PROUST. These revisions resulted in improved accuracy performance by PROUST in 12 of the 39 student programs. To give the reader an idea of just how minor these revisions were we will explain one in detail. The specific revision we will discuss accounted for all of PROUST's increased performance in 4 of these 12 student programs.

PROUST's difficulty with these four programs came from its inability to recognize the stopping value in the main loop of the program (a solution to the Rainfall Problem should stop asking for new data after the user has entered the sentinel value 99999). Only one very weak bug rule was in PROUST's bug library to cover cases in which students used the wrong sentinel value as the stop condition for the main loop. Specifically, the bug rule that PROUST had would check to see if the sentinel value used was 9999 if PROUST couldn't find exactly the expected value. In the four programs PROUST had problems with, the students had used 999999 as the sentinel value. To fix PROUST we simply beefed-up the bug rule so that it could handle 9, 99, 999, 9999, 999999,

9999999, etc. This allowed PROUST to identify the 999999s as buggy sentinel values.

After this and other similarly small fixes, we re-ran PROUST on the same data. The result was almost a 20% increase in PROUST's accuracy: after tweaking, PROUST was able to correctly identify 61.4% of the bugs in students' programs. Figure 14 shows the bug counts for the initial and and tweaked versions of PROUST for our data and for that of Johnson (1985).

Although tweaking did not make PROUST perfect, it did dramatically improve its accuracy rating. It is difficult to interpret the implications of this result. One would hope that, with increased usage, small glitches (like the one described above) would get worked out and that tweaking would become unnecessary. However, this result does highlight the fact that PROUST's bug rules can be fragile and idiosyncratic. We have discovered a way of dispensing with bug rules that is summarized later in this chapter when we describe CHIRON.

Figure 14 also contains the results Johnson obtained for PROUST before and after his tweaking. Again, we see that Johnson's small revisions (different from ours, but also small) resulted in a dramatic improvement in PROUST's bug identification abilities: from 52% before tweaking to 77% after tweaking.

Data source:	Sack & Soloway		Johnson	
Proust Version:	Initial	Tweaked	Initial	Tweaked
Bugs Identified:				
True bugs	100	146	196	289
False bugs	38	59	25	35
Bugs Missed:	136	91	182	89
Bugs found by Human Coders:	236		378	

Figure 14: Bugs identified and missed by the initial and tweaked PROUST in two studies.

The likely source of difference between our accuracy figures and those of Johnson seems to be the following: Both our group and Johnson (1985, p.230) noticed that it is difficult for an isolated individual to find all of the bugs in student programs. Several people working together will usually be able to identify all of the bugs. Consequently, an accuracy rating based upon a single person's bug count will be more optimistic than an accuracy rating based upon a group's bug count, simply because a single person's bug count will document fewer bugs for PROUST to find. We had four expert graders to identify bugs in the student programs, while Johnson worked alone. We found 6.1 bugs/program, while Johnson found about 5.0. If his programs were actually equally buggy, he should have found around 465 errors instead of 378. Using this total, tweaked PROUST found 42%, of the bugs, and tweaked PROUST 62%, results essentially identical with ours.

How can PROUST's knowledge-base be improved in order to improve its bug identification accuracy?

The weakness with both of the preceding analyses is that, even though both of them provide us with a more detailed understanding of PROUST's bug identification abilities, neither provides suggestions for making PROUST better at the task of finding bugs. To get at this issue we try to identify specific inabilities of PROUST that hinder it in its task of finding bugs. Specifically, in this micro-analysis we will show one way in which PROUST's knowledge base could be improved.

PROUST's Lexical Inabilities

Lexical cues in programs (i.e., the meaning of variable names and output messages) can provide people who read a program with a lot of information about the program author's intentions. For example, consider a statement to use the current day's rainfall, RAIN, to update the value, MAX, of the maximum amount of rainfall that fell on any given day. As a first attempt, we have seen students write

```
MAX := RAIN
```

instead of

```
If (RAIN > MAX) Then MAX := RAIN
```

PROUST's knowledge-base does not contain any lexical information in it; consequently, to PROUST, the assignment

```
MAX := RAIN
```

looks like

```
X7 := Z12
```

where `X7` and `Z12` might be any meaningless symbols. Our panel of four expert graders looked through the bugs that PROUST had been unable to identify and found that 38 (16%) of the student bugs missed by PROUST and 12 (32%) of its false alarms could have been avoided through use of lexical information.

Of course, these estimates are only guesses about what PROUST might have been able to do had it known more. But, we believe the observation that an automatic program debugger should be able to utilize lexical knowledge is a good observation. In order to test how feasible it would be to provide an automatic debugger with a useful amount of lexical knowledge, we examined our 39 student programs more carefully. In particular, we wanted to know if a simple mechanism (like pattern matching on commonly occurring variable names) would suffice to improve PROUST's performance. We went through the student programs to determine two properties of the variable names:

- *Variability*: We wanted to know how many different name instances were associated with each of variables in the Rainfall Problem, and how frequently students used the same name instance.
- *Discriminability:* We wanted to know how often a name chosen by one student to denote a particular variable was used by other students to denote different variables. We used two criteria: 100% (a name used by no other student) and 80% (a name not used by more than 20% of students) to mean something *other* than its central meaning.

Results

What we found (Figure 15) was rather surprising. First, students use a limited range of variable names in the Rainfall Problem, and many students use the same names. Second, if a name is used for one variable, then it is rarely used (by any student) for a different variable. In other words, an automatic debugger equipped with a simple matcher and short lists of the variable names usually associated with particular Rainfall Problem variables, could, in principle, take advantage of the lexical cues contained in variable names.

	Number of Students Using:				
	Most common name		One of most common two names		Number of names used
Discriminability:	100%	80%	100%	80%	
Variables:					
Total Rainfall	12	16	24	28	12
Average	16	16	24	24	9
Day Count	16	16	20	20	19
Maximum	8	8	16	20	14
Rainfall Input	8	8	12	16	15
Rainy Day Count	4	4	8	8	23

Figure 15: Variable names used in student programs.

Discussion and Extensions

Our analysis of PROUST's lexical inabilities is the clearest illustration we have of PROUST's knowledge deficiencies. We performed other analyses of this sort. For example, our panel of 4 expert graders found that 71 (30%) of the bugs missed by PROUST and 16 (42%) of the false alarms could have been avoided had PROUST been able to perform data and control flow analyses of the sort commonly used in many optimizing compilers (Aho, Sethi, Ullman, 1986)[1].

[1]The results of a *control flow* analysis shows the order in which statements will be executed in a program. *Data flow* analyses allow one to determine which READLN or

However, these other micro-analyses did not suggest simple additions to PROUST like the simple pattern matching suggested by the lexical micro-analysis. Even though adding a component to PROUST to perform data and control flow analyses would not be difficult, it *is* difficult to decide when and where PROUST would make use of the flow analyses; and, it is difficult to see exactly how flow analysis knowledge could be inserted into the knowledge representation languages used in PROUST. Questions like these have pushed us to design and build a completely new bug identifier in order to test out our speculations. We will describe our answers to these knowledge-base questions in the upcoming section on CHIRON.

In its interpretation process, PROUST fetches the goal of the problem specification and then decides which plan, that satisfies the current goal, best describes the manner in which the student has tried to fulfill the current goal in their program. If none of the plans listed under the goal can be matched to the student's code without mismatches and no set of bug rules can explain the mismatches, then PROUST's interpretation process is stopped cold: it cannot proceed to the next goal before finding some interpretation for the current goal. This goal-by-goal approach makes PROUST vulnerable to giving up its interpretation completely if it cannot find a plan for the first goal of the problem specification. Almost all of PROUST's *incomplete* interpretations occurred when it was unable to match the first goal.

Although this result illustrates the fact that PROUST's interpretation process should be more flexible, the result does not reveal what strategy should be implemented to allow the kind of flexibility necessary.

CHIRON: ANSWERS TO QUESTIONS RAISED BY PROUST

In this section we describe the manner in which CHIRON will interact with students. Next, we explain how we think our current and proposed work on CHIRON addresses questions raised in the PROUST evaluation. We are describing a prototype version of CHIRON that has not yet been used by students. Many parts of CHIRON are still under development. For example, we are developing the machinery necessary for CHIRON to not only identify errors, but to fix them as well. Collected together in this section is a summary of our current formulation of CHIRON's bug identification techniques. A more detailed description of the bug identification techniques used in CHIRON can be found in Sack (1989).

---

assignment statement is responsible for a given variable's value in a given segment of a program.

What CHIRON does

CHIRON prompts the user for a name of a file to be analyzed, which the student types:

```
Input the name of the file that you would like analyzed.
<<< Waiting for input >>> "program_filename.pas"
```

CHIRON first checks the program's syntax. If it is syntactically correct, CHIRON performs control and data flow analyses and then starts its goal and plan analysis.

After CHIRON has finished its goal and plan analysis, it outputs a general description of the errors found and then enters a loop from within which a student can ask questions. The student can terminate interaction with CHIRON by typing `quit`, return to a text editor, make changes to the program, and then reinvoke CHIRON for further advice.

To illustrate what CHIRON does, Figure 17 shows a buggy solution to the following problem. Figure 18 shows how CHIRON answers questions after it has analyzed this program, and Figure 19 lists examples of the types of questions CHIRON can answer.

> Average problem: Read in numbers until 99999 is input. Prompt the user before each number is read. Calculate and output the average of all the numbers input except the 99999.

Figure 16: The Average problem.

How CHIRON Answers Some of the Questions Raised by PROUST's Evaluation

PROUST's evaluation raised the following problematic areas, each of which is addressed in a planned or prototyped improvement of CHIRON over PROUST.

Interface:	What type of interface would make an automatic debugger a better aid to debugging and a better teacher of the skills of debugging than PROUST?
Knowledge base:	How can we incorporate lexical, data, and control flow knowledge into a debugger's knowledge base of programming plans and goals?
Bug description:	How should bugs be represented so that the debugger's knowledge of errors is more general, and specific "tweaks" are less necessary?

Control structure: What type of control structure would allow a debugger's interpretation process to be more flexible than PROUST's, and allow it to recover gracefully from a failure to match a first goal?

CHIRON's improvements over PROUST can be summarized as follows. First, CHIRON's interface allows the student to ask questions. Second, the layering and hierarchy of CHIRON's knowledge base both allowed us to include lexical, data, and control flow knowledge, and to perform bug identification without a bug catalog. CHIRON focuses on finding the correct parts of the student program, rather than the incorrect; bugs are simply the parts or attributes of the student program that are not correct. Finally, CHIRON's more robust control structure owes its strength to the use of machine learning techniques for plan identification.

The following sections describe CHIRON's improvements in each of these four areas.

```
PROGRAM Average (INPUT, OUTPUT);
VAR Count:  INTEGER;
Sum, New, Avg: REAL;
BEGIN
    Sum := 0;
    Count := 0;
    WRITELN ('Input a number');
    READLN (New);
    WHILE (New <> 99999) DO BEGIN
        SUM := Sum + New;
        Count := Count - 1;
(* Bug 1: counter augmented by "-" not "+" *)
        Count := Count - 1;
(*Bug 2: counter augmented twice *)
        READLN (New) ;
        WRITELN ('Input a number');
    END;
    IF (Count > 0) THEN BEGIN
        Avg := Sum / Count;
        WRITELN ('The average is ', Avg);
    END;
END
```

Figure 17: A buggy solution to the averaging problem.

;;; CHIRON analyzes the student program and reports that
;;; there is a problem with the COUNTER plan.

1. <<< Waiting for input >>> What's wrong with my COUNTER?

* Your COUNTER does not work correctly, specifically
* your COUNTER UPDATE does not work correctly, specifically
* I expected to find a
* +, but I was only able to find an
* ADDITIVE_OPERATOR.

2. <<< Waiting for input >>> Explain what an ADDITIVE_OPERATOR is.

* An ADDITIVE_OPERATOR is an operator that accepts two numbers
* and combines them in some way. + and - are
ADDITIVE_OPERATORs.

3. <<< Waiting for input >>> I want to quit so that I can fix my program

* Goodbye!

;;; CHIRON reanalyzes the student program after the <->s in
;;; the counter updates get changed to <+>s

* Parsing my_program.pascal.
* Done with goal/plan analysis.
* There is something wrong with the COUNTER implemented in
your program.
* Ready for questions. Type QUIT to quit session with
CHIRON.

4. <<< Waiting for input >>> What errors do I have in my COUNTER plan?

* Your COUNTER does not work correctly, specifically
* the COUNTER UPDATE->UPDATE relation is not implemented

5. <<< Waiting for input >>> What is the UPDATE->UPDATE relation of a COUNTER?

* A COUNTER UPDATE->UPDATE relation specifies that there is
* data flow from the UPDATE back to the UPDATE.

6. <<< Waiting for input >>> What piece of my program implements a COUNTER UPDATE?

* A COUNTER UPDATE is implemented by
* the ASSIGN on line 11, and
* the ASSIGN on line 12.

Figure 18: Dialog with CHIRON about the buggy average program.

Goal / Plan Information

Terminology Questions

Explain what a counter is.

Explain what a counter update is.

Implementation Questions

How is the counter implemented in my program?

How is the counter update implemented in my program?

Error Questions

What is wrong with my counter?

What is wrong with the counter update?

Control / Data Flow Information

Control Flow Questions

Does control flow from the assignment statement on line 8 to the writeln on 25?

How does control flow from line 8 to line 25?

Why doesn't control flow from the assignment on line 8 to the writeln on 25?

Data Flow Questions

Is there data flow from the assignment statement on line 8 to the writeln on line 25?

Does the value given to X in the assignment on line 8 survive between the assignment on line 10 and the writeln on line 25?

How does data flow from line 8 to line 25?

Why doesn't data flow from line 8 to line 25?

Low Level Data Flow Questions

What is the [GEN or KILL or IN or OUT] set of the assignment statement on line 8?

Guard / Symbolic Value Information

What guards exist between all of the definitions of the variable X and the writeln on line 25?

Is the writeln on 25 explicitly guarded against the case in which X <=0?

Figure 19: Examples of questions that CHIRON can answer.

CHIRON's Interface Allows the Student to Ask Questions

As a first step toward constructing an interface better than PROUST's we have implemented an interactive, question-answering, interface for CHIRON. CHIRON's simple natural language interface parses English questions typed by the students using a semantic grammar (Brown, Burton, and de Kleer, 1982). Figure 19 shows the types of questions that CHIRON is designed to answer.

We believe that a question-answering interface will be more effective than PROUST's output which consists merely of a list of the errors found in the program. The PROUST interface (see Figure 3) provides no interaction with the student about the program analyzed.

Letovsky (1986) studied verbal protocols gathered from professional programmers engaged in the task of understanding correct programs. He observed a small set of recurrent behaviors that included asking certain questions of the code and documentation and making certain types of conjectures about the code. We are trying to develop CHIRON's interface so that it supports the type of question-asking/conjecture-formulation that Letovsky saw, and we are trying to expand on Letovsky's question types so that questions about incorrect code can also be supported.

At the very least, an interactive interface will be useful to us, the future evaluators of CHIRON, simply because an interactive question-answering interface will provide us with an automatic method for collecting more information about students; student transcripts will show the types of questions the students asked CHIRON.

Hierarchy and Layering in the Knowledge Base

CHIRON's plan knowledge is arranged in hierarchical, tree structures. Plans are defined as specializations of more general plans. For example, finding the maximum of a sequence of values is a specialization of a more general plan called an accumulator. Figure 20 shows several CHIRON plans, with downward lines running from general plans to their specializations. All accumulator plans accept a sequence of values from another part of the program (called an enumerator), combine the sequence together using some operation, and then return a single result.

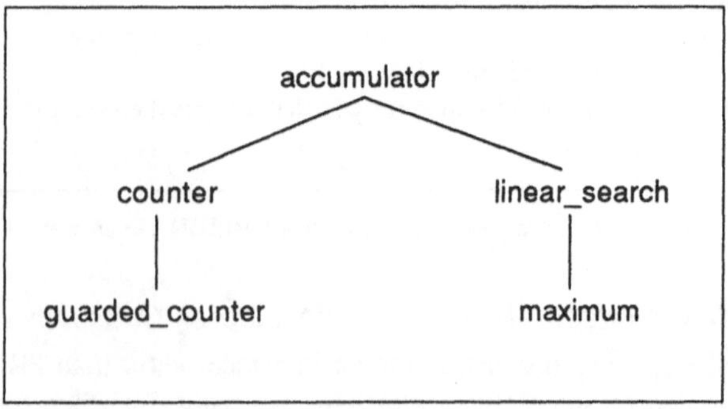

Figure 20: Plan definitions in CHIRON's knowledge-base with generalization / specialization relationships.

An accumulator plan has the parameters listed in Figure 21. These parameters must obey the constraints shown in Figure 22. The definition of the accumulator plan is then simply a function which associates the parameters with the constraints.

Once the accumulator plan is defined, plans for specializations are relatively simple. For example, a counter is a special type of accumulator in which the ?UpdateExpr increments the value of ?Var. A guarded_counter is a special type of counter in which the count ?Var is updated if and only if ?GuardTest is true. A maximum is a special type of linear_search in which the ?Var is updated if and only if ?EnumVar's current value is greater than ?Var's current value. A linear_search is a special type of accumulator in which the ?Var is updated by replacing its previous value with ?EnumVar's current value, and in which ?Var is updated if and only if ?GuardTest is true.

Hierarchically Arranged Non-Plan Knowledge. Some of CHIRON's non-plan knowledge is also arranged hierarchically. For example, <+>, <->, <*>, and </> are specializations of the <arithmetic_operator>. Another general pattern <boolean> has specific operators like = and <>. Language specific statements, like PASCAL's <READ>, <READLN>, and <:=> statements are all specific ways of giving a variable a value and so they are all grouped under a language-independent pattern called <variable_gets_value!>. Lexical knowledge can also be included in hierarchies of the same format. For example, variable names like MAX, MAXIMUM, MAXM could all be grouped under the general pattern <variable_name_for_mamixum>, which in turn could be declared to be a specialization of <variable_name>. Although our current CHIRON does not contain lexical knowledge, generalization and specialization hierarchies of this sort are the manner in which we intend to include lexical knowledge.

Layered Plans. CHIRON's plans specify the following three layers (similar to the plans used in the Programmer's Apprentice Project (c.f., Rich, 1981)).

1. Template Layer: patterns that can directly match code in the students' programs (e.g., ?update part of the counter plan).
2. Flow Layer: descriptions of data and control flow between the pieces of the template layer, for example, that data must flow from the :init part to the :update part (e.g., init->update part of the accumulator plan).
3. Input/Output Layer: information about the type of data produced and consumed by the parts of the template layer (e.g., enum_update ->update step of the accumulator plan).

?Var	variable into which the result of the accumulation is collected.
?InitExpr	an expression describing the value to which ?Var is initialized.
?Init	the part of the program in which ?Var is given the result of ?InitExpr.
?UpdateExpr	the part of the program describing how ?Var is updated.
?Update	part of the program in which ?Var is given the result of ?UpdateExpr.
?EnumVar	successively contains each of the sequence of values that are to be accumulated.
?EnumInit	part of the program in which ?EnumVar is initialized.
?EnumUpdate	part of the program in which ?EnumVar is updated to its next value.
?GuardTest	a boolean expression, true when ?Update can legally be executed, false when it cannot.
init	constrains ?Init to be a type of statement in which ?Var is given ?InitExpr's value.
update	constrains ?Update to be a type of statement in which ?Var is given ?UpdateExpr's value.

Figure 21: Parameters of the accumulator plan.

Name	Requirement
init->update	data flows from ?Init to ?Update
init->enum_update	?Init is executed before ?EnumUpdate
update->update	data flows from ?Update back to ?Update
enum_init->update	data flows from ?EnumInit to ?Update
enum_update->update	data flows from ?EnumUpdate to ?Update

Figure 22: Constraints of the accumulator plan.

Bug Description = Correct Description + Generalizations

PROUST's objective is to determine what is *wrong* with a student's program by explaining discrepancies using bug-rules: knowledge about typical programming errors. In contrast, CHIRON's objective is to explain what is *right* about a student's program by explaining discrepancies using generalization mechanisms: knowledge about the elaboration and simplification of typical programming plans and plan components. CHIRON's use of generalization knowledge to describe bugs allows CHIRON to locate buggy pieces of code in a student program without using bug rules that might be too idiosyncratic or weak (as sometimes is the case with PROUST's bug rules).

From a PROUST perspective there are two problems with the counter plan implemented in the buggy program shown in Figure 17: `COUNT := COUNT - 1;` was found instead of the expected `COUNT := COUNT + 1;` and, instead of just one statement, there are two matching the counter update pattern.

In contrast, when CHIRON determines that the <+> operator does not exist in the `COUNT := COUNT - 1` statements, it replaces its expectation with a more general operator (here `<additive_operator>`) stored in the operator hierarchy. The buggy lines 11 and 12 of Figure 17 are then matched by CHIRON's expectation. Figure 18 shows how CHIRON uses this generalization in explaining the bugs.

If lines 11 and 12 had been of the form `COUNT := COUNT * 1`, then even the more general `<arithmetic_operator>` would be used. For a *Read for Increment* bug (writing `Read(COUNT)` instead of `COUNT := COUNT + 1)`, CHIRON would replace <:=> with the generalization `<variable_gets_value!>`.

CHIRON could also use its hierarchies to find buggy tests in which, for example, the student had written `(TOTAL >= 0)` instead of `(TOTAL > 0)`, while PROUST needs a special bug rule: the Sloppy Guard bug rule shown in Figure 9.

In this short introduction to CHIRON's bug description method we have shown how just a small piece of generalization/specialization knowledge about operators could be used to replace four different bug rules that PROUST would have to have in order to find the same errors in students' programs. We are incorporating generalization/specialization knowledge about, not only operators, but plans, data and control flow relations, variable names, and various other objects and relations. An extensive knowledge about generalizations and specializations will allow CHIRON to find errors in student programs without a pre-enumerated catalog of bugs like PROUST has.

A Control Structure that can Never Stall

Roughly, CHIRON's bug identification control structure consists of the following algorithm:

```
repeat
    if  no unmatched student-program parts
    then
        exit, returning matches of student-program parts to
        exact and generalized specification parts
    else
        get an unmatched specification part;
        attempt to match to a student-program part.
    If match fails
    then
        if generalization of specification-part exists
        then
        generalize that part
    else
        match student-program part to <anything>
```

Because, the symbol `<anything>` is predefined to be the generalization of everything in the knowledge base, it will match anything, and this control structure can never stall. Pragmatically, CHIRON would still be able to tell the student that an error had occurred in the particular part of the program matched to <anything>.

CONCLUSIONS

Before evaluating PROUST we knew that we wanted our next debugger to be better than PROUST. But, it is only now, after the evaluation, that we have some inkling of what a "better" debugger is. This evaluation has focused our attention onto a concrete set of PROUST's strengths and weaknesses. We started our testing of PROUST with two general questions: (1) Can PROUST explain to students the errors it has found, and (2) Can PROUST identify bugs in novices' programs? We sharpened both of these questions using micro-analyses to uncover *why* PROUST was able to explain and identify errors in students' programs. Our newest debugger, CHIRON, is an effort to synthesize our evaluation results into a "better" debugger.

Bug Explanation

We found that students who had access to PROUST when they were doing their programming assignments performed modestly better on a midterm examination specifically designed to exercise bug identification and repair skills.

At a finer level of interpretation, we saw that PROUST helped students identify *idiosyncratic* (but not *common*) bugs in their own programs. And, we found that students who succeeded in fixing particular bugs on their programming assignments were significantly better at repairing similar bugs on the midterm.

The particularity of these results showed us the utility of making hair splitting distinctions between different kinds of bugs: even bugs that are seemingly only slightly different on the surface can be caused by very different factors, and these causal factors can determine how easy it is for a bug identifier to explain a bug to a student. In order for a bug identifier to more ably reason about different kinds of bugs, it is arguably necessary for it to have a depth of knowledge that is deeper than PROUST's in at least two dimensions: (1) knowledge about *programming* and, (2) knowledge about the *student*. CHIRON's three-layered plan language is two layers deeper than PROUST's plan language and represents a push to put more knowledge about programming into our new debugger. Studies by Spohrer (1989) have given us new insights into novice programmers' reasoning and problem solving strategies. However, it is still not exactly clear how this deeper knowledge about students can be used to increase a bug identifier's effectiveness at diagnosing and explaining bugs to students.

Letovsky (1986) showed us that programmers tend to ask questions and formulate and investigate certain types of conjectures about the code they are reading. Consequently, it seems that PROUST's "edict-style" output could be improved upon. CHIRON's interface is being developed to allow the student to pursue a more natural question-and-conjecture-style inquiry about the errors in their programs. Also, in this evaluation, as evaluators, we found that PROUST's output style did not allow us to determine which parts of PROUST's output, if any, students actually read or understood. Hopefully, students' dialog transcripts with CHIRON will give a more accurate trace of what kinds of remedial advice students ask for, understand, and use. We hope that Littman's (1989) studies of tutorial dialogs will shed further light on the issue of how to make CHIRON educationally effective.

Bug Identification

Both our evaluation and the evaluation conducted by Johnson (1986) showed that, overall, PROUST was only able to identify about one half or less of the bugs present in the student programs submitted for analysis. We conducted a number of micro-analyses to cast more light on PROUST's overall accuracy rating: to pinpoint when and why PROUST was (in)accurate in identifying bugs. We found that PROUST was very accurate when it was able to give a *full* interpretation to a student program and very inaccurate when it was only able to give a *partial* or *incomplete* interpretation.

During our evaluation and Johnson's evaluation various small changes were made to PROUST, like strengthening key bug rules. Both we and Johnson found that these "tweaks" to PROUST could make it much more accurate in identifying errors: about 20% better. We are trying to build CHIRON so that it doesn't need "tweaking" by ridding it of PROUST's weaknesses and temperamental parts. For example, CHIRON has a control structure that can't get stalled on the first goal the way PROUST often is; and, in CHIRON we have devised a way to find buggy code in a student's program without using bug rules.

We performed several speculative analyses to determine how our new debugger might benefit from a richer knowledge of the lexical content of program variable names, control flow, and data flow analyses. None of this kind of information is used by PROUST in its analysis of student programs, but CHIRON will because we estimate that using this knowledge will make the new debugger more accurate at identifying bugs than PROUST. The extra layers in CHIRON's plan representation language will allow CHIRON to use this information about student programs.

Our experience with PROUST (and also its predecessor, MENO II (Soloway, et al., 1983)) has convinced us that intelligent tutoring system design is an empirical, engineering endeavor. An ITS designed in the laboratory will inevitably take a beating from the rigors of the classroom. Here, we have tried to illustrate how one might profit from a close examination of an ITS's failures. We see our work as a first step towards the articulation of some principled techniques for testing ITSs so that they fail in ways that inform the design of their successors.

ACKNOWLEDGEMENTS

Our evaluation of PROUST was done at the Yale University Computer Science Department within Elliot Soloway's Cognition and Programming Project (CAPP). We owe our thanks to many former members of CAPP. An earlier technical report (Sack, et al., 1986) contained most of the material that we reported here as our section on the educational evaluation of PROUST. We would like to thank David Littman and Jim Spohrer for their guidance in shaping the form and content of the earlier technical report and, by precedent, the form and content of that section of this paper. Lucian Hughes, Scott Fertig, and Andrew Lilies were also co-authors of the earlier technical report and contributed several months of their time to gathering statistics and critiquing earlier drafts of this paper written in 1986. In particular the data on variable names was Lucian's work. Lewis Johnson lent his expertise to our evaluation efforts when we started in 1985. Stan Letovsky and Rob Rist gave us some pivotal ideas in several 1985 meetings on PROUST. We thank Drs. Eva Baker and Nancy Atwood of the UCLA Center for the Study of Evaluation: they provided critically important moral and technical support for this evaluation effort. Thanks to Prof. Harald Wertz for his advice and support during Warren's year at the University of Paris 8. Drs. Jill Larkin and Ruth Chabay extensively edited several drafts of this chapter. We thank them for the many insightful contributions and improvements they made to its form and content.

REFERENCES

Aho, A., Sethi, R., & Ullman, J. (1986). *Compilers: Principles, Techniques, and Tools*. Reading, MA: Addison-Wesley.

Anderson, J. R. (1988). The Expert Module. In M. Polson & J. Richardson (Eds.), *Handbook of Intelligent Training Systems*. Hillsdale NJ: Lawrence Erlbaum Associates, 21-53

Bachant, J. & Soloway, E. (1989). The Engineering of XCON, in V. Barker & D. O'Connor, Expert Systems for Configuration at Digital: XCON and Beyond, *Communications of the Association for Computing Machinery* 33 (3), 311-317.

Brown, J. S., Burton, R., & de Kleer, J. (1982). Pedagogical, natural language and knowledge engineering techniques in SOPHIE I, II and III. In D. Sleeman, & J. S. Brown (Eds.), *Intelligent Tutoring Systems*. NY: Academic Press.

Clancey, W. J. (1982). Tutoring rules for guiding a case method dialogue. In D. Sleeman, & J. S. Brown (Eds.), *Intelligent Tutoring Systems*. NY: Academic Press.

Cullingford, R. E. (1978). *Script application: Computer understanding of newspaper stories*, Ph.D. Dissertation, Research Report #116, Computer Science Department, Yale University.

Doyle, J. (1977). *Truth Maintenance Systems for Problem Solving*. (Technical Report No. 419). Massachusetts Institute of Technology: Artificial Intelligence Laboratory.

Fikes, R. E., & Nilsson, N. J. (1971). STRIPS: A new approach to the application of theorem proving to problem solving. *Artificial Intelligence*, 2, 189-208.

Johnson, W. L. (1986). PROUST: *Intention-Based Diagnosis of Errors*, Los Altos, CA: Morgan Kaufmann.

Letovsky, S. (1986). Cognitive Processes in Program Comprehension. In E. Soloway & S. Iyengar (Eds.), *Empirical Studies of Programmers*. NY: Academic Press.

Littman, D. (in preparation). Forthcoming dissertation, Yale University: Department of Computer Science.

McDermott, J. (1982). R1: A rule-based configurer of computer systems, *Artificial Intelligence* 19 (1).

Miller, M. (1982). A structured planning and debugging environment for elementary programming. In D. Sleeman, & J. S. Brown (Eds.), *Intelligent Tutoring Systems*. NY: Academic Press.

Newell, A., & Simon, H. (1972). *Human Problem Solving*. Englewood Cliffs, N.J: Prentice-Hall.

Rich, C. (1981). A Formal Representation for Plans in the Programmer's Apprentice, *IJCAI Proceedings*, 1981, 1044-1052.

Sacerdoti, E. (1974). Planning in a hierarchy of abstraction spaces. *Artificial Intelligence*, 5, 115-135.

Sacerdoti, E. (1975). *A structure for plans and behavior*. Technical Note 109, AI Center, SRI International Inc., Menlo Park, CA (Ph.D. Dissertation).

Sack, W. (1988). Finding Errors by Overlooking Them, *Proceedings of International Conference on Intelligent Tutoring Systems*, Montreal, Canada.

Sack, W. (1990). Finding Errors by Overlooking Them, *Intelligent Tutoring Systems: At the Crossroads of Artifial Intelligence and Education*, C. Frasson & G. Gauthier (Eds.), Norwood, NJ: Ablex Publishing Corp.

Sack, W., Littman, D., Spohrer, J., Lilies, A., Fertig, S., Hughes, L., Johnson, W. L., & Soloway, E. (1986). *Empirical Evaluation of the Educational Effectiveness of PROUST*. (Cognition and Programming Project Report No. 55). Yale University: Computer Science Department.

Shortliffe, E. H. (1975). *MYCIN: A rule-based computer program for advising physicians regarding antimicrobial therapy selection*, Ph.D. Dissertation in Medical Information Sciences, Stanford University.

Soloway, E., Rubin, E., Woolf, B., Bonar, J., & Johnson, W. L. (1983). MENO II: An AI-Based Programming Tutor. *Journal of Computer-Based Instruction*, 10 (1&2), 20-34.

Spohrer, J. (1989). *MARCEL: A Generate-Test-and-Debug (GTD) Impasse/Repair Model Of Student Programmers*. (Technical Report No. 687). Yale University: Department of Computer Science.

Spohrer, J., & Soloway, E. (1986). Novice mistakes: are the folk wisdoms correct? *Communications of the ACM*, 29 (7), 624-632.

Stallman, R. M. and Sussman, G.J. (1977). Forward reasoning and dependency-directed backtracking in a system for computer-aided circuit analysis. *Artificial Intelligence* 9(2): 135-196.

Wilensky, R. (1978). *Understanding goal-based stories*. Ph.D. Dissertation, Research Report #140, Computer Science Department, Yale University.

Wilensky, R. (1981). PAM, In Inside Computer Understanding. In R. Schank and C. Riesbeck (Eds.), Inside computer understanding: Five programs plus miniatures. Yale University Press and Lawrence Erlbaum Associates, Hillsdale, N.J.

AUTHOR INDEX

PROGRAM INDEX

SUBJECT INDEX